Jurassic Park
and Philosophy

Popular Culture and Philosophy® Series Editor: George A. Reisch

VOLUME 1 *Seinfeld and Philosophy: A Book about Everything and Nothing* (2000)

VOLUME 2 *The Simpsons and Philosophy: The D'oh! of Homer* (2001)

VOLUME 3 *The Matrix and Philosophy: Welcome to the Desert of the Real* (2002)

VOLUME 4 *Buffy the Vampire Slayer and Philosophy: Fear and Trembling in Sunnydale* (2003)

VOLUME 5 *The Lord of the Rings and Philosophy: One Book to Rule Them All* (2003)

VOLUME 9 *Harry Potter and Philosophy: If Aristotle Ran Hogwarts* (2004)

VOLUME 12 *Star Wars and Philosophy: More Powerful than You Can Possibly Imagine* (2005)

VOLUME 13 *Superheroes and Philosophy: Truth, Justice, and the Socratic Way* (2005)

VOLUME 19 *Monty Python and Philosophy: Nudge Nudge, Think Think!* (2006)

VOLUME 25 *The Beatles and Philosophy: Nothing You Can Think that Can't Be Thunk* (2006)

VOLUME 26 *South Park and Philosophy: Bigger, Longer, and More Penetrating* (2007)

VOLUME 30 *Pink Floyd and Philosophy: Careful with that Axiom, Eugene!* (2007)

VOLUME 33 *Battlestar Galactica and Philosophy: Mission Accomplished or Mission Frakked Up?* (2008)

VOLUME 35 *Star Trek and Philosophy: The Wrath of Kant* (2008)

VOLUME 36 *The Legend of Zelda and Philosophy: I Link Therefore I Am* (2008)

VOLUME 38 *Radiohead and Philosophy: Fitter Happier More Deductive* (2009)

VOLUME 39 *Jimmy Buffett and Philosophy: The Porpoise Driven Life* (2009) Edited by Erin McKenna and Scott L. Pratt

VOLUME 41 *Stephen Colbert and Philosophy: I Am Philosophy (And So Can You!)* (2009) Edited by Aaron Allen Schiller

VOLUME 42 *Supervillains and Philosophy: Sometimes, Evil Is Its Own Reward* (2009) Edited by Ben Dyer

VOLUME 43 *The Golden Compass and Philosophy: God Bites the Dust* (2009) Edited by Richard Greene and Rachel Robison

VOLUME 44 *Led Zeppelin and Philosophy: All Will Be Revealed* (2009) Edited by Scott Calef

VOLUME 45 *World of Warcraft and Philosophy: Wrath of the Philosopher King* (2009) Edited by Luke Cuddy and John Nordlinger

Volume 46 *Mr. Monk and Philosophy: The Curious Case of the Defective Detective* (2010) Edited by D.E. Wittkower

Volume 47 *Anime and Philosophy: Wide Eyed Wonder* (2010) Edited by Josef Steiff and Tristan D. Tamplin

VOLUME 48 *The Red Sox and Philosophy: Green Monster Meditations* (2010) Edited by Michael Macomber

VOLUME 49 *Zombies, Vampires, and Philosophy: New Life for the Undead* (2010) Edited by Richard Greene and K. Silem Mohammad

VOLUME 50 *Facebook and Philosophy: What's on Your Mind?* (2010) Edited by D.E. Wittkower

VOLUME 51 *Soccer and Philosophy: Beautiful Thoughts on the Beautiful Game* (2010) Edited by Ted Richards

VOLUME 52 *Manga and Philosophy: Fullmetal Metaphysician* (2010) Edited by Josef Steiff and Adam Barkman

VOLUME 53 *Martial Arts and Philosophy: Beating and Nothingness* (2010) Edited by Graham Priest and Damon Young

VOLUME 54 *The Onion and Philosophy: Fake News Story True, Alleges Indignant Area Professor* (2010) Edited by Sharon M. Kaye

VOLUME 55 *Doctor Who and Philosophy: Bigger on the Inside* (2010) Edited by Courtland Lewis and Paula Smithka

VOLUME 56 *Dune and Philosophy: Weirding Way of the Mentat* (2011) Edited by Jeffery Nicholas

VOLUME 57 *Rush and Philosophy: Heart and Mind United* (2011) Edited by Jim Berti and Durrell Bowman

VOLUME 58 *Dexter and Philosophy: Mind over Spatter* (2011) Edited by Richard Greene, George A. Reisch, and Rachel Robison-Greene

VOLUME 59 *Halo and Philosophy: Intellect Evolved* (2011) Edited by Luke Cuddy

VOLUME 60 *SpongeBob SquarePants and Philosophy: Soaking Up Secrets Under the Sea!* (2011) Edited by Joseph J. Foy

VOLUME 61 *Sherlock Holmes and Philosophy: The Footprints of a Gigantic Mind* (2011) Edited by Josef Steiff

VOLUME 62 *Inception and Philosophy: Ideas to Die For* (2011) Edited by Thorsten Botz-Bornstein

VOLUME 63 *Philip K. Dick and Philosophy: Do Androids Have Kindred Spirits?* (2011) Edited by D.E. Wittkower

VOLUME 64 *The Rolling Stones and Philosophy: It's Just a Thought Away* (2012) Edited by Luke Dick and George A. Reisch

VOLUME 65 *Chuck Klosterman and Philosophy: The Real and the Cereal* (2012) Edited by Seth Vannatta

VOLUME 66 *Neil Gaiman and Philosophy: Gods Gone Wild!* (2012) Edited by Tracy L. Bealer, Rachel Luria, and Wayne Yuen

VOLUME 67 *Breaking Bad and Philosophy: Badder Living through Chemistry* (2012) Edited by David R. Koepsell and Robert Arp

VOLUME 68 *The Walking Dead and Philosophy: Zombie Apocalypse Now* (2012) Edited by Wayne Yuen

VOLUME 69 *Curb Your Enthusiasm and Philosophy: Awaken the Social Assassin Within* (2012) Edited by Mark Ralkowski

VOLUME 70 *Dungeons and Dragons and Philosophy: Raiding the Temple of Wisdom* (2012) Edited by Jon Cogburn and Mark Silcox

VOLUME 71 *The Catcher in the Rye and Philosophy: A Book for Bastards, Morons, and Madmen* (2012) Edited by Keith Dromm and Heather Salter

VOLUME 72 *Jeopardy! and Philosophy: What Is Knowledge in the Form of a Question?* (2012) Edited by Shaun P. Young

VOLUME 73 *The Wire and Philosophy: This America, Man* (2013) Edited by David Bzdak, Joanna Crosby, and Seth Vannatta

VOLUME 74 *Planet of the Apes and Philosophy: Great Apes Think Alike* (2013) Edited by John Huss

VOLUME 75 *Psych and Philosophy: Some Dark Juju-Magumbo* (2013) Edited by Robert Arp

VOLUME 76 *The Good Wife and Philosophy: Temptations of Saint Alicia* (2013) Edited by Kimberly Baltzer-Jaray and Robert Arp

VOLUME 77 *Boardwalk Empire and Philosophy: Bootleg This Book* (2013) Edited by Richard Greene and Rachel Robison-Greene

VOLUME 78 *Futurama and Philosophy: Bite My Shiny Metal Axiom* (2013) Edited by Courtland Lewis and Shaun P. Young

VOLUME 79 *Frankenstein and Philosophy: The Shocking Truth* (2013) Edited by Nicolas Michaud

VOLUME 80 *Ender's Game and Philosophy: Genocide Is Child's Play* (2013) Edited by D.E. Wittkower and Lucinda Rush

VOLUME 81 *How I Met Your Mother and Philosophy* (2014) Edited by Lorenzo von Matterhorn

VOLUME 82 *Jurassic Park and Philosophy: The Truth Is Terrifying* (2014) Edited by Nicolas Michaud and Jessica Watkins

IN PREPARATION:

The Devil and Philosophy (2014) Edited by Robert Arp

Leonard Cohen and Philosophy (2014) Edited by Jason Holt

Homeland and Philosophy (2014) Edited by Robert Arp

Adventure Time and Philosophy (2014) Edited by Nicolas Michaud

Girls and Philosophy (2014) Edited by Richard Greene and Rachel Robison-Greene

Justified and Philosophy (2014) Edited by Rod Carveth and Robert Arp

Dracula and Philosophy (2015) Edited by Nicolas Michaud and Janelle Pötzsch

For full details of all Popular Culture and Philosophy® books, visit www.opencourtbooks.com.

Popular Culture and Philosophy®

Jurassic Park and Philosophy

The Truth Is Terrifying

Edited by
NICOLAS MICHAUD and
JESSICA WATKINS

OPEN COURT
Chicago

Volume 82 in the series, Popular Culture and Philosophy ®, edited by George A. Reisch

To order books from Open Court, call toll-free 1-800-815-2280, or visit our website at www.opencourtbooks.com.

Open Court Publishing Company is a division of Carus Publishing Company, dba Cricket Media.

ISBN: 978-0-8126-9847-3

Library of Congress Cataloging-in-Publication Data

Jurassic Park and philosophy : the truth is terrifying / edited by Nicolas Michaud and Jessica Watkins.
　　pages cm. — (Popular culture and philosophy ; VOLUME 82)
　ISBN 978-0-8126-9847-3 (trade paper : alk. paper) 1. Jurassic Park (Motion picture)
　　I. Michaud, Nicolas. II. Watkins, Jessica.
　PN1997.J833J87 2014
　791.43'72—dc23

2013047450

Contents

Thanks   ix

We Spared No Expense   xi

I Present at the Creation   1

1. Damn You, Michael Crichton!
   NICOLAS MICHAUD AND JESSICA WATKINS   3

2. Let the Raptors Run!
   GREG LITTMANN   11

3. The Past in a Petri Dish
   DAVID FREEMAN   21

4. Runaway Memes
   BRENDAN SHEA   29

5. Beer and Dinosaurs
   ADAM BARKMAN AND NATHAN VERBAAN   39

II Life Has Lost Its Way   51

6. Why Not Play God?
   VINCENT BILLARD   53

7. Is the Essence in the Amber?
   EVAN EDWARDS   63

8. Bring Back the Dinosaurs!
   JOHN R. FITZPATRICK   73

9. Flea-Market Capitalism
   TIMOTHY SEXTON   81

10. Do Dinosaurs Really Scare Us?
    MICHAEL J. MUNIZ   91

III Unnatural Selection 99

11. What's It Like to Be a *T. rex*?
    RICK STOODY 101

12. Feathering the Truth
    BRANDON KEMPNER 111

13. Raptor Rights
    JOHN V. KARAVITIS 121

14. If Dinosaurs Were People . . .
    SKYLER KING 131

15. Who Gets a Second Chance?
    LISA KADONAGA 143

IV Staying Alive 153

16. Superiority Is Our Weakness?
    CRISTOPHER KETCHAM 155

17. You Monkeywrenching Bastard!
    SETH M. WALKER 167

18. What We Leave Behind
    TIM JONES 177

19. It's Only Natural to Blame Technology
    DANIEL KOKOTZ 187

20. Decline of the Meatosaurus
    KENN FISHER 197

21. How Ethics Can Save You from Being Eaten
    ROGER HUNT 209

V Death Is My Destination 217

22. When You Go Extinct, *You* Don't Get to Come Back
    NICOLAS MICHAUD 219

23. Playing God in Jurassic Park
    JEFF EWING 229

24. How Much Are Your Grandchildren Worth?
    JANELLE PÖTZSCH 239

25. Chaos and the Inevitable Collapse
    DAVID L. MORGAN 249

26. A *T. rex* Swallowed My Pride
    MICHAEL D. STARK AND A.G. HOLDIER   257

27. How to Avoid Extinction
    TRIP MCCROSSIN   267

Velociwriters   275

Genetic Markers   281

Thanks

The task of putting new life into old ideas (mixed in with some new ones) is monumental, as Hammond's team would attest. We'd like to thank a few of the many people who helped conceive and hatch this book:

Thanks to David Ramsay Steele and George Reisch for their guidance in this work and for making sure it's as tasty and tender to our readers as a certain hated attorney was to a certain beloved *Tyrannosaurus rex*.

Thanks to our authors, who shared their passion about the many worlds of philosophy. We couldn't ask for better authors. Their diligence and effort made this project a pleasure and brought this book to the next level of awesome!

Thanks especially to our families, who no doubt are glad to see this project completed. Powell Kreis, Jacob May, Justine Watkins, Ross Houston, Steve Edwards—thanks for listening to us and for sharing your expertise. Jake, especially, thanks for always humming the *Jurassic Park* theme as we hiked our trails and for being our rereading (and rewatching and regaming) buddy—you helped this project take on a life of its own!

Thanks to our students and colleagues, who have patiently dodged some hissing spit when our deadlines wore our patience thin, and who are likely to tranquilize us if we make so much as one more dinosaur analogy.

Thanks to our readers for holding hope in human triumph over ourselves, and for enjoying the flawed experiment so much that you want to learn more about it. You make Jurassic Park a real possibility.

Thanks to all of our teachers who ever made us gape in wonder at the universe around us and ache to know more. Thanks, also, to the ancient and contemporary philosophical and scientific heroes from Democritus to Neil deGrasse Tyson, who remind us that life without wonder is no life at all.

We Spared No Expense

Michael Crichton changed the world. Monsters that had once been reserved for B-horror flicks and low-budget cult movie classics came charging to life in *Jurassic Park*. There's a good chance you remember the theater where you first heard the seat-rattling roar of Spielberg's *Tyrannosaurus rex*, and all of us—and we do mean *all* of us—got just a little misty when we looked up in awe with Dr. Sattler at the majestic arching neck of our first live brachiosaurus.

Crichton's books, and the movies that came from them, didn't just become a pop-culture phenomenon; they inspired generations of thinkers to dream of what was once impossible. Crichton and Spielberg did more than give us a thrill-riddled roller coaster ride of a movie to lose ourselves in while we shovel popcorn and candy into our mouths . . . they gave us *hope* (along with the cavities). Crichton didn't just imagine these terrific monsters, and Spielberg didn't just put them on the big screen; they showed us how it might be done—how it *could* be done.

It's true; we are a long way away from bringing back dinosaurs. It may turn out to be impossible. Current scientific thinking suggests that, sadly, it is not going to be feasible in the precise way described by Crichton. But the inspirations of science, the dreams of ingenuity, the passions that drive progress, are not held back by little things like "reality."

It was thousands of years after the first philosopher dreamed up the idea of an atom before we discovered them— and our atomic reality bears little resemblance to his ancient dreams. So, it may be a thousand years before we can bring back dinosaurs, and, maybe, the way we do it will have little in common with Crichton's vision. But that still puts Crichton in pretty good company. Crichton imagined a possibility, and then he didn't just put it down on paper. . . . He poked, and prodded at it, he tried to *understand* the range of possibilities. He had no way to test his idea; he could only imagine it. He wasn't doing science—he was doing *philosophy*.

And that's where this book starts. Crichton wanted us to do more than just enjoy the book, or gorge ourselves on tasty theater treats. He wanted us to *think*. And he had good reason to do so. Whether inspired by his work or not, scientists are trying to bring dead species back from extinction, while humanity itself seems to enjoy consistently teetering on the brink of oblivion.

It may well be that in the near future we will look up in wonder as the Passenger Pigeon, brought back from extinction, blackens out our skies again (and again coats thousands of acres of land with an inch-thick layer of droppings), and immediately afterward we evaporate ourselves with some impressive, but unfortunately effective, doomsday weapon. *Jurassic Park* goes far beyond where science—mad or otherwise—can go . . . it goes into the worlds of ethics and metaphysics; it makes us ask what we *should* do with science. Because what we *can* do and what we *should* do are two very different things.

So, this is where we explore what *Jurassic Park* reveals to us about God, creation, morality, science, language, reality, and our bright or *bleak* future. We spared no expense—it's all up for questioning, because when Ian Malcolm asks us whether we should bring these tyrant lizards back from the dead, that question isn't the end. . . . It's just the beginning.

Crichton's message seems pretty clear—he wanted us to think because, when we don't, people *die*. *Jurassic Park* does something even the scariest of our horror movies can't do; it reaches not *away* from reality but *towards* it to remind us that we are very, *very* edible. No ghosts, no goblins, no magic—just *nature*.

We like to think, like John Hammond, that we have control, but we don't. In the end, we would be little more than bloody smears on the teeth of a *T. rex*, or disemboweled and paltry playthings for a young velociraptor.

The ground is shaking, the future is coming, and our little worlds tremble before the tremendous possibilities confronting us. Will we survive it? Probably not. This may well be the last book you read before the unimaginable and unpredictable future arrives.

So call your mom. Tell her you love her. And then sit back, relax, and let us take you on a tour of something surprisingly real and deadly dangerous. . . . Welcome to *Jurassic Park and Philosophy.*

I

Present at the Creation

1
Damn You, Michael Crichton!

NICOLAS MICHAUD AND JESSICA WATKINS

That's right. We said it! Well, we *wrote it*, and that's almost worse. We're unhappy with Michael Crichton, writer of numerous bestsellers, visionary behind *Jurassic Park*, and hero to millions. . . . Why? Actually, for a very good reason! Crichton's work, though profound, beautiful, engaging, and brilliant, is also scary (and a bit addicting). After all, if his world weren't so engaging, you wouldn't have spent money on this book, would you?

You're probably thinking, "Well, what's so bad about all that? He's created a beloved saga that has continued to live on beyond him. He should be well respected and acknowledged for his brilliance, not harassed by some shaggy-looking, ill-tempered philosophers!" Fair enough, but hear us out. What if Crichton has actually done us some harm? What if, by creating a world that enraptures us, he created a picture for us that makes us just a little *too* afraid? And when we say afraid, we don't just mean of dinosaurs (though, yes—if you run into an actual cloned *Tyrannosaurus rex*, . . . RUN!), we mean, maybe he's made us just a little too afraid of *science*.

In this book, you see a lot of very bright work from some brilliant philosophers. Most of them, if you've noticed, give a grateful nod to the warnings of *Jurassic Park*. . . . "Don't get cocky," "Don't play God," "Don't screw with nature," "Don't bite off more than you can chew," . . . yada yada yada. We seem pretty comfortable thanking Crichton for this advice. After all, *Jurassic Park* isn't just a monster movie; it's a story that warns us about how dangerous our technologies can be, and how very delicate we are when we're in the jaws of a *T. rex*.

But that's just our point! We're *delicate*. Dr. Ian Malcolm reminds us constantly that "life finds a way." . . . Sure, *other* life. Dinosaurs go extinct and suddenly a bunch of small, furry, smelly mammals take their place. But those dinosaurs are D-E-A-D, *DEAD*. And that wasn't even the worst cataclysm to hit the Earth. There've been bigger extinctions; the one that killed the dinosaurs is just our favorite one!

What we mean to say is, some life (in fact *most* life) *doesn't* find a way, even if life as a whole succeeds; life forms, species, and ecosystems are pretty darned vulnerable. We see that vulnerability all through *Jurassic Park*. We're vulnerable, our society is vulnerable (our economy is *really* vulnerable—and not just to those deadly beasts). Humans developed science and technology specifically to deal with that vulnerability. And now, thanks to Mr. Crichton and his Dr. Malcolm (who, as you can hear echoing throughout this book, believes scientists should be more concerned with whether we *should* act than if they we're *able* to act), we're all just a little more timid about using the one thing that helps us stay a step ahead of all the stuff out there trying to kill and eat us!

BOOM

Let's face it. The sun's gonna explode. —And we're not scientists, but we're pretty willing to guess that at that point life on Earth will cease to exist. This, of course, doesn't mean that all life everywhere will cease to exist, but when the Earth is enveloped in the unimaginably hot plasma of the sun's supernova, life on Earth will disappear—along with the Earth itself!

Life is vulnerable. That's one of the terrifying realizations of science, and we think it's part of why we often want to reject scientific thought. Before it became predominant, humans were pretty comfortable with the idea that we were the center of the universe and pretty comfortable with the idea that everything revolved around us. In other words, we believed that we were special, and that we mattered. But science really challenges that idea.

We tend to think that science makes us arrogant. It seems that Crichton certainly thinks so; he paints a picture of science where corporate jerks and blind scientists run amok, resurrecting the dead in all kinds of really suicidal ways. But this is a pretty terrible picture of scientists. Scientists are actually generally really careful, and spend their whole lifetimes focusing on developing one hypothesis to the best of their abilities.

Rather than making us arrogant, science actually humbles us. Unlike previous pictures of the world where humans beings are basically beamed down from heaven, placed in charge of all of the "inferior" animals, and are the center of the universe, science paints a picture in which we owe our ancestry to the same muck and mire inhabited by the simplest bacteria, are closely related to apes, and are clinging by our fingernails to a small and unimportant rock whizzing around the sun at nineteen miles per second. So, we think Crichton is pretty wrong here, as is Dr. Malcolm. Science isn't what lets us play God. It's what reminds us that we *are not* gods and that we are just another part of creation—a very vulnerable part of creation.

So we realize that if (as science teaches us) we aren't really all that special in the universe, then we could suffer the same fate as everything else in it. In other words, just like a whole lot of other species who've kicked the bucket, we may, maybe even through no fault of our own, find ourselves also very, very dead. The Permian extinction took out ninety percent of life on the planet. And with regularity we hear about some just-discovered meteor that is about to whiz past us. Why aren't we busy building a super-sophisticated anti-meteor program around the globe? We're glad to hear that UN talks are *finally* starting on this subject, but we suspect it might be worth our while to hedge our bets by putting Bruce Willis out there with a hammer, or some dynamite, or something.

Being Eaten Sucks

Look, we're not saying that Crichton got it *all* wrong. In a lot of ways his book is about how we're very, very vulnerable. While Malcolm is "finding a way," dinosaurs that find humans crunchy and darned easy to catch are picking everyone else off. In fact, isn't Crichton warning us that we could bring about our own extinction through our stupidity? It's bad enough that there is—somewhere out there—a meteor with our name on it, but we seem to be trying pretty hard to do ourselves in.

Humans are very short-sighted. We've forgotten that being eaten *sucks*. Maybe that's what Crichton was trying to get at:

that we have become so comfortable in the world that we've created with science that we have forgotten what it was like to be hiding in the tall grass while something large, toothy, and hungry hunts us down. The fact is, though (as Crichton reminds us), we're still quite edible.

But that idea isn't contrary to science; it's *proclaimed by science*! Many people avoid this fear because they have a belief in a soul. Now, the idea of a soul is pretty unscientific. —That isn't to say that the soul doesn't exist, but that it isn't something that science has a whole lot of evidence for. Isn't a soul really a kind of "being eaten insurance?" Wouldn't having a soul basically make dying not so bad, because after you die you still get some sort of existence somewhere else?

Science flies in the face of that way of thinking. Our realizations through our investigations of the world grab us, shake us, and scream, "Seriously! You are really fragile . . . cancer, heart disease, velociraptors! There are, like, a zillion things that could kill you, just in your neighborhood!" Science is our way of acknowledging—rather than ignoring—danger, and then, trying to confront that danger.

Why Being in the Restroom when *T. rex* Eats You Is a Good Idea

Okay, so let's look at it like this. Maybe Crichton's criticism of science is that it makes us think we have control. And that's why we keep coming back to the "god" analogy. We gain so much unearned personal power through science that we forget we don't have the control we think we do. So we become arrogant, and then start doing stupid stuff.

Fine, but is a rejection of science really going to change human arrogance? Let's think about someone like Jean-Jacques Rousseau. This guy was pretty anti-Enlightenment; he thought that the whole push towards science was a bad idea, moving us away from the natural world and our place in it. He thought we should go back to nature, accept our place in it, and be happy.

Honestly, we see absolutely no reason to believe that giving up science-mindedness would suddenly make us *more* humble. For example, there are plenty of people who believe that their ability to pray gives them some control of the world. They believe, without a doubt, that because they have the right connection to God, they have nothing to worry about. Suicide bombers have to be pretty sure that they chose the right god, the right belief, and the right ideology to blow themselves up to kill other people. We—as a species—are very good at misusing all sorts of ideas in order to defend our own arrogance.

Sure, science can be something that some nuts allow to go to their heads, but it's actually pretty hard to perpetrate those atrocities when our discoveries keep reminding us how small and un-special we are. To a *T. rex,* we're just another tasty treat. And in the history of the Earth, we're just a blip on the map.

Which is really the more arrogant perspective: the idea that Earth is 13.72 billion years old, and we have barely been around for any of it, or the idea that Earth was created in six days and we were the final and grandest creation? The fact is, you don't see a whole lot of people going to war over their belief in something scientific, because science *always allows for the possibility that we're wrong.* Science isn't what we should fear.

You see, Hammond was a *very bad* scientist. He was so sure that he couldn't be wrong that his actions verged on the extreme beliefs of a suicide bomber. He had no doubt that his plan would work, and in fact, he was so sure that he was willing to test the thing out on his grandkids. Not many scientists would do that. (Can you imagine it? "Come here Suzie, this cure for cancer totally works; we haven't tested it yet, but what could go wrong?")

What Is a *T. rex?*

Science isn't a thing that we need to be careful of; it's a way of viewing the world. Think of a *T. rex,* for example. There are a few ways we could view Hammond's creation:

1. an atrocious monster that is a spit in the eye of God,

2. a grand achievement of human intellect over nature, or

3. a dangerous animal that we barely understand and want to study very carefully in order to avoid being eaten by it.

The third option is pretty clearly the most scientific one. In fact, scientists are pretty brave, though not full of bravado. They would not run away from the *T. rex*—nor would they act like they *know* they can control it; they would seek to understand it so they could better live with it.

What really bothers us most is the knowledge that people treat science like it takes all of the wonder out of the world. The going rationale is, "Well, if you can create a *T. rex*, haven't you taken the *magic* out of it?" When we learn that Santa isn't real, the Easter Bunny is a sham, and the Tooth Fairy is just a con, we learn that scientific reality just destroys dreams and hopes. Humans want to believe that the world is magical, amazing, and if we just wish hard enough, maybe we could make something miraculous happen. Damn science. It takes all of that away. No magic, no fun, no fantasy. Just blunt, hungry reality, constantly trying to eat us. Shouldn't we, like Rousseau, reject science so that we can return to a wonder of nature, and the universe? Wouldn't that be true humility?

No. The idea that the universe is more wonderful when it matches our fantasies is true arrogance. Scientific inquiry forces us to try to understand the world, rather than try to make it match our dreams and hopes. That's why it's so powerful! If we really learn it, we learn how to manipulate the actual world, and not just our imaginations.

—And as for wonder, scientists like Neil deGrasse Tyson, Stephen Hawking, and Albert Einstein would be horrified to hear someone suggest that science kills wonder. Whether made by God, or some random unexplained event, the universe is amazing . . . even without Santa! As Einstein said, "The most beautiful thing we can experience is the mysterious. It is the source of all true art and all science."

When we really reflect on the world and our place in it, how can we not be in wonder of it? We are compilations of trillions of atoms that are constantly being lost and exchanged for new ones. We're part of a galaxy that is moving at about 185 miles *per second,* and we can't even feel it. The sun is so large that even at 93 million miles away, we can see it. And we can feel its heat even though at 185,000 miles per second, its light takes eight minutes to reach us. Take time to study a leaf—to really *study* a leaf: understand how it turns light into usable energy, and then uses that light/energy to create flowers that make *more plants. The universe is wondrous!*

Carl Sagan made a point that we think is actually very, very humbling. He realized that if we are made up of "star stuff," then there's no difference between us and the rest of the universe. Stars and dinosaurs are made up of protons, neutrons, and electrons and *so are you.* In other words, we're arrangements of *stuff* that can think and feel! Sure, we could just shrug our shoulders and say, "Oh, well, that's 'cause I have a soul." Or we could realize the tremendous fact that we are just lucky arrangements of matter in the universe that *realize they are the universe!*

Which do you think is the more humble thought? On the one hand, you have the idea that you're separate and distinct from nature because you have a special something that nothing else does, and on the other, you're just the universe becoming conscious of itself for a brief instant before a *T. rex* eats you. The more humble thought may also be the more wondrous.

Don't Burn Crichton's Book . . . or This One!

When we say all of this, we don't mean that Crichton is wrong or that we shouldn't be humble before the divine; we just lament that he only gave us half the story. Where are all of the scientists who would be working to fix what Hammond and his team did so horribly wrong? All we get to see, for the most part, are scientists who are overwhelmed by corporate greed. The few other scientists who are "good" detach themselves from the park and its creations. But that really isn't how it would work, even in Crichton's narrative.

Think about all of the scientists who would be working day and night to protect us from those dinosaurs. Think about the botanists working to use those plants to find cures for diseases that couldn't be cured before. Think about the zoologists who would be studying the animals to understand aging, genetics, and physiology, which would also help us in thousands of different unpredictable ways. There would be scientists who would be working to figure out (somewhat sadly) how to kill those dinosaurs in case the hypothetical threat they pose were ever to be realized. And think about the scientists who would be working hard to figure out a way for us and the dinosaurs to live together in peace.

So, really, the message we should take away from *Jurassic Park* isn't that we should be afraid of science. Nor is it that we should just do whatever we want with the power we gain from it. Maybe the lesson is that life is fragile, *we* are fragile, and science is the shield and the sword we use to help ourselves survive in a very hostile but beautiful world.

Whether we choose to use those tools to do harm is entirely up to us; in the end, if we do something stupid because we're arrogant or greedy, let's not blame science . . . because it was science that was whispering in our ears, "You really aren't that special. Be careful! There's a very, *very* big world out there, and almost everything in it could kill you."

2

Let the Raptors Run!

GREG LITTMANN

You get your first look at the six-foot velociraptor as you enter a clearing. He moves like a bird, lightly, bobbing his head. You stare at him, and he just stares right back. And that's when the attack comes. Not from the front, but from the side—human beings selling merchandise. Want a velociraptor hat? A bucket of edmontosaurus meat to toss to the tyrannosaurus? Or perhaps you would like to make a donation to save the giant orthocone? That's a thirty-foot squid that became extinct millions of years before the first dinosaur appeared, and you can't get more endangered than that. . . .

What would you give to see a velociraptor eye to eye, separated by the bars of a steel fence, but close enough to make out the saliva on its serrated teeth as it sizes you up as a meal? What about the chance to see a wooly mammoth stamping the ground, and to hear it trumpet its defiant return to the Earth? The movie *Jurassic Park* and its sequels may be science fiction, but biologists are already planning to revive extinct species and are steadily improving their ability to do so. The red-breasted passenger pigeon, the Pyrenean ibex, and even the gigantic wooly mammoth that once sent our spear-wielding ancestors screaming in terror are just a few of the species being targeted for new life, a process often known as "de-extinction."

Dinosaur DNA has long ago decayed past the point from which we can recover it, so we can't just drain a mosquito preserved in amber and clone some tyrannosauruses to thrill the kids. Still, potentially being able to resurrect species from the past few tens of thousands of years is an extraordinary prospect, and advances in genetic engineering may one day allow us to recreate more ancient species yet, even if we have to redesign them gene by gene.

Just like Hammond's geneticists in *Jurassic Park* filling in the gaps in dino genetic code with frog DNA, real scientists are likewise attempting to artificially fill in missing pieces of DNA in order to recover species that have not left behind a complete genome. Geneticist George Church of Harvard University suggests recreating the passenger pigeon genome by splicing manufactured genes that replicate fragments of passenger pigeon DNA into the genome of a rock pigeon. It can only be a matter of time before geneticists explore replicating species as best they can without using any of that species's original DNA. It may be debatable whether a tyrannosaurus designed from scratch by geneticists without any original dinosaur DNA qualifies as a real tyrannosaurus, but that, too, may one day be in the cards.

So we stand ready to reintroduce extinct species and might even one day be able to construct reservations for the animals of prehistory, like Jurassic Park. Of course, the fact that scientists have learned *how* to do something doesn't automatically mean that it *ought* to be done (we could put on history's greatest fireworks show by detonating all the nukes at once, but let's not).

Should We Raise the Dead?

You did it. You crazy son of a bitch, you did it.

—Dr. Ian Malcolm

Why might we want to revive extinct species? The most obvious reasons are much the same as for why we should want to conserve species that are alive today. One powerful motivation is simply that we *like* to know that other species exist. Throughout recorded history, humans have delighted in nature, and there is a sense of loss, at least for many of us, when a species goes out of the world forever. We want elephants to keep existing because elephants are, to put it bluntly, very, very *cool*.

This motivation for conservation is also a motivation for the reintroduction of lost species. If the elephant is cool, then so is the mammoth, and so are the other vanished species of history and prehistory. The meteor strike and other global catastrophes of 65 million years ago that wiped out the dinosaurs allowed for the evolution of large mammals like us, but it was in some ways a terrible tragedy. Magnificent animals of the late Cretaceous, like the ferocious tyrannosaurus, the three-horned triceratops, and the mace-tailed ankylosaurus were wiped from the planet. We may be glad that their extinction allowed humanity to evolve, and even glad that they're not free to terrorize us today as they once terrorized our shrew-like ancestors. Still, the awful fact that *there are no tyrannosauruses* makes the universe that much less wonderful, just as the loss of the last elephant would. We can all sympathize with the joy and awe Drs. Alan Grant and Ellie Sattler feel in *Jurassic Park* as they gaze on a vista of towering brachiosaurs striding majestically through the river. As every young child intuitively understands, dinosaurs, too, are *cool*.

In the case of species conservation, people frequently don't just want to know that the species exists; they want to *experience* it, too. For example, people like to see elephants, and they like it even more if they can get within close range, such as at an animal park or zoo. Similarly, in the case of reintroducing extinct species, our motivation may not simply be for the species to exist, as on the isolated dinosaur reservation on the island of Isla, but for the species to be accessible to us. We might even want to build equivalents of Jurassic Park itself, with prehistoric animals on display as we drive by in our cars.

Other motivations for species conservation are more practical. One is that having a wide variety of animal and plant species available for study is incredibly valuable for the advancement of science and technology. Most obviously, every species is a unique resource for biology or botany, and all the fields that stand to benefit from their research. Not only could we learn by the study of the species reintroduced, but also from the process of learning how to produce them. In *Jurassic Park*, Hammond's scientists use frog DNA to fill in gene sequence gaps in their dinosaur DNA, learning more about DNA and how to manipulate it along the way. In the real world, each new experiment with life improves our understanding.

Perhaps the most popular motivation for species conservation is that humans depend on the health of the ecosystem.

The loss of any species that is part of the system threatens the stability of the system itself, and that threatens *us*. For that reason, it would be smart to reintroduce many lost species. Reintroducing the species into their old ecosystems could have a stabilizing effect as they step into the role in the ecosystem that they used to play. Mammoths once helped to keep the steppes of Siberia a grassland instead of an icy tundra, by breaking up and fertilizing the soil. It may well be that reintroducing the mammoths could help to restore the land. Genetic engineering is often condemned as unnatural, but it may be that de-extinction will prove to be an invaluable tool for healing nature of the damage we've done.

Beyond Ecology and into the Theme Park

Dr. Grant, my dear Dr. Sattler, . . . Welcome to Jurassic Park.

—Dr. John Hammond

However, not all de-extinction is likely to help the ecosystem, with the *Jurassic Park* films offering a prime example. Even if we could bring back dinosaurs, as Hammond does, life has changed so much in the last 65 million or more years since these species were around that the ecological roles they once played have long ago been made obsolete. Releasing velociraptors back onto the plains of Mongolia would be a disaster. In the unlikely event that the raptors survived at all in an environment they didn't evolve to live in, the harm that a thriving raptor population would do to established species would be enormous (though it would make picnics *much* more exciting!).

De-extinction without ecological benefit is far more morally controversial than de-extinction with ecological benefit. There are certainly people who sneer at attempts to protect the ecosystem, but almost always, it's because they don't believe that the ecosystem is under threat, not because they don't care if it collapses. Keeping the ecosystem working is essential according to almost every moral theory, since almost every moral theory forbids harming something on which billions of people depend to live. Many people believe that we have moral duties that extend beyond humanity—duties to animal or even plant life—which make protecting the ecosystem even more important.

On the other hand, recreating species purely for human scientific advancement and personal pleasure won't be any sort of benefit to non-humans, a fact which forces us to ask whether there's anything exploitative or otherwise inappropriate about using non-human life in this way. There are clearly cases where treating non-human life as a tool for our benefit is morally okay. Growing corn requires manipulating nature for our own benefit, but doesn't constitute corn abuse. On the other hand, there are also clearly cases in which treating non-human life as a tool for our benefit is wrong. If Hammond had entertained the public by pitting his dinosaurs against each other in combat to the death, it would have been an abuse of his power (and if your sympathies don't extend to a confused stegosaurus being gored by a raging triceratops, consider the immorality of staging fights between dogs or bears or monkeys).

What isn't clear is exactly what distinguishes a morally *acceptable* use of nature from a morally *unacceptable* one. How should we decide whether we're acting morally or not when dealing with non-humans, especially when we bring back lost species to roam the Earth?

Equal Rights for Gigantic Carnivorous Extinct Reptiles Now!

What's so great about discovery? It's a violent, penetrative act that scars what it explores. What you call discovery, I call the rape of the natural world.

—Dr. Ian Malcolm

One straightforward way to extend our moral concerns to other species would be to value all life equally. An influential account along these lines was offered by Norwegian philosopher Arne Naess (1912–2009), who in 1973 drew a distinction between what he identified as the "shallow" and "deep" ecology movements. Naess characterized the shallow ecology movement as being focused on the "fight against pollution and resource depletion" with the central objective of "the health and affluence of people in the developed countries."[1] The deep ecology movement, on the other hand, treats the natural world as having value in itself, apart from any benefits it provides to humans.

In particular, the deep ecology movement recognizes *"the equal right to live and blossom"* of all living organisms. To limit our concerns only to humans is viewed as straightforward discrimination against life that is unlike us. Naess's idea of the deep ecology movement evolved over time, but the notion that all life has a right to live and flourish remains an important value.

It all sounds very egalitarian, but will extending our moral concerns to non-humans in this way help us with the issue of de-extinction? Unfortunately not. We still have no guidance on key questions. Do extinct species, like the tyrannosaurus, have a right to live, and if so, does this give us a moral duty to revive them if we are able? Do our duties to an extinct species depend on whether the species was driven to extinction by human beings—like the Neanderthal, the Dodo, and the Tasmanian Tiger—rather than killed off before humans arrived on the scene, like the dinosaurs? (Malcolm sure thinks that it makes a difference: "This isn't some species that was obliterated by deforestation, or the building of a dam. Dinosaurs had their shot, and nature selected them for extinction," he protests.) Can a *species* even have rights, or can only *individual* organisms have them? If only individual organisms can have rights, then does any consideration of rights help us determine whether to reintroduce extinct species, since no *individual*, specific animal or plant is going to be brought back from the dead? The notion of a universal right to life and flourishing doesn't give us any clear guidance.

Worse yet, in insisting on an "equal right to live and blossom," we are projecting human interests onto nature, even while we attempt to avoid the assumption that human interests are the only ones that matter. Why think that an organism has the right to "live and blossom" rather than, say, a right to "die and wither"? For humans and many other animals, it's because we have a passionate desire for life and what life has to offer. An animal like a lion may not understand what death is; but, given the effort it expends on activities like hunting

---

[1] Arne Naess, "The Shallow and the Deep, Long-range Ecology Movement: A Summary," *Inquiry* 16:1 (1973), p. 95.

food and finding nice places to lie in the sun, there are clearly things that a lion wants that only life provides.

A plant, however, has no desire for anything. Lacking a brain, it also lacks thoughts, feelings, and consciousness. It's easy to interpret the way that a plant responds to its environment as striving to survive—they sink roots into the soil where the water is and sprout leaves that will turn towards the sunlight and soak it up—but the mere fact that something in nature *does* something doesn't mean that it *intended* to do that thing. A raindrop doesn't desire to fall; it just falls in accordance with the laws of physics. Likewise, a plant grows in a way that makes it likely to survive not because it wants to survive, but just because that is how it has evolved to grow.

A Future of Scientific Wonders

We've made living biological attractions so astounding that they'll capture the imagination of the entire planet.

—JOHN HAMMOND

What we need is a theory that acknowledges responsibility to non-human organisms, but doesn't project our attitudes and desires onto them. In my view, the best fundamental approach to environmental ethics doesn't come from recent work but from the beginnings of the animal rights movement in the nineteenth century. The English philosopher John Stuart Mill, in his book *Utilitarianism* (1861), laid out what he thought was the ultimate moral rule. Utilitarianism is the view that "actions are right in proportion as they tend to promote happiness; wrong as they tend to produce the reverse of happiness." Mill recognized that animals are capable of happiness and suffering and saw this as giving us a moral responsibility toward them. Like animal rights advocates today, Mill believed that the law should intervene to prevent animal abuse, arguing that we have the same reason to stop abuse of animals as we have to stop the abuse of children.

Utilitarianism gives us a moral framework that allows us to interact with the natural world in a way that doesn't arbitrarily limit our moral concerns to humans. At the same time, it avoids projecting our preferences onto organisms that have no preferences of their own. Utilitarianism also gives us guidance regarding de-extinction. Utilitarianism recognizes no specific right to life of any organism—not even you. All that matters is that happiness is maximized and suffering kept to a minimum, regardless of who (or what) is experiencing them. Under utilitarianism, it will be morally right to bring a species back from extinction when doing so is likely to produce more happiness than suffering.

Since utilitarianism only values total happiness and not the distribution of happiness between species, it doesn't matter how many species become extinct per se or are brought back from extinction. Having said that, humanity could benefit both scientifically and from the sheer joy of sharing the world with strange and marvelous species from the past.

There will probably still be no benefit to non-humans, since restored species are unlikely to be much *happier* than presently living species. However, using other organisms for our own benefit is acceptable under utilitarianism, provided that the total happiness that results outweighs the total suffering. We must, of course, make sure that if members of a restored species can feel pleasure or suffering, we provide them with the sort of life that's satisfying for them.

A plant has no well-being on this model, since it can't suffer, and so we may treat the plant as we like. A mammoth, on the other hand, would have an ability to suffer and this would give us obligations towards it. A mammoth would likely want to roam around grazing, rather than, say, living in a cage or fighting in an arena, and if we do revive mammoths, we have to respect such desires. Tiny-brained reptiles like the dinosaurs resurrected in the *Jurassic Park* movies may well not be capable of suffering in the ways that a mammoth or humans could suffer, but their mere ability to feel physical pain makes them morally important.

Not only are dinosaur fights out of the question; so is killing them just for the thrill of it—like hunter Roland Tembo from *The Lost World: Jurassic Park*. He views the animals as mere tools to make himself feel alive—as objects to which he owes no moral concern. Justifying his ambition to kill a Tyrannosaurus, he explains simply, "Somewhere on this island is the greatest predator there ever lived. The second greatest predator must take him down." Even Dr. Ellie Sattler falls into the trap of treating the well-being of the animals as irrelevant compared to the well-being of humans. Dismissing Hammond's concerns for the dinosaurs as Jurassic Park collapses into chaos, she insists: "The only thing that matters now are the people we love." If we are to resurrect an extinct animal species, then we must take a more sympathetic attitude. We may use other species for our own benefit, and even bring them back from extinction for our own knowledge and amusement, but only if we remember to be kind.

So there's nothing wrong, in principle, with Hammond's dream of a wildlife park filled with species resurrected from the dead. With biologists already working on the reintroduction of extinct species, decisions about de-extinction without ecological benefit will increasingly need to be made, including, perhaps, whether to permit reserves like Jurassic Park for allowing the public to encounter exotic forms of life from the past. With the recent discovery of liquid blood in a frozen mammoth corpse in Siberia, and with plans already underway by Russian and Korean scientists to attempt cloning it, it may not be long before a Pleistocene Park is up and running, giving a safe and happy home to these refugees from the last ice age. In time, ambitious geneticists may even attempt to follow Hammond in reconstructing more ancient and astonishing species yet.

Of course, unlike Hammond, we'd better make sure that the security system keeps the carnivores firmly on the other side of the fence. To a pack of velociraptors, you are the fattest, juiciest damn tree-shrew they ever saw.

3
The Past in a Petri Dish

DAVID FREEMAN

> DR. ELLIE SATTLER: So, what are you thinking?
> DR. ALAN GRANT: That we're out of a job.
> DR. IAN MALCOLM: Don't you mean extinct?
>
> —*Jurassic Park*

Dr. Alan Grant strolls along the stage, gazing out into the sea of faces in the auditorium. "Dinosaurs lived sixty-five million years ago. What is left of them is fossilized in the rocks and it is in the *rocks* that *real* scientists make *real* discoveries! What John Hammond and InGen did at Jurassic Park is create genetically engineered theme park monsters, nothing more and nothing less." But just eight years earlier, he had dropped to his knees on the grassy plains of Isla Nublar, staring up in astonishment at a living, breathing brachiosaurus munching on a tree branch high above him. What happened?

Aside from the whole getting-chased-by-hungry-dinosaurs thing, which kind of puts a downer on any island vacation, what has caused Grant to change his mind from awe, to contempt? Sure, running out in front of a rampaging *Tyrannosaurus rex* is maybe not the best way of testing the theory about motion-based vision, but this is his life's work we're talking about here! He was so full of questions for game warden Robert Muldoon back on the island, so how come he's suddenly given up even thinking of these animals as dinosaurs brought back from the remote past via the wonders of genetic engineering?

Grant's change of mind is likely because he has come to two realizations:

1. A cloned dinosaur is not *really* a dinosaur

and

2. A cloned dinosaur won't even *act* like a real dinosaur.

Unsolved Mysteries in Paleontology

There are many unanswered questions in paleontology that could be solved if we had any real, live dinosaurs to provide answers for us. Paleontologists have no idea what color dinosaurs were or what texture their skin was and the illustrations you see in books are generally educated guesses, mostly based on living reptiles.

There are two main kinds of evidence paleontologists use in piecing together what dinosaurs looked like: body fossils (fossilized bones and teeth) and trace fossils (indirect evidence of dinosaur activity, like fossilized tracks in the mud). They can generalize what dinosaur behavior might have been like, using comparisons from living animals and examining dinosaur diet from evidence like coprolites (fossilized dino poop). But most available evidence is very incomplete and paleontologists come to their conclusions largely through careful deduction—in other words, educated guesswork.

So why go to a museum to look at bones or dig up fossils in the deserts of Montana when you can just go to Costa Rica and see the real thing in the flesh? At first glance, Jurassic Park would provide a wonderful opportunity for paleontologists to fill the gaps in the fossil record—but, as Grant eventually realizes, the only gaps cloned dinosaurs are going to fill are the ones in their stomachs.

Chickenosauruses and the Dino Double Helix

Let's start at the top and ask what it actually means for something to be a dinosaur. Technically speaking, birds are dinosaurs. The "official" scientific definition of a dinosaur is any animal that is a descendant of the most recent common ancestor of *Megalosaurus* and *Iguanodon*. The only group of animals still alive today in that family tree just so happens to consist of blue jays, emus, penguins, and chickens, among thousands of other species.

Birds are avian dinosaurs. But this isn't really what we mean when we think of dinosaurs. We mean a group of non-avian dinosaurs that come from a much earlier part of the same family tree. They were (mostly, but not always) enormous and lived anywhere between 65 and 230 million years ago.

So, part of what it means to be a dinosaur is to be extinct—but since there are still dinosaurs alive today, it's not a deal breaker for a dinosaur to be alive today. What we're looking for is a way to combine the two definitions so that we can have a non-avian dinosaur of the kind we are thinking about when we typically talk about dinosaurs, but one whose definition does not include being dead for millions of years. Either way, it should *look* like a *T. rex*, or a raptor, or a brachiosaurus, or one of the other kinds of animals that we mean when we talk about dinosaurs.

In his book *How to Build a Dinosaur*, famed paleontologist (and adviser on the *Jurassic Park* movies) Jack Horner looks at a real-life *Jurassic Park* type of scenario being played out by Canadian paleontologist Hans Larsson at McGill University.[1] Larsson is using the techniques of molecular biology to try to build a dinosaur out of a chicken embryo.

While it sounds a bit fantastic, the basic idea behind it is surprisingly simple. After all, a chicken is technically a dinosaur anyway. It's not quite the same thing as what we're thinking of in our revised definition of what it is to be a dinosaur, but a chicken is at least descended from the extinct variety of dinosaurs and carries some of the same genes that extinct dinosaurs had. The tricky part is figuring out how a chicken develops chicken characteristics and how to turn on different genes to make it develop dinosaur characteristics instead.

In theory, it's possible—and a lot easier than trying to find dino DNA in amber. But even Horner thinks that a successful "chickenosaurus" would not actually be turning a chicken into a dinosaur. It would just be growing a chicken that looks more like

---

[1] Jack Horner and James Gorman, *How to Build a Dinosaur* (New York: Plume, 2010).

one of its ancestors. I am descended from my grandparents and carry many of their genes, but having my grandpa's eyes or nose does not make me my grandpa. For me to be my grandpa, or a chicken to be a non-avian dinosaur, we need to have a genetic similarity to our ancestors that goes far beyond just sharing certain similar features. We need to have the right DNA.

Imagine you're a Jurassic Park scientist working on a sample of real, complete *T. rex* DNA. You decide to tinker with the DNA to help you figure out how to patch up the gaps in the DNA of the other species you have available. You alter just a single strand of DNA and grow it to see what happens—is the new baby still a *T. rex*? Well, it sure looks like a *T. rex* and it still wants to eat you. Minor mutations happen to DNA all the time, so surely changing one strand wouldn't create a whole new species. And if one strand doesn't make a difference, changing a second strand shouldn't matter either. Or three, or fifty, or a hundred. But at some point you must change enough DNA to turn the *T. rex* into something else.

Alter just a percent or two of our DNA and you wind up with a chimpanzee instead. Alter 40 percent of it and you get a fruit fly! (Jeff Goldblum already learned that lesson long before he was chased by raptors. . . .) So, when do we decide whether we've got a new species or not? The species problem presents a lot of difficulties for biologists. They need to classify very similar animals as being one species or another so they know what label to slap on the sample. If this is tricky when you have a whole, living animal, then imagine how hard it is when all you have is a fossilized tooth and a few broken limb bones.

This is the problem with Jurassic Park dinosaurs. We don't have a complete sample of dino DNA so it is necessary for InGen's genetic engineers to fill the sequence gaps with DNA from living animals (in the movies they use frog DNA, but in the book it's a combination of amphibian, reptilian, and avian DNA). They are behaving as though they're just replacing a bit of missing DNA with the same stuff from another creature. But the problem is that differences in DNA *do* matter. DNA contains loads of complex instructions for forming certain parts of a living animal. Jurassic Park dinosaurs are genetically different from their extinct predecessors and we have absolutely no way of knowing just *how* different. But I think we can pretty confidently say that extinct dinosaurs did *not* have modern frog DNA inside them!

The genetic differences may be very minor—but they might also be very dramatic. And without a specimen of the original species, we can't know for sure if our genetically modified dinosaur is anything like the real thing. So visiting Jurassic Park isn't really going to tell you any more about what color dinosaurs were or what a *Tyrannosaurus* roar sounded like than the imaginative deductions of museum curators in building animatronic models for display (plus you won't have to pay $2,000 a day to visit a museum and the animatronic displays can't eat you).

This is obvious to geneticist Dr. Henry Wu in an exchange he has with John Hammond in the *Jurassic Park* novel. Wu is contemplating the idea of engineering further batches of dinosaurs to be more docile to fit with the public's expectations of how dinosaurs move. He thinks they move too fast to seem "real" to visitors:

> "Why not push ahead to make exactly the kind of dinosaur that we'd like to see? One that is more acceptable to visitors, and one that is easier for us to handle? A slower, more docile version for our park?"
>
> Hammond frowned. "But then the dinosaurs wouldn't be real."
>
> "But they're not real now," Wu said. "That's what I'm trying to tell you. There isn't any reality here." (Michael Crichton, *Jurassic Park*, Ballantine, 1990, p. 122)

As Wu tells Hammond, "I don't think we should kid ourselves. We haven't *re-created* the past here. The past is gone. It can never be re-created. What we've done is *reconstruct* the past—or at least a version of the past" (p. 122). Jurassic Park dinosaurs are a version of the past and without an example of the original we can never know how accurate our version really is.

They Do Move in Herds . . .

Alright, so maybe we need to revise our definition of a dinosaur again. Maybe a dinosaur doesn't need to be genetically *identical* to the extinct version, as long as it at least acts the same way the dead ones would have. If it runs and growls like a dinosaur, it's a dinosaur. If it tries to bite your legs off too, it's a *carnivorous* dinosaur. The paleontologists in the books and movies have a series of "Aha!" moments every time a dinosaur does something that validates or contradicts an academic theory about its behavior (you could base a drinking game on this).

But there's a problem with this. Not only are we creating dinosaurs out of a random mishmash of DNA belonging to all kinds of different animals, we're throwing them into a totally different ecosystem. Dinosaurs don't belong in our world—they belong to a world that is long gone. Our world is populated by a whole range of different animals, insects, plants, and bacteria that evolved long after dinosaurs made their exit. While the movie hints at West Indian lilac being responsible for the sick triceratops, the novel confirms that the dinosaurs have been eating the poisonous berries. In the *Lost World* novel, disease caused by contaminated food will ultimately kill all the dinosaurs.

The Jurassic Park dinosaurs simply aren't equipped to cope with a modern ecosystem. It runs the other way as well—we can't truly create a suitable environment for the dinosaurs to live in without re-creating the extinct insects and bacteria that lived alongside them millions of years ago. The whole reason given in the book for creating so many compys was to clean up after the larger dinosaurs—it turned out the bacteria that broke up dino droppings was long extinct so the park was filling up with enormous mounds of poop, which the compys will apparently happily eat in the absence of any ancient bacteria to do the job. And while all the grassy plains might provide a spectacular backdrop for dinosaur-watching, real dinosaurs never saw grass—they died out before it even evolved!

Okay, so maybe it will take the dinosaurs some time to adjust to the environment but ultimately they spend all their time with other dinosaurs, not with modern animals. Sooner or later, social structures will be formed and old rivalries reignited just like old times, right? Except that many of the dinosaurs have never seen each other before either—some of the species on the island come from wildly different times and places. *T. rex* may have met his ultimate match in spinosaurus but in reality the two dinosaurs lived on the other side of the world from each other—and 30 million years apart! Almost 100 million years separates *T. rex* and stegosaurus, which is nearly twice the distance in time between *T. rex* and us!

Even the social structures within species might turn out to operate totally differently in the park than they did in the past. In *The Lost World* novel, the raptors don't even care for their young because they don't know how, having been raised in isolation without a pre-existing social structure to guide their development. There are no infants in the raptor nest and the few juvenile raptors are already battle-scarred and starving, fighting each other for scraps of food in their pig-sty of a nest, surrounded by carcasses and smashed eggshells. Malcolm muses on their fate in one of his frequent morphine-induced monologs:

> Millions of years ago, in the now-vanished Cretaceous world, their behavior would have been socially determined, passed on from older to younger animals. . . . But on this island, the velociraptors had been re-created in a genetics laboratory. . . . These newly created raptors came into the world with no older animals to guide them, to show them proper raptor behavior. They were on their own and that was just how they behaved. (Michael Crichton, *The Lost World*, Arrow, 1995, pp. 361–62)

Beyond this, there's one more thing that can alter the dinosaurs' behavior—the presence of people on the two islands. Outside of the Creation Museum in Kentucky, dinosaurs and humans have never co-existed. As much as Sarah wants to keep the human impact on Site B as minimal as possible, Malcolm reminds her that's a "scientific impossibility" because of Heisenberg's Uncertainty Principle—"what you study, you also change." By trying to observe and document the behavior of the dinosaurs, paleontologists would inadvertently affect the responses of the creatures. We are utterly unlike anything they've ever seen before and so are our cars and modern equipment. Dieter Stark learns this the hard way in the *Lost World* movie—amazed and unsettled that the compys don't fear people, he callously gives them something to fear—only to find out later what their response to fear actually is when they doggedly hunt him down for lunch.

Even Wu had never paid much attention to the behavior of the dinosaurs when he engineered them. He was more interested in the predictable things that he could control: proteins and enzymes. But deep down something bothers him about the dinosaurs: "He was never sure, not really sure at all, whether the behavior of the animals was historically accurate or not. Were they really behaving as they had in the past? It was an open question, ultimately unanswerable" (*Jurassic Park*, p. 334).

You Do Plan to Have Dinosaurs on Your Dinosaur Tour, Right?

So what are we to make of all of this? We have some genetically engineered animals that are clones of dinosaurs—kind of—and may or may not behave anything like the dead ones buried in the sand used to. They also may or may not actually be able to cope with the world we've brought them into. If Jurassic Park actually existed, it's probable that paleontologists *could* learn some things about real dinosaurs from genetically engineered ones but it's not the same as studying a real dinosaur. They would be studying a genetically modified animal interacting with an entirely different ecosystem in an artificial environment that doesn't belong to them, millions of years in the future. Theme park monsters. Not real scientific research any more than you learning about the dietary habits of sharks by taking the Jaws ride at Universal Studios.

A dinosaur theme park might provide tantalizing clues and even valuable insights to the field of paleontology, but this knowledge is still incomplete, just like the fossils buried beneath the rocks. We may be able to reconstruct something *like* the past in a petri dish, but to recover true history, we'll need a time machine, and that's altogether a different movie.

4
Runaway Memes

Brendan Shea

Things go horribly wrong in Jurassic Park. It's no wonder that the few surviving characters decide that John Hammond's plan was a bad idea, as being hunted and eaten by a pack of out-of-control raptors would not make most people's list of "things I'd like to do over my summer vacation."

What *exactly* was wrong with Hammond's planned theme park, though? And what can we learn from his mistake (well, other than *Don't invite your grandchildren to a monster filled island!*)? After all, while the prospect of a resurrected *Tyrannosaurus rex* still seems a bit "out there," most of us (as voters, shareholders, or simply as concerned citizens) have to make tough decisions about the risks and benefits of less exciting but just as deadly sorts of biomedical research.

Right now, we're all making decisions about genetically modified organisms (GMOs), cloned animals, and gene-based therapies. It's certainly tempting to say something like, "What Hammond did was unnatural," or "Hammond was playing God." But these vague statements, even if accurate, don't tell us much about what distinguishes Hammond's monster-filled theme park from the "good" sorts of genetic research that have helped to increase food production, treat diseases, and to generally help humans lead happier, healthier lives.

Here's the deal. The disaster at Jurassic Park was due, at least in part, to Hammond's failure to follow some simple rules of thumb dealing with humans and evolution. The fact is that we need some rules, and we'll need to follow them now because we're working to bring back extinct animals and create new animals right *now*. Should we pursue research on bringing back passenger pigeons? Neanderthals? Wooly mammoths? What about infectious viruses and bacteria? And if we *do* pursue this research, *who* should we allow to do it, and *how* should we regulate it? These are the kind of questions you don't want to be asking yourself as you look in your side-view mirror into the gaping mouth of an angry *T. rex*.

How Tough Can It Be?

Everything about this park is meant to be isolated. Nothing gets in, nothing out. The animals kept here are never to mix with the greater ecosystems of Earth. They are never to escape.

—IAN MALCOLM[1]

As Malcolm and the other visitors quickly realize, InGen's creation of Jurassic Park is a *hugely* ambitious undertaking. To start with, there's the resurrection of the dinosaurs: Each dinosaur's genetic code might contain tens of thousands of genes, or chunks of DNA that serve as a recipe for manufacturing proteins. Those proteins contain *billions* of individual chemical molecules. The process of turning these genetic codes into dinosaur embryos is just as tough, since they have to find cells that "know" how to turn dinosaur DNA into dinosaur embryos. And I'm betting that the process of growing and incubating eggs takes a complex mixture of hormones and nutrients.

But wait! There's more! From here, things don't get any easier, as InGen must make sure that Jurassic Park is an adequate *environment* for the young dinosaurs. Along with controlling for things like climate, this means that each species must be placed with the right mix of *other* species of dinosaurs, plants, insects, and bacteria, and so on (and notice they don't do a great job of *that*). Since many of the species that the dinosaurs originally lived with are also extinct, this will require either finding suitable modern replacements (which may be difficult or impossible) or bringing back the extinct species. This also leads to the problem Malcolm notes—*isolating* Jurassic Park from all the plants, animals, bacteria, and insects of the outside world.

---

[1] Michael Crichton, *Jurassic Park* (Random House, 2012), p. 101.

This is all crazy complex, and so I think Hammond's team, however smart, was destined to screw up somehow. There's too much room for a mistake, and the overwhelming odds are that this mistake will have bad consequences: the genetic codes will be meaningless gibberish, the embryos won't grow, or the park environment will simply self-destruct (and it sure does, doesn't it?). As Malcolm states elsewhere, complex ecosystems seem to be *inherently* unpredictable, at least for mere humans. This sort of unpredictability doesn't necessarily mean that we should never build these systems, but we need to be much more careful and thoughtful about it than Hammond and InGen.

Not-So-Special Creation

LEVINE: God is in the details.
IAN MALCOLM: Maybe your God. . . . Not mine. Mine is in the process.

Until a few hundred years ago, almost everyone, even the philosophers, believed that the first members of each species had been individually created by a super-powerful, super-knowledgeable creator. There seemed to be good evidence for this because living beings are *vastly* complex systems, and the environments in which they move and interact are even *more* complex. To most educated people, it simply seemed obvious that systems of this complexity must have been *designed* by a supremely powerful, exceptionally intelligent being—God. According to these thinkers, our world is essentially a much larger (and much more competently designed!) version of Jurassic Park, with each species tailor-made to flourish in its environment niche. A version of this "argument from design" was even defended by Richard Owen (1804–1892), the British biologist and paleontologist who coined the term "dinosaur" to describe the fossils he uncovered.

This sort of thinking is powerfully criticized by David Hume (1711–1776). He creates a character, Cleanthes, who compares the world to a finely tuned, highly complex "machine" that seems like (though far exceeds) the sorts of machines that are designed and built by humans.[2] Cleanthes concludes that our world (and all things that live in it) was itself designed by an

---

[2] *Dialogues Concerning Natural Religion* (Penguin, 1990), part 2.

intelligent creator. Unfortunately for Cleanthes and Owen, there are severe problems with this argument—the world of intelligent design is like Hammond's dream of Jurassic Park, but the *real* world is a lot nastier, more like Malcolm's chaos.

Hume created another character to address those problems, Philo. Philo argues that, even if we *assume* that the world was designed, there isn't much reason to believe that the creator was anything like the all-perfect Judeo-Christian-Islamic God. After all, while the world has lots of pretty neat stuff in it (like we might think about Jurassic Park) it also had a lot of awful things in it, including huge amounts of needless death and suffering. (In real life, unlike in Jurassic Park, the innocent kids often don't survive.)

All this, says Philo, gives us reason to believe that, if the world *was* designed, the designers were probably a *group* of relatively ignorant (or perhaps even malicious) beings. Basically, when you look at Jurassic Park, you don't just think "intelligent designer." You think, "intelligent designer who really *really* screwed up!" When we look at the world, if it was made by an intelligent designer, it's hard to believe it was a well-thought-out design with all the volcanos, tsunamis, and mass death and whatnot.

Where Did the Dinosaurs Come From?

The history of evolution is that life escapes all barriers. Life breaks free. Life expands to new territories. Painfully, perhaps even dangerously. But life finds a way.

—Ian Malcolm

Around the same time that Richard Owen was discovering and classifying the first species of dinosaurs, Charles Darwin was hard at work formulating his Theory of Evolution by Natural Selection. Darwin's *Origin of Species* proposed two new ideas. The first idea ("evolution") was that the first members of each species were *not* created by an individual act of creation. Instead, all living creatures were descended from a common ancestor. This means, among other things, that dinosaurs are our distant cousins. While this idea was controversial, many biologists of the day (including Owen) had suspected that something like this might be the case.

Darwin's far more controversial idea concerned the main *reason* that evolution was happening, which he called "Natural Selection." According to Darwin, Natural Selection occurred whenever there was a *variation* among traits, some traits promoted *fitness* betterness than others, and the traits could be *inherited*.

For an example of how evolution by natural selection works, let's consider the raptors living in Jurassic Park. While they all start as genetically identical "clones," difference arises slowly from genetic mutation and then (once male raptors appear) rapidly from sexual reproduction. These genetic differences lead to differences in height, weight, speed, intelligence, and a thousand other less visible traits. The raptors' environment (Jurassic Park) makes it so that some of these are *advantageous*, while others are not. For example, if the park raptors' primary food source ended up being human children, small, fast raptors may be more likely to survive and reproduce than larger, slower raptors. Finally, these traits are inherited—the small raptors will, on average, have small offspring.

As Ian Malcolm argues, complex processes such as evolution by natural selection often cannot be accurately *predicted*. But, we can be confident that "life will find a way"—given enough time (sometimes billions of years), evolution will stumble upon a solution to the challenges posed by a particular environment. In the case of the dinosaurs living in Jurassic Park, this happens with terrifying speed, with males quickly appearing in an all-female population and the young raptors sneaking onto the mainland. And, of course, there's no guarantee that evolution will make things "better" or "more advanced"—if things had gone terribly wrong on Jurassic Park, it may have ended up that relatively intelligent humans were wiped out by stupid dinosaurs. Evolution is not "trying" to get anywhere in particular, and the vast, vast majority of species that have ever existed have eventually gone extinct.

This brings us to our first rule of thumb that John Hammond violates: *Don't assume that evolution "wants" humans to survive.* As we've seen, evolution doesn't care whether humans survive conflicts with other species, whether these are naturally occurring bacteria or genetically designed dinosaurs. With this in mind, humans ought to aggressively continue to develop and apply new scientific theories to solve problems as they arise. In some cases, these new solutions might involve the creation of new species (either directly by genetic engineering or indirectly by affecting which organisms reproduce). When doing this, however, we can't assume (as Hammond does) that humans can *control* these new species, or that the overall effect will be beneficial for humans.

Where Did You Get That Idea?

. . . the Earth would survive our folly. Life would survive our folly. Only we think it wouldn't.

—Ian Malcolm

Darwin knew that variability and inheritance happened, but he didn't know *why*. This question was partially answered by the Austrian monk Gregor Mendel (1822–1884), who discovered that there were *units* of biological inheritance that controlled traits like "being tall" or "being short." We now know that these "genes" are made out of the chemical compound DNA. This provides a new way of looking at evolution by natural selection: instead of thinking about populations of *organisms* competing to survive and reproduce, we can think about populations of *genes* competing in the same way.

This change of perspective helps answer some evolutionary puzzles. For example, many organisms (including humans and dinosaurs) are willing to sacrifice their *own* lives to save the lives of their children. This sort of "instinctive altruism" might seem to be contrary to evolution to natural selection—after all, how can the desire to sacrifice my own life increase my "fitness"? Once we shift to the gene's-eye view, though, the answer is easy. We simply note that children probably contain copies of the many of the same genes that the parents have, and that the parent's genes "want" the child to survive.

Somewhat surprisingly, this same idea can help us answer an important question about Jurassic Park: "Why do humans often pursue such obviously bad ideas such as the construction of a theme park filled with packs of human-eating raptors?" The answer, it turns out, involves *memes*.

So what are "memes"? Just as a *gene* can be defined as a "unit of biological inheritance," a *meme* is a "unit of cultural inheritance." Basically, a meme is any idea or activity that can be copied from one human mind to another. So, for example, the characters in *Jurassic Park* are carriers for countless memes, including computer programming, paleontology, evolutionary biology, chaos theory, genetic engineering, theme parks, baseball, and capitalism. Over the course of the story, we see the characters "infect" one another with the memes—Dr. Grant teaches the children memes related to surviving in a crisis situation, Malcolm helps spread the chaos theory meme, and Hammond tries (and fails) to spread the meme of a dinosaur-themed amusement park.

Just as genes can help us explain why dinosaurs will die for their children, memes can help explain why Hammond and InGen create Jurassic Park. Instead of asking, "How does the construction of something like Jurassic Park benefit humanity?"—after all, it clearly doesn't!—we can ask, "What features of the dinosaur-theme-park meme allowed it to infect the minds of the InGen investors?"

The answer to *this* question probably includes factors such as the promise of profit, the desire for fame, and the urge to do something important. Biological evolution has "built" human minds to desire these sorts of things (since, in the past, these sorts of desires helped our ancestors to survive and reproduce), but they can also be taken advantage of by dangerous memes such as Jurassic Park.

Jurassic Park, then, is a product of both genetic evolution and memetic evolution. Biological evolution produced the *original* blueprint for dinosaurs, as well as the human minds that created the park. Memetic evolution, by contrast, produced the *scientific theories, cultural values,* and *technological skills* that "infected" the minds of the creators. And both sorts of evolution continue throughout the events described in *Jurassic Park*, as the park's environment "selects" against various genes (such as those carried by the dinosaurs and humans who die) and memes (such as the ideas carried by John Hammond at the time of his death).

We've now arrived at a second rule of thumb that Hammond breaks: *Don't assume that more complex means better adapted.* While evolution predicts that relatively complex organisms like humans or dinosaurs must have had simpler creatures as their distant ancestors (and complex *memes* like calculus must have been preceded by simpler memes like algebra), it does *not* follow that more complex creatures or ideas are "better" or "more evolved" than their simpler competitors. For example, the fact that Jurassic Park was a more complex meme than Disney World does *not* mean that it was a better one. Similarly, the fact that dinosaurs are "simpler" than humans doesn't mean that evolution will make sure that humans win.

The Evolution of Jurassic Park

We have been residents here for the blink of an eye. If we are gone tomorrow, the Earth will not miss us.

—Ian Malcolm

In the beginning, biological evolution produced organisms that served as carriers for various genes. Along the way, it produced at least one sort of thing (human brains) that could *also* serve as carriers for memes. This started a new branch of the evolutionary process which led to, among other things, the development of language, science, art, and (eventually) the sort of genetic engineering that led to Jurassic Park. All along, though, it was the memes and genes that were doing the *real* work, with us humans serving as unwitting carriers. In an important sense, Jurassic Park is *itself* a product of evolution, just like humans and dinosaurs.

This brings us to our final rule of thumb: *Never underestimate the power of evolution by natural selection.* While the InGen scientists are brilliant, they're limited in the way that all humans are limited—they have short life spans, limited information, and prejudiced thinking that prevent them from seeing "the whole picture." The evolutionary process, by contrast, has none of these limitations. It has *billions* of years to solve problems, and it can operate on the sorts of traits that are "invisible" to humans. Finally, its method of *randomly* generating "solutions" ensures that it is immune to the sorts of biases that plague humans. And while the evolutionary process often operates over long time periods, it can also operate quite quickly, and with devastating results. For example, the development of antibiotic-resistant bacteria, anti-viral resistant HIV viruses, and chemotherapy-resistant recurrent cancer are all due to the same basic evolutionary process.

Hammond's failure to observe this third rule, more than anything else, dooms his project to fail. He intentionally creates highly dangerous organisms that he *knows* will be subject to evolutionary forces. The risk of his failure is increased by the sheer number of organisms he creates, by his almost total ignorance about their abilities, and by the badly thought-out methods by which he creates them ("It looks like frog DNA works! Let's use it!"). Even in the face of these problems, he assumes that he can outsmart evolution and maintain absolute control over these organisms (and that he can do so with a tiny number of staff!). As Ian Malcolm realizes almost immediately, this assumption is false, and it's inevitable that Hammond's control will break down *somewhere*, and that the results are likely to be bad (though even Malcolm could not have predicted just *how* bad).

While there's no way of guaranteeing the success of something like Jurassic Park, Hammond's team might have done better had they followed these three rules of thumb.

- **First, InGen ought *not* to have assumed that "attractive to investors" meant "an idea that is likely to succeed." Instead, they needed to take seriously the possibility that Jurassic Park was a bad (though very attractive!) meme.**

- **Second, they ought to have taken the possible negative consequences more seriously, and not simply *assumed* that things would work out as planned.**

- **Finally, if they did decide to carry out the project, they ought to have proceeded much more carefully and slowly, and to have gathered as much information as possible. Among other things, this would require that InGen stop being so secretive, and instead allow independent researchers to evaluate each stage of its work.**

While Hammond's mistake is (thankfully) a fictional one, the errors that he makes are tempting, and we need to be on guard to avoid making them in real life. This requires that we, as citizens, do our best to stay informed about important scientific matters, and that we take seriously our responsibility to help decide the laws and policies that will ultimately decide whether (and how) ideas like Jurassic Park ever become reality.

5
Beer and Dinosaurs

ADAM BARKMAN AND NATHAN VERBAAN

Setting: A student bumps into his philosophy professor in a local pub.

Aristotleosaurus

STUDENT: Hello, Professor.

PROFESSOR: Oh, hi there! You look confused [*smiles*] . . . What class are you coming from?

STUDENT: Not from a class, but from the movie theater. I just watched *Jurassic Park 3D* and it got me thinking.

PROFESSOR: That's good. About what?

STUDENT: Well, I was wondering if John Hammond's dream is ethical.

PROFESSOR: Good question! I think there are actually two distinct questions here. First, is the cloning of dinosaurs ethical? And second, is it ethical to control them the way they were controlled in *Jurassic Park*?

STUDENT: That makes sense. Even if cloning is okay, it doesn't mean it's okay to treat clones like theme park attractions!

PROFESSOR: Well, let's tackle the first question first. Let's start it with this question: Is it okay to clone animals, in general?

STUDENT: I'm not sure. It depends.

PROFESSOR: Well let's narrow it down. . . . Do you think animals have souls?

STUDENT: What?! I thought we were discussing cloning? How does a discussion of the *soul* fit into this?

PROFESSOR: [*laughs*] I see your point, but just follow me for a moment . . . Suppose you were able to create a perfect replica of yourself through cloning—let's call him Student #2. If Student #2 did not have a soul, he would just be a hollow shell. He would look like you in every way down to the smallest code of DNA, but he still wouldn't be you, right?

STUDENT: Right, because he doesn't have a soul.

PROFESSOR: Exactly. Now, if he did have a soul, would he be you?

STUDENT: No, because we would be in two different places at the same time. We'd be having two different experiences at the same moment, so we would have to have different minds. We've already talked about that in class; you said it was like a "me-ness."

PROFESSOR: A "this-ness" property. Right! In other words, "me"—*this* [*points at himself*] thing that is speaking with you—has a distinct me-ness property that makes it *this* and not *that*. You and I, for example, have two distinct centers of consciousness.

STUDENT: Okay, I'll buy that.

PROFESSOR: So we can agree that you do not share a consciousness with Student #2. But, he would still be a clone of you?

STUDENT: Yes.

PROFESSOR: So now we go back to our first situation, in which he does not have a soul. Would Student #2 still be a clone of you?

STUDENT: I'm not sure. He would look like me and be made from my DNA but he wouldn't have a soul.

PROFESSOR: Nor would he be alive.

STUDENT: Wait; so the soul is necessary in order to be alive? I thought you said he would be like me in every way?

PROFESSOR: I said that he would *look* like you in every way, not *be* like you in every way. Looking and being are separate things. A pair of twins may look identical, but act very differently.

STUDENT: Well, that's because twins are two different people.

PROFESSOR: Just like you and your clone, remember?

STUDENT: Oh I see. But you still haven't answered my question, is the soul necessary to being alive?

PROFESSOR: Well, according to Aristotle, yes. In *De Anima* the Philosopher says, "The soul is, so to speak, the first principle of living things." This means that the very first thing a being needs in order to truly live is a soul. Without the soul a plant, animal, human, or dinosaur would just be an empty shell.

STUDENT: Wait, Aristotle thinks plants and animals have souls? I thought that was only a characteristic of humans?

PROFESSOR: Yup! Aristotle believed that plants, animals, and humans all have souls. Their souls just have different properties and capabilities.

STUDENT: Okay, so let's say a living being needs a soul in order to be really alive, but what exactly does this have to do with the ethics of cloning dinosaurs? I still don't see it.

PROFESSOR: Fair question. Think about it like this. Do souls—specifically animal souls—exist independent of bodies? And if so, is that how they ought to function?

STUDENT: I remember reading something about this in class, but . . .

PROFESSOR: Although some have thought so, most, including Aristotle, have said no. Animal souls, though distinct from animal bodies, do not at all function well without bodies. In fact, they don't function at all. That would include dinosaur souls!

STUDENT: I understand; so it's impossible to talk about a cloned body being *alive* without the implication that the soul has also been cloned or somehow added? So if we cloned a dinosaur, and like in the movie it was alive, we would know it had a soul.

PROFESSOR: Correct. But remember, the "this-ness" property is unique to every soul and therefore cannot be replicated. So how could the soul be cloned?

STUDENT: It . . . can't be.

PROFESSOR: Right, but perhaps the soul emerges when the physical ingredients are in place, and brings with it certain unique properties. The soul isn't cloned, but emerges, and then animates the body.

STUDENT: This is a bit over my head. But it seems to me that this—the emergence of a soul—is a good thing, isn't it?

PROFESSOR: Is it better for a thing to exist or not exist?

STUDENT: Well I would rather exist!

PROFESSOR: Okay; so you have partially answered your question why animal—and hence dinosaur—cloning can be seen as ethical: it helps to bring about a living thing, which is good in and of itself. And, notice, if souls don't exist, the same argument still works. Cloning a living thing would still be creating new "existing" life! So, either way, it seems that Hammond would be doing a good thing!

STUDENT: [*a bit confused*] I think I need another drink . . .

PROFESSOR: [*laughs*] Okay, let's get another round, before we hit the next question!

The Divine Dino-Slayer

STUDENT: I understand now how cloning in general is a good thing because of its relation to a soul, but what about dinosaur cloning more specifically?

PROFESSOR: Well, there are two opposing views we should consider. The first is that it is ethical to clone dinosaurs because we are bringing back to life an extinct species—calling forth life from nothingness, so to speak. And the second is that dinosaurs are extinct for a *reason*, and we should not mess around with this.

STUDENT: In other words, we shouldn't play God, right? In fact, I think this is exactly the debate that took place in the movie between Ian Malcolm and John Hammond—

PROFESSOR: —Hammond basically tells Malcolm that he isn't giving his scientists enough credit for doing something amazing and Malcolm replies that they were so busy figuring out if they *could* do it that didn't ask if they *should* do it.

STUDENT: Right, and doesn't Hammond say something about birds?

PROFESSOR: Yes, Hammond argues that condors are near extinct, and if he had created them, instead, no one would complain. Malcolm has a pretty good response, though arguing that the dinosaurs weren't killed off because of something humans did. "They had their shot." And nature decided time was up.

STUDENT: They didn't see eye to eye, did they?! [*laughs*]

PROFESSOR: No. No, they did not. What Hammond thinks of as discovery, Malcolm calls "the rape of the natural world."

STUDENT: So to say that Malcolm was adamantly against cloning dinosaurs is an understatement.

PROFESSOR: To put it mildly, yes. This argument between the characters continues for a while in this scene and comes back to haunt Hammond later on in the movie.

STUDENT: When everything falls apart.

PROFESSOR: Precisely. So, what do you think?

STUDENT: Well, going back to our discussion of the soul, we said that it was—all things being equal—better to exist than not to exist, right?

PROFESSOR: Yes, we did.

STUDENT: Couldn't we extend that to an entire species?

PROFESSOR: Sure we could.

STUDENT: Then bringing the dinosaurs back from extinction would be a good thing simply because we are allowing a species to exist that went extinct in the past.

PROFESSOR: Your logic does you credit, but how would you respond to Malcolm? How would you respond to people who say there must be a *reason* that they went extinct, whether—by God, nature, or some other force?

STUDENT: [*looks into his glass glumly*] That's where I get stuck. The movie gives such a graphic image about what happens when we try to take nature into our own hands. It's hard to say it's good when we see all the bad things that could happen.

PROFESSOR: As Ellie Sattler says, "You never had control; that's the illusion! I was overwhelmed by the power of this place. But I made a mistake, too, I didn't have enough respect for that power and it's out now."

STUDENT: So how would we respond to peoples' accusations about the dangers of bringing back dinosaurs?

PROFESSOR: Well, as you know, we can't simply say we'll keep them under control because, as Malcolm says, "Life finds a way."

STUDENT: Exactly my point. I don't know how we can say it's right, even though we just said it was the right thing to do! [*throws his hands in the air*]

PROFESSOR: [*smiles*] Don't worry! Remember, you and I can't *actually* clone dinosaurs; the worst that might happen here is we'll spill a drink!

STUDENT: [*looking serious*] But I don't see how we can say it's good unless we say the goodness of a thing existing trumps all the bad things that could happen.

PROFESSOR: And that's a very tough thing to argue.

STUDENT: Yes, what about all the lives that would be lost or scarred from Jurassic Park? Would saying, "But the fact that they exist is a good thing," really outweigh all of the death and   destruction it causes?

PROFESSOR: No, it wouldn't. But let me ask you this: what was the *reason* the dinosaurs went extinct?

STUDENT: An asteroid?

PROFESSOR: No, that was the secondary cause. Here I am asking about the primary cause—the greater cause or agent that decided the fate of the dinosaurs.

STUDENT: I'm not sure what you mean. . . .

PROFESSOR: There are many theories about *how* the dinosaurs went extinct, but only a few discussing *why*. And the *why* is a much more interesting question . . .

STUDENT: Alright, I'm listening.

PROFESSOR: There are two main theories about why the dinosaurs went extinct. The first is natural selection by means of unguided evolutionary causes, and the other is divine intervention, by either direct means or by way of natural selection. Let's begin with the first theory—that the dinosaurs went extinct simply because of their own inability to survive change.

STUDENT: If this theory is true, then the dinosaurs didn't go extinct because nature "selected" them, right? They just went extinct because they were no longer able to survive after the asteroid changed the environment too much— like it became too cold.

PROFESSOR: Right. If dinosaurs were not strong enough to survive, then what is the harm in bringing them back? The reason they died off is their inability to survive, but by bringing them back we're giving them a second chance at life.

STUDENT: Okay, so unguided evolutionary theories don't give us any reason not to clone dinosaurs, and Malcolm would have been smart enough to know that. Perhaps when he talks about nature "selecting dinosaurs for extinction," he means divinely guided nature?

PROFESSOR: You might be right. To speak about nature "choosing" things is to give nature reason, intentions and choice, and this—for some—is another way of speaking about God. So, let's assume (perhaps with Malcolm here) that there is a divine being who, using natural selection, destroys the dinosaurs. Here we must work under the assumption that this divine being knows what is best for the world. And, let's assume that this divine being also knows everything that is possible in this world. This is to say, all of the technological capabilities—past, present and future—within this world are known by this divine being.

STUDENT: So this divine being did not want the dinosaurs on the planet and so it wiped them out, correct?

PROFESSOR: Yes, many ancient myths tell of the divine dragon slayer—Marduk, Ra, Apollo, and others—and perhaps the truth in these myths is that there is a divine being who slew the dinosaurs. As I said, if this divine being has the power and knowledge to wipe out the dinosaurs because it was better for the planet, it's a given that this divine being will also know everything that is capable of being done with the resources on this planet.

STUDENT: That's a fair statement.

PROFESSOR: My question to you, then, is this: if this being could wipe out the dinosaurs, could this being prevent a specific technological advancement from being invented?

STUDENT: Easily, right? I mean, it would have to be a super powerful being, so it could stop anything it wanted.

PROFESSOR: And if this divine being wanted to destroy the dinosaurs, to wipe them out from existence entirely, would this divine being prevent the technological advance that gave us the ability to bring them back?

STUDENT: Possibly; *probably*, even. Why would the divine being let us undo what's best for the planet?

PROFESSOR: Exactly. If a divine being destroyed the dinosaurs and did not stop us from achieving the ability to clone them, then it's at least possible that this being is fine with dinosaurs coming back onto the planet *at this time*. Otherwise, this technological advance would never have happened.

STUDENT: So you're saying that if the divine being wanted the dinosaurs to stay extinct, then we would never be able to clone them in the first place?

PROFESSOR: Yes; why would the divine being destroy the dinosaurs and still allow their return if they were never supposed to return?

STUDENT: I see your point; but then why would the divine being destroy the dinosaurs in the first place?

PROFESSOR: Simply because it was what was best for the world *at that point in time*.

STUDENT: Okay, wait. So you're saying if it was by unguided natural selection that the dinosaurs went extinct, then there would be no ethical problem bringing them back. And if dinosaurs were destroyed by a divine being and if it *is actually* possible to bring them back, then the divine being would probably have made it so, and, again, there would be no problem with us bringing them back.

PROFESSOR: Yup. [*raises his glass, smiling*]

STUDENT: Okay, so let's say you're right and not only is it not wrong to bring back the dinosaurs, but it is the *right* thing to do, what about the second question you mentioned? Is it ethical to treat dinosaurs the way they were in Jurassic Park? After all, they were really not much more than gimmicks to Hammond.

PROFESSOR: We'll get into that in a minute; right now I think it's time for a third round. . . .

The Form of the Dinosaur

PROFESSOR: Now for the final part of your question, is Hammond's dream ethical—is it ethical to put dinosaurs in a theme park?

STUDENT: Based on what we've said about existence being good, and cloning dinosaurs being something that we should do, then couldn't Hammond argue it's basically just like a zoo?

PROFESSOR: Really? What do you think?

STUDENT: So . . . What? Now we're going to say containment of animals at a zoo is unethical?

PROFESSOR: Not quite, though if you recall, Dale Jamieson in "Against Zoos" takes this position. But, no; even if we don't go as far as Jamieson, we should still focus on the difference between containment and controlling.

STUDENT: I don't know what you mean.

PROFESSOR: Well, at a typical large zoo in North America an animal is contained, not controlled. The animal's fed, taken care of, and generally treated with a sense of respect for its being. But at Jurassic Park, the dinosaurs, though certainly fed, were not so respected. They were genetically controlled, and as you pointed out, treated really only like "attractions," not just contained for their own safety and ours.

STUDENT: Okay, so containment has to do with holding, but controlling has to do with manipulating the very genetic makeup of a species?

PROFESSOR: Yes. And this is actually what's brought up in the movie as well.

STUDENT: When is that?

PROFESSOR: There are two major sections in which this happens. The first is once again with Malcolm in the same argument we discussed before. Malcolm states, "Genetic power is the most awesome force the planet's ever seen, but you wield it like a kid that's found his dad's gun." The second is the lysine contingency. Remember, they alter the dinosaurs in order to make them dependent on lysine—the scientist think they've made animals that will die without Jurassic Park giving them the lysine they need.

STUDENT: That does seem to go beyond just cloning, which seems generally ethical—respectful, even—to something a bit more perverse and unethical.

PROFESSOR: I'm inclined to agree with you. But why? Why exactly is genetic manipulation of this sort unethical?

STUDENT: I suppose because we're preventing the dinosaurs from functioning the way they're supposed to.

PROFESSOR: Bingo! By preventing the dinosaurs from reproducing and being able to survive without the park supplying lysine, Hammond is probably being unethical—he is treating dinosaurs not as dinosaurs—not as they ought to be treated, not according to their natures—but like toys or tools.

STUDENT: So, the dinosaurs in Jurassic Park—the genetically controlled dinosaurs—are not properly actualized dinosaurs, but are shadows of what they could and should be? Would Plato have argued that the dinosaurs in Jurassic Park do not have a full grasp of their reality so-to-speak until "life found a way" and they could act more fully as themselves?

PROFESSOR: I think so.

STUDENT: What about people who neuter their pets? In our argument, wouldn't that be "controlling"? And second, are we saying that we're in favor of cloning dinosaurs, but containing them in large cages to prevent them from excessive breeding?

PROFESSOR: Well, as to your first question, sterilizing an animal that never has a chance to breed may well be rather unfair to them. In Jurassic Park, the dinosaurs were never given the chance to breed—not even once— and that, to me, is controlling in the negative sense. As for your second question, we have simply asserted that cloning dinosaurs is ethical and that some form of containment for some of them seems permissible. Certainly we'd want to control the breeding of the dinosaurs that are contained in a zoo, but we'd do this by introducing males and females to each other at certain times, and not through other means—this seems a bit more natural. And, of course, I'm not at all opposed to cloning *some* dinosaurs and releasing into the wild to do as they will, but that is another issue.

STUDENT: [*checking his watch*] Wow, it's getting late. Alright, so, what's the final answer? Was John Hammond's dream ethical?

PROFESSOR: Yes and no. Doesn't his dream of bringing the dinosaurs back from extinction seem ethical because it's giving an extinct species another chance at life? But it also seems his dream is *un*ethical because he is altering the genetic makeup of the dinosaurs, preventing them from becoming all that they are capable of becoming, and not providing them with a world where they can flourish. So I'm not sure we can say for sure.

At this moment a tall man, unnoticed in the shadows until now steps forward, pulls up a chair, turns it around, and drops his leg over it casually. He's been listening in on their conversation for some time. Leaning forward, his eyes intent, the man pours himself a drink. He looks frazzled and tired.

DR. IAN MALCOLM: Yes, um, well. Let me tell *you* why cloning dinosaurs is *definitely* a very bad idea. . . .

II

Life Has Lost
Its Way

6
Why Not Play God?

VINCENT BILLARD

The lights dim, the theater hushes, and there on the screen we see a dream come true—real dinosaurs! Looming before us, majestic and beautiful, are the massive creatures that died out over sixty-five million years ago. For a moment, we sit back in awe. . . . And, then, they start terrorizing us! Not only are the characters on the screen being eaten alive, but those of us watching the movie walk away thinking, "Well! Bringing dinosaurs back to life was a *very* bad idea!"

Isn't this strange? We take great pleasure in watching dinosaurs brought back to life on the screen, while the whole project of bringing dinosaurs back to life seems condemned by the movie's most important characters! This schizophrenic situation definitely needs some explanation.

The human mind is undeniably attracted to the idea of seeing near-mythical creatures walk. Somewhere in the back of our minds we've all got a mental image (remembered from real life or a movie) of a child wearing dinosaur pajamas. The link between dinosaurs and childhood is a strong one, relating to dreams, magic and ancestral fears. So it's logical that in *Jurassic Park*, two of the most important characters are young children, a boy and a girl, both as cute and smart as you would expect. Because of their presence, we feel the beauty and majesty of the dinosaurs. Through their innocent eyes, we can enjoy this encounter with giant, extinct animals and also be frightened by the terror they inspire.

Nightmares

What exactly is it that fascinates us about these big creatures? The origin of the word "dinosaur" provides a clue: *deinos-sauros* means *terrible lizard.* "Terrible," in the sense of "awesome," "mighty," "fearfully great." Dinosaurs are attractive because they're huge and imposing, so we want to play with them like a child plays with figurines and scary toys.

We can think of them as ancient patterns, exposing the oldest fears and hopes of mankind; the fear of returning to the animal state has become one of mankind's secret and profound fears. If this theory is true, dinosaurs definitely belong to our collective unconscious; they represent not only the most impressive and threatening of animals, but also the most fascinating and mysterious.

This idea helps us understand why we feel so concerned by the fate of the dinosaurs: they are in fact part of our dreams; they have haunted the imagination of mankind since the mists of time. If by magic we had the possibility of resurrecting them, how on earth could we turn the invitation down? How could we tell the child we all hide in our hearts that we wouldn't take this opportunity? On the other hand, doesn't *Jurassic Park* show us how selfish and immature that dream is? How many people have to die so we can recreate nightmares from our misty past?

But, wait a minute. . . . Is bringing back dinosaurs really such a childish or awful goal? Are we wrong to entertain dreams of recreating extinct species? It's actually not totally clear whether or not such an action would turn out to be a mistake. At the very least, the idea deserves some discussion.

Jurassic Park begins with a childish fascination for dinosaurs. The scientists are totally stunned when they meet their first diplodocus in the flesh. Gazing at the dinosaurs, the mathematician Ian Malcolm says, "You did it. Crazy son of a bitch, you did it." Their excitement is extreme, the scientists smiling like children in front of their Christmas gifts.

Then, jokingly, Malcolm speaks against de-extinction. When Dr. Alan Grant, the leading paleontologist, confesses that now he is "out of a job," Ian Malcolm answers: "Don't you mean 'extinct'?" The dialog is amusing, but something sounds off—it is a warning.

Life Finds a Way

An important argument between mathematician Malcolm and geneticist Dr. Henry Wu (who believes he can control whether animals can mate and their access to lysine) introduces the best argument against de-extinction. The whole Jurassic Park project consists in dominating and controlling nature, but is that actually possible?

A large part of philosophy is devoted to controlling our own lives. A common aim of philosophy is to teach us how to live our lives better, but this is not always possible. According to ancient philosophy, our passions prevent us from firmly controlling our lives. In many cases, it's because we can't control our passions that we end up being unhappy and sad.

One school of philosophy in ancient Greece, the Stoics, argued that there are two reasons for human unhappiness: we tend to seek satisfaction in possessions that we cannot have, and we try to avoid misfortunes that are inevitable. Philosophy teaches us that we cannot really control what happens to us, so we need to free ourselves from our passions and view any misfortune that happens to us with wisdom.

In *Jurassic Park*, what's at stake is not our power over *our* lives, but the power of humans over life in general. Human control is seen as an illusion because "life will always find a way" to restore itself, despite human restraint. During the entire movie this idea is constantly emphasized, claiming that the adaptability of life always allows it to flourish and defy our wish to master it—life (or nature) is cleverer than we are.

What does this tell us? Is it proof that we can't control the process of recreating extinct species? First, the kind of problems encountered by the team of scientists in Jurassic Park are not impossible to solve. They just went too fast, without taking enough time to think about all the problems; we don't know for sure that they couldn't have solved them.

Secondly, if the weather (in the form of a hurricane) and Nedry hadn't betrayed them, the scientists would have had enough time to take stock of the security issues and try to remedy the situation. Similar problems occurred when scientists tried the first ever revival of an extinct species in 2003 by cloning a bucardo (an Iberian wild goat that had gone extinct three years earlier) by inserting its DNA (taken from frozen bucardo skin) into the eggs of an existing goat. A cloned bucardo was born, but then unfortunately it died just ten minutes later. A first attempt is never perfect. Finding solutions to these problems is just a question of time, not an insurmountable obstacle.

If the Pirates of the Caribbean Break Down in Disneyland, They Don't Eat Tourists

The second kind of argument against de-extinction in *Jurassic Park* concerns the kind of animals that have been brought back because the animals concerned are very dangerous species. For instance, at the end of the argument between Malcolm and Wu, when the baby dinosaur starts whimpering, Grant asks: "What species is this?" Wu answers: "It's a velociraptor." "You bred raptors?" asks a surprised and worried Grant. The same surprise and anxiety occurs later when the visitors of the park discover that there is *Tyrannosaurus rex* inside the building.

It's a very specific problem: if the scientists had only bred herbivorous and placid dinosaurs, none of the fatal problems would have occurred. But this argument against the de-extinction of dangerous animals is not so clear-cut, because dangerousness is a subjective concept. Shouldn't we also avoid bringing back the saber-toothed tiger—because it was probably more dangerous than living lions? We ought to remember their dangerousness when we breed these animals so that we'll be more careful, but it does not mean that we have to give up the idea of breeding them at all; otherwise, we would never keep any dangerous animals in zoos at all. The problem we're really facing is more about our confidence in technology, not that de-extinction is impossible or impossible to do safely.

In *Jurassic Park*, not only the animals are dangerous, but also the conditions in the park itself. During the visit we immediately realize the number one problem of this kind of park: How is it possible to see the dinosaurs? They're hidden in their natural surroundings, and the closer we are to them the more we're in danger. If we want to watch living dinosaurs we need to be close to them, which is more dangerous, but if we want to be totally safe we can't see them. This doesn't prove that de-extinction itself is a problem, just that we need to figure out better logistics.

But the most dangerous aspect of the animals of Jurassic Park lies probably not in their claws or in their jaws, but in their intelligence. The raptors are smart—*very* smart. They figure out how to escape cages, open doors, and trap humans. We can't be sure whether we're totally capable of outwitting the raptors. Human intelligence can never be sure of winning out against the intelligence of nature. Above all, this problem leads us to the most important criticism of any de-extinction project. Wanting to dominate nature itself, are the men exceeding their abilities? Are they trying to play God?

Playing God

Once again, it's Malcolm who expresses his opinion firmly: "They were so preoccupied with whether they *could* they didn't stop to think if they *should*." In *Jurassic Park III* Grant answers the question, "This is how you make dinosaurs?" with a pointed, "No, this is how you play God." Both men are less afraid of the dinosaurs than they are of humans' tendency to warp and twist the world around them.

Jurassic Park raises a number of ethical questions, and "Should we be playing God?" is certainly one of the most important. The fact is, we do it already! Throughout history, species have been going extinct (though there have been more or less extreme periods). According to scientists, there have been at least five great episodes of mass extinctions in the past, during which anywhere from 60 to 96 percent of existing species became extinct. Indeed, the massacre has been so intense that 99 percent of all existing species that have ever existed are now extinct.

But the big difference between those mass extinctions and recent extinctions is that humans are the cause of Earth's sixth mass extinction event. It is due to our actions and our impact on the planet—causing habitat loss and modification, the spread of invasive species and climate change. Nature or God is not responsible anymore: it's our fault, because we have already been playing God. Because of this, we should now consider it our moral duty to bring back extinct species, to undo the harm humans have caused.

We have to make a clear distinction, though: as Malcolm notes, where some species are extinct because of mankind, that's not the case with the dinosaurs. For example, the passenger pigeon disappeared at the beginning of the twentieth century because of us, as did the Tasmanian tiger, while the Tasmanian devil will soon disappear because of us once again. But it's absolutely not the case with dinosaurs: they "had their shot" and "nature selected them for extinction." So what? Is it bad to de-extinct a species if we are not responsible for their extinction?

Neo-Dinosaurs

First of all, we'll never actually recreate dinosaurs! Even if we found enough DNA and technology could allow us to create a creature from it, it would not be a copy of the extinct animal. It wouldn't be a complete de-extinction, because most of the extinct species being discussed have at best left only fragments of DNA. Even if scientists manage to modify, for instance, velociraptor DNA in the direction of bird or lizard DNA, they will never know if they have succeeded completely. For this reason we shouldn't call them "velociraptors." Really, they are "neo-velociraptors" with the "best qualities" of velociraptors and birds. The process is less like raising a species from the dead than it is building a brand-new one.

This makes a huge difference, because then we can claim that we wouldn't be *resuscitating* the dinosaurs (only God can do that) but creating new animals. So, we're not really playing God; we're just doing what humans have always done, merging species, enhancing them, crossbreeding. If that's playing God, then we're the kind of species which plays God naturally, doomed by our nature to play with nature.

In *Jurassic Park III*, Grant acknowledges (although negatively), "Dinosaurs lived 65 million years ago. What is left of them is fossilized in the rocks. And it is in the rocks that real scientists make real discoveries. Now, what John Hammond and InGen did at *Jurassic Park* is create genetically engineered park monsters. Nothing more and nothing less." Alan Grant speaks of "monsters," but we could say that all new species created by mankind are monsters, from dogs to the plants and flowers we come across every day. By making *neo-dinosaurs* we would be, in a sense, making what we're used to: we would only be creating new forms of life.

Ian Malcolm sums up what is going on in the Park by saying, "God creates dinosaurs—God destroys dinosaurs—God creates Man—Man destroys God—Man creates dinosaurs . . ." But he's not absolutely right, because Man does not "create" dinosaurs, he creates "neo-dinosaurs." The argument's wrong. . . .

At an even deeper level, we could say that nature is now our own creation.

Enhancing Nature

When we look at it closely, we realize that actually there's no such thing as nature or wilderness anymore, if by nature we mean something completely apart from humans. In fact, human hands have touched all the landscapes we see in the majority of countries in the world: forests and even lakes and rivers. This means that when we talk of nature versus mankind, we are mistaken; the world we live in is already partly the result of our will. So in wanting to reintroduce a newly-engineered species into the wild, we would not be doing something radically different to what we have been doing for centuries.

But what about what some call "Transhumanism" or "Post-humanism"? What does it mean? Trans-humanism is a new movement that seeks to develop technologies that eliminate aging and greatly enhance human intellectual, physical, and psychological abilities. Transhumanist thinkers study the benefits of new technologies that could overcome fundamental human limitations. With the aim of achieving a new human, transformed into a being with such greatly expanded abilities that she merits the label "post-human."

Creating neo-dinosaurs could simply be considered to be following in the wake of this movement. De-extinction would involve re-creating extinct species and creating new ones. This revival would not only bring back species already extinct, but it could help prevent the extinction of further species by allowing science to increase the population numbers of threatened species, and by studying and fixing the things that made other extinct species vulnerable in the first place.

An example which speaks for itself is that of the Tasmanian devils, which have a large population plagued by a transmissible facial cancer. If we can perfect the revival process and gene manipulation, we could theoretically repress the gene causing the cancer and make them immune to the virus. For many species in similar situations, genetic deficiencies could be quickly bred out of existence as more and more animals reproduce with enhanced or corrected genes. This would certainly help ensure that our current wildlife populations would continue to flourish and, in this way, we could avoid any further extinctions. We would not re-create extinct species with their deficiencies, but create new ones with fewer problems (*Insert maniacal laughter here*).

The Ethics of De-extinction

So can we control nature, in the end? In *Jurassic Park* we're warned that we can't. Dr. Ellie Sattler, the paleobotanist and Dr. Grant's friend says: "You've never had control. That's the illusion. I was overwhelmed by the power of this place. I made a mistake, too. I didn't have enough respect for that power, and it's out now." I think that we could be less pessimistic.

Let me ask a question: why on earth would technology give us the power of de-extinction, if it is not to be used? There is a kind of mystery in modern technology: no human in the ancient world or during the middle-ages ever imagined that a human could walk on the moon or speak to and see another human from hundreds of kilometers away. Can we really believe that this power has been given to us not to use it? In fact, with it available, it may actually be our *duty* to do it, whatever difficulties we may encounter along the way.

And now I think the last problem is ethical. In order to create one living dinosaur (or passenger pigeon, or Tasmanian tiger), several modern female animals will need to be impregnated in order for one to give birth to offspring that survives more than a few days. How many modern and extinct animals need to be sacrificed in order for this method to become reliable? Who is willing to make a decision that will most likely end the lives of so many animals, in some cases that are already under threat of extinction?

De-extinction will not be possible if it requires violating any reasonable standard of humane treatment, and this raises the question of whether de-extinction is compatible with animal welfare. My suggestion is that cloning and de-extinction are only beginning, and we can expect processes to be improved with time. It's not only *exciting* experiencing so many of the amazing creatures that have been lost to our world; it's our duty to do so if technology gives us this power.

If Jurassic Park becomes possible, future generations will be given the opportunity to experience some of the most remarkable creatures that have lived on our earth. Currently, many of the world's most marvelous creatures can only be found in encyclopedias, but by reviving these missing species, by de-extincting them, science could redefine attitudes toward the natural world. We could once again view *T. rex* (well, "*neo T. rex*"), woolly mammoths, saber-toothed tigers, passenger pigeons, and dodo birds.

It's the kind of magic that technology can provide us with, if we believe in it.

7

Is the Essence in the Amber?

Evan Edwards

Alright folks, let's admit it: for better or worse, the human race is *kind of like* a mass murderer. Over the course of the couple of million years that we have been slowly but surely colonizing the planet, we've put a lot of other species out of commission. Completely. As in, we've annihilated entire groups of animals forever. So now we're trying to bring them back. As if we were some real life scientists of *Jurassic Park*.

In the late nineteenth and early twentieth centuries, humans began to think that the wholesale extermination of large predators and pests, not to mention the more human-friendly beasts, might be a moral failing. It's a rather recent development in moral thought to even consider killing other animals off to be a problem. And today, the question of whether driving other species to extinction is immoral or not has reached a fever pitch. We have entered a period of species anni-hilation as great as any mass extinction in the history of the planet.[1]

There are the two well-known responses to such a crisis: First, the typical "right-wing" response. This point of view sees the crisis as either manufactured or blown out of proportion by "the left," and is dismissed as a result. Second, there is the typ-ical "liberal" response. This plan of action views the problem as very real, and is taken by groups like the Sierra Club, who

---

[1] Eldgridge, Niles. "The Sixth Extinction." *actionbioscience.org*. American Institute of the Biological Sciences, n.d. Web. 4 Aug 2013. <http://www.action-bioscience.org/newfrontiers/eldredge2.html>.

draft letters to Congress or lobby on behalf of the pool of species on Earth slowly drying up.

Besides these responses, however, there is one more bizarre and perhaps less well-known: the gene bank.[2] Rather than dismissing the problem or trying to prevent extinction, the gene banks of the world save their genetic materials so that if we do happen to extinguish a species, future scientists will have the information needed to recreate it with the appropriate technology. The rise in popularity of gene banks in the last decade has led to the creation of a new term in the extinction debates: "de-extinction." Rather than just thinking that a species is either alive or dead, humans now have at least the theoretical possibility of blurring those lines, of bringing a species that has died to live once again. In *Jurassic Park*, InGen, at least with its projects on the islands of Isla Nublar and Isla Sorna, operates a fictional gene bank not incredibly unlike the ones in the real world.

Setting aside the moral issues surrounding the concept of a "gene bank," what I wonder is whether the goals envisioned by these organizations' "bankers" are even *possible*. When we think deeply about what it means to "de-extinct" a species at all, we realize that what we need when trying to keep a species alive is something basically *more* than just genetics. The gene banks of the world will not save the various species of the planet.

Beyond the 'Real' World with Genes and Gene banks in Jurassic Park

Ian Malcolm, the quirky chaos mathematician, also thinks that species are more than their genes. In the story, Malcolm acts like the devil's advocate against characters like Grant, Sattler, and Hammond. Hammond, and his chief geneticist Henry Wu, believe they can create dinosaurs using slightly altered genetic code, because apparently genes are the essence of a species. Malcolm is of an entirely different opinion: genetics are just a tiny piece in the puzzle of life. So many other pieces, like the environment in which animals are born, the history of those

---

[2] Lamb, Robert. "How Gene Banks Work."*HowStuffWorks*. N.p.. Web. 4 Aug 2013. <http://science.howstuffworks.com/life/genetic/gene-bank.htm>.

animals' ancestors, and so on, are far more important than fine tuning DNA.

At the time of the movie's release, the concept of de-extinction sounded a bit far-fetched, the sort of thing you'd *only* find in a science-fiction story. Today, however, scientists are in the process of reviving species like the wooly mammoth, the dodo bird, and the passenger pigeon.[3] They even successfully birthed a kid from an extinct species of Spanish goat.[4] Perhaps it is as good a time as any to think more seriously about Crichton's novel as a way of giving ourselves guidance on the way forward into this strange new world of extinction and "de-extinction."

Scientists have criticized the novel on the grounds that while it is possible to reconstruct DNA which has gaps, it's only possible if the genetic material is taken from the same species as the one being reconstructed. They point out that if we were to put amphibian DNA into a broken strand of, say, *T. rex* DNA, then the thing produced would be *an entirely different species*; that is, even if that thing roared, ate, and had the same funny little arms as a *T. rex*.

While it may be the case that the genetic material would be different, and even that the animal or plant produced might behave differently because of that genetic material, the biologists' argument has a fatal flaw, because it relies on the assumption that genetics is the determining factor that tells us what something is. This is a problem because it relies on an underlying assumption that the essence of a thing is isolated, written in a genetic code which will produce the same results in any time period. Developments in science and philosophy over the last two hundred years or so have piled up a lot of evidence against assumptions like this.

To say that the plants and animals produced in *Jurassic Park* are impossible reproductions from a genetic point of view is not the best way of thinking about the problem. In fact, it

---

[3] Landers, Jackson. "Scientists look to revive the long-extinct passenger pigeon." *The Washington Post*. The Washington Post, 08 Jul 2013. Web. 4 Aug 2013. <http://articles.washingtonpost.com/2013-07-08/national/40434945_1 _passenger-pigeon-woolly-mammoth-de-extinction>.

[4] Zimmer, Carl. "Bringing them Back to Life." *National Geographic*. Apr 2013: n. page. Web. 4 Aug. 2013. <http://ngm.nationalgeographic.com/2013/04/ 125-species-revival/zimmer-text?source=hp_dl2_ngm_reviving_species _2130325>.

might be downright wrong. Even if we *could* find or create the exact DNA of a *T. rex*, and not just substitute it with amphibian genes, we *still* wouldn't have the same beast that stalked the Earth during the Cretaceous.

While this may seem like a point dreamed up in the disconnected world of the university, the concern of white collar university types, this actually has some pretty important real-world consequences. Instead of worrying ourselves with the preservation of genetic materials in a laboratory, if we really want to fulfill some sort of moral obligation to not wipe out other species once and for all, what we *actually* ought to be concerned with is preserving the natural habitats of these animals in the first place! —For that is what makes an animal be what it really is.

I Wanted to Show Them Something that Wasn't an Illusion

Philosophy begins and ends with a Greek man who lived over two thousand years ago. His name was Plato (427–347 B.C.E.). He had the same desire as John Hammond, who tells us that he just wanted to show people "something that wasn't an illusion. Something that was real." This very same desire is at the very heart of all of Plato's works. His most famous and most important contribution to thought is his theory of Forms. According to Plato, the things that we see around us in the normal world are not, strictly speaking, *real*. Rather, they are all appearances of things which have a higher reality, a more true reality—specifically, the Forms.

Take, for example, the chair you're sitting on. Plato would ask you (if he were still alive) to explain *how* you know it's a chair. You may answer any number of ways: "It's made of wood and is for sitting," "I bought it in the chair section at Walmart," and so on. In the end, though, these only tell what the chair is *like*, not what it *is*. For Plato, instead, the chair is only *real* if it is the appearance of the perfect form of "Chair." While individual chairs come into existence and disappear, the 'form' of chair has a real lasting existence.

According to Plato, these forms exist outside of space and time, and imprint themselves onto the world that we see around us. The Greeks thought that anything that is in time and space is corruptible, or able to wither and die, so the forms must exist in a separate kind of reality. Plato thinks this is the case because we immediately know what a chair is, and if that idea of a chair were to become something else, then it wouldn't be a chair anymore. The idea (or form) of a chair *must therefore be constant*, because the idea must exist outside of time and space.

Life Finds a Way, Even without Forms

This way of thinking dominated philosophy for more than two thousand years, until Darwin and his followers began to develop evolutionary theory in the nineteenth century. In his book, *The Phenomenon of Life*, Hans Jonas (1903–1993) argues that up until the time of Darwin, the way that humans normally thought about the essence of things was as if they had unchanging God-given forms, like in Plato's philosophy. When Darwin's book *On the Origin of Species* was published, Jonas says that things changed completely. Instead of thinking that there are unchanging forms of species, Darwin and his followers showed us that the definitions of groups of animals that we hold together as a "species" are in fact the result of an almost random series of events in the course of time that *could have been different.*

If we look at the evolutionary history of the animals of *Jurassic Park,* for example, we can see this idea at work. During the ages of the dinosaurs, mammals were mostly tiny, unimportant creatures. When the great lizards were put out of commission, however, mammals thrived in the new environment. All the amazing varieties of mammals today, from chinchillas to kangaroos, could not have made their appearance on the planet without the random event of a meteor crashing into Earth. Life, in other words, finds a way to thrive without necessarily being tied to an *essence* of a thing lying behind the scenes. The environment, and the conditions of the world itself, create species.

Hans Jonas writes of the discovery of evolution: "In the history of life, *conditions* take the place of *essence* as the originating principle. In the shape of environment, condition becomes so much a necessary correlative to the concept of organism that it enters into the very derivation of its being."[5] What he means

---

[5] Hans Jonas, *The Phenomenon of Life* (Northwestern University Press, 2001), p. 46.

here is that to assume there is an "essence" or a "form" of human that has always been and will always be in the future is crazy. Rather, the sort of things in the environment at the time we were evolving made it more helpful to have the characteristics that we now think of as 'essentially human' than to not have those characteristics.

Instead of taking essence as the most important factor in determining what a thing *is*, today we instead think of the sort of things that went into making that thing possible in the first place. If in the older, Platonic way of thinking, the specific organization of genes is what makes a species really be *what it is*, then after Darwin's discoveries genes are just the result of a weird chain of events and are less important than the environment that went into making those genes the way they are in the first place. In other words, we've gone past the Platonic viewpoint, taken by today's genetic bankers who think that by isolating a species's DNA, they can re-make that animal in the future.

Genes are, in this way, the modern, scientific version of Platonic forms. It's almost like they were saying: "It doesn't matter when or in what environment we reproduce this species; as long as we have the genetic code, we can say it's the same animal." As we learned from Jonas and the Darwinists, the genes may produce an identical critter when we spawn it in the laboratory, but it isn't really the *same* in the sense that the environmental conditions that made it be the animal that it once was are gone. It would be like taking Mona Lisa's smile and putting it on the face of the person in Edvard Munch's *The Scream*. It just doesn't fit. The creepy little compys who munch on characters in the *Lost World* are, despite appearances, entirely new critters.

Just as that suggestive smile from Michelangelo's masterpiece doesn't convey the same feeling if it is put on the terrified man's face in *The Scream*, if we were to put a wooly mammoth into the wilds of Mongolia or the American Midwest (where they once roamed by the thousands), *it just wouldn't work*. They would be outside of their place, and most likely die off or produce some unexpected disaster in their adopted habitat. It's for this reason that thinking about de-extinction as a problem for geneticists doesn't make as much sense as thinking about the question from an ecological or biological point of view. If, as

Jonas and countless others have argued, Platonic forms are out of date in the modern thinking person's world, then why do we still hold so dearly to the work of genetics?

It's Still the Flea Circus. It's All an Illusion

The older, Platonic way of thinking argues that there was a single, unchanging essence or "Form" which let us say that a *T. rex* was different from a velociraptor, or a passenger pigeon was different from a rock pigeon. Nowadays, we can say that, sure, the two are different, but the difference is more because they evolved in different conditions to fit different places in ecosystems, and that is *really* what makes them different from one another.

In the conversation that happens between Dr. Wu, Jurassic Park's chief geneticist, and Malcolm, Wu represents a Platonist and Malcolm represents a Darwinist following the line of thought put forward by Hans Jonas.

MALCOLM: Surely not the ones that are bred in the wild?

WU: Actually they can't breed in the wild. Population control is one of our security precautions. There's no unauthorized breeding in Jurassic Park.

MALCOLM: How do you know they can't breed?

WU: Well, because all the animals in Jurassic Park are female. We've engineered them that way.

MALCOLM: But again, how do you know they're all female?

WU: We control their chromosomes. It's really not that difficult. All vertebrate embryos are inherently female anyway, they just require an extra hormone. . . . we simply deny them that.

MALCOLM: John, the kind of control you're attempting simply is . . . it's not possible. If there is one thing that the history of evolution has taught us it's that life will not be contained. Life breaks free, it expands to new territories and crashes through barriers, painfully, maybe even dangerously. . . .

WU: You're implying that a group composed entirely of female animals will . . . breed?

MALCOLM: No, I'm, I'm simply saying that life, uh . . . finds a way.

This is the same argument that exists between Plato and Darwin. Wu argues that by making a particular genetic code and remaking it in its 'perfect' form, the park can continue on with its normal operations without worries. The 'form' of the velociraptor, programmed by the geneticists with very specific guidelines, is supposed to be impossible to change. As long as these animals have the genetics with which the scientists provide them, there is no possibility of problems arising. Malcolm argues that there are more important things than genetics that make an animal be what it is. Life, the environment, the way that evolution works, and so on, have more to do with the production of animal life than the genetic code, which (as we saw above) is the *result* of these more important factors.

When Malcolm says, "If there is one thing that the history of evolution has taught us it's that life will not be contained," he is essentially arguing for Hans Jonas's philosophy. Forms, the Platonic version of genetic codes, cannot contain the wild factors that go into determining what a thing is. So, it's *not enough* to keep a species's DNA cryogenically frozen in a gene bank. Even if we were to have a Jurassic Park, actually engineer it, we would be dealing with entirely different lizards than the ones that lived so many millions of years ago.

Hammond wanted to give the world a real experience of the world of dinosaurs. He didn't want to cheat people with what he viewed as the illusory world of the flea circus; he wanted to make the fleas *really jump*. At the end of the movie, when everything has crumbled, Dr. Sattler reminds John that the park itself is still an illusion. The deeper point that Ellie makes in pointing this out is that John can *never* create a real world of the dinosaurs. We can't recreate the dinosaurs because the world which produced them is long gone. We don't have, and will never have, the power to bring the dinosaurs back except in an illusory way.

God Help Us, We're in the Hands of Engineers

So what does this all mean, really? After all the talk of Plato, and Darwin, and the fantastic story of *Jurassic Park*, what have we really learned? What was the heart of their thoughts, and why were they important?

For thousands of years, we looked at the world, thinking that there was an unchanging ground of forms, which we could count on to guarantee life even if we screwed up. When Darwin realized that species change when we mess with the environment, we were all of a sudden placed face to face with the fact that we don't have as much innocence as we used to think we had. We haven't really gotten over this terrifying realization. *Jurassic Park* shows us how we're still dealing with it.

At one point in the film, Malcolm exclaims in horror that "We are in the hands of engineers." We should feel the same horror when we realize that instead of tending to the extreme violence that we are inflicting on the natural world, we are entrusting its preservation to the very people who still cling to an outdated way of thinking which got us into this mess in the first place.

8
Bring Back the Dinosaurs!

JOHN R. FITZPATRICK

Comparing the book and movie versions of *Jurassic Park* is one weird experience. What's odd, at least to me, is that the movie is a far more *vivid* experience. Now, I'm pretty used to this when the book is mediocre (or just plain bad); a good film adaptation can change it for the better. But what's strange is— and if you've read the books you probably agree—Michael Crichton's books aren't mediocre at all; in fact, they're pretty good!

Usually, when we try to present a novel in two hours or less, so much gets cut that the movie can never pack the same punch. But the film *Jurassic Park* breaks this general rule. The movie's visuals add *something* in a way that makes the books seem, well, tame. But this is to be expected; if a picture is worth a thousand words, then who knows how many words are needed to match a moving picture? And make no bones about it—the dinosaurs are the stars here.

Think about the scene in the first *Jurassic Park* where the scientist, Ellie, is first exposed to actual dinosaurs in the wild. The description in the book is gripping!

> Her first thought was that the dinosaur was extraordinarily beautiful. Books portrayed them as oversized, dumpy creatures but this long-necked animal had a gracefulness, almost a dignity about its movement. . . . The sauropod peered alertly at them, and made a low trumpeting sound, rather like an elephant. A moment later, a second head arose above the foliage, and then a third, and a fourth. "My God" Ellie said again.

Well played, Michael Crichton! But the movie's scene is . . . magical. The overwhelming beauty of the creature, and the look of awe and wonder on Ellie's face can't be captured with the written word. *Jurassic Park* is a monster movie, and these creatures can also be truly terrifying. But my thoughts during this scene are simple—seeing is believing, and these creatures are magnificent. It's been years since I have experienced this scene on a movie screen large enough to capture the full impact of it all. But even on TV the scene is beyond powerful: these creatures are a joy to behold.

If we could bring these marvelous creatures back to life, how could we *not* want to? It would seem almost immoral not to bring them back; how could it be right to deprive people of the experience of these creatures in the flesh? If one of the things that makes human lives valuable is our ability to experience awe and wonder at the majesty of nature, depriving ourselves of experiencing dinosaurs in the wild would be wrong! It seems wrong in the same way that forcing poor people to live in concrete jungles is wrong. It seems wrong in the same way our indiscriminate destruction of unique environments seems wrong. Perhaps any serious attempt to show respect for people must include showing some respect for nature. And any respect for nature would include allowing us to see these marvelous creatures beyond the movie screen and in reality!

Good Intentions Get People Eaten

In much of the public's mind, the launching of the environmental movement began with Rachel Carson's book *Silent Spring*. Her fear was that the "scientific" use of pesticides was harmful to many creatures; the short-sighted misuse of chemicals was largely misunderstood. Carson imagined a future where our own folly would lead to the extinction of higher animals, including many songbirds. We faced a future where we could no longer experience the pleasure of hearing these magnificent creatures sing their elaborate songs in the spring. Scientists, hand in hand with "scientific" agriculture, developed products because they were able to, without asking whether or not they should.

To Carson, scientists overestimate their ability to control nature and underestimate the unintended consequences. But they have good intentions; isn't this enough? Crichton's answer is a loud, "*No!*" The short-sighted scientist with good intentions is common to many of Crichton's books and screenplays, and, boy, is this lesson clear in *Jurassic Park*! Perhaps the most vivid condemnation is found in the skeptical mathematician, Ian Malcolm, and his repeated insistence that the whole project of trying to contain and control dinosaurs was doomed to fail. Malcolm suggests that martial artists train for years before they develop deadly skills, and by then they're mature enough to use them wisely. But many scientists rely on skills developed by others, and so they never really had to *earn* their knowledge. As a result, they lack maturity, wisdom, and prudence.

Malcolm sounds a lot like the nature writer Aldo Leopold, who argued that our current limited ways of understanding human action and fear of nature result in us not giving nature the full value it is due. He called for an expansion of our ethics that gives moral concern to nature. Environmental ethicists who follow in Leopold's tradition would find experiments like Jurassic Park to be both impractical and entirely immoral. Thinkers like Leopold share Crichton's skepticism that we can ever understand nature well enough to make plans to control it in a positive sense; even if we could, institutional pressures (like government and business) would undermine our ability to keep our experiments safe and controlled.

Crichton has also criticized our actual attempts to "manage" Yellowstone National Park. As Crichton views the history of land management, he sees well-meaning people who do far more harm than good. They try to control predators, and end up with their overpopulated prey. They try to re-introduce a species, but the evolved ecosystem is no longer able to accommodate it successfully. Yes, the managers of Yellowstone had good intentions. They tried to help but ultimately did irreparable harm. And even if we knew how to do this, powerful interests might well frustrate our best intentions, as we see in current debates over the farm bill.

Who Cares?

... And what should they care about? Moral philosophers have attempted for centuries to expand our idea of who counts. In the late eighteenth and early nineteenth centuries a group of radical English philosophers challenged the idea that the lives of the rich were more valuable than others. The idea that the happiness of illiterate and landless peasants should be considered on a par with that of the rich was shocking in an era barely beyond feudalism. When Jeremy Bentham advocated for the consideration of anyone who could feel pain, including non-human animals, it was outrageous that anyone cared about them. When John Stuart Mill argued in behalf of working class women and black slaves, what offended his contemporaries is that white male aristocrats should have to change their behavior in response to claims that came from outside of their class. And when the contemporary philosopher, Peter Singer, similarly began arguing in the 1970s for massive increases in aid to the developing world, vegetarianism, and the ending of factory farms, his opponents were outraged that they should care about the well-being of animals or the developing world's poor. These thinkers ask us to expand our definition of the moral community—in other words they are asking us to expand our idea of who counts and who deserves respect. We are being asked to consider the suffering of those we previously did not consider victims.

We see this idea in *Jurassic Park* when humans arm themselves with non-lethal weapons when trying to contain even the most vicious dinosaur predators. They're facing off against a fearsome opponent like *T. rex* with *dart guns*! True, this is partly because the animals are *expensive*. But this is also standard procedure in today's zoos, even for animals that are not of great monetary value. We often try to not kill them when we can just stun them.

In the 1950s, Leopold began arguing that our moral imagination suffers because it lacks enough consideration for nature. He begins his argument in his *A Sand County Almanac* by recalling a section of the *Odyssey* where the great Greek poet Homer describes Odysseus's decision to execute twelve slave girls on a whim. This raises no issues of propriety for Homer's Greek audience, since back then (like now) the dominant view was that one can do what one wants with one's property, and in the ancient Greek view, slaves are property. However, this is shocking to us today because we find the casual execution of humans terrible and the practice of slavery to be barbaric.

Humans are not property. But Leopold raises the issue to question the moral premise at its core. Is it really morally justifiable to do anything I want with my property? Leopold didn't think so. He called for a land ethic that holds that "a thing is right when it tends to preserve the integrity, stability, and beauty of the biotic community. It is wrong when it tends otherwise." In Leopold's ethic, ecosystems themselves are intrinsically valuable. Leopold has the same awe and wonder for natural wilderness that Ellie had for the dinosaurs. Even a desert can be an entity of intrinsic value that's worth our protection and care, and even a river can have rights because the land itself is valuable.

I imagine that many cheered at the end of one of the versions of the first *Jurassic Park* when the bombers came in and firebombed the island, but Leopold would have been saddened if he had lived to read this. If someone adopts a land ethic, then the destruction of this ecosystem to prevent only hypothetical dangers to humans can only be seen as an act of barbarism similar to the rape of Nanking or the firebombing of Dresden.

Faking Respect

There's an old vaudeville line that goes like this: "Once you can fake sincerity, the rest is easy." One could say the same about "faking respect." Robert Elliot, in his famous article, "Faking Nature," argues against what he calls the "restoration thesis." Elliot claims that nowadays many industrialists and developers think it is morally allowable to damage nature as long as we clean up our mess when we are done. He imagines a case where a mining company wishes to mine a beach for some chemical not essential to the ecosystem (perhaps it is too deeply imbedded in the ground to really impact the ecosystem). So, in theory, we could tear up the beach, take out the chemical, and restore with new plants, animals, insects, and so forth. Humans have use of the chemical, and nature is restored. Heck, why not?

The first problem is that we really can't "restore" nature in more than a superficial sense. Since humans are incapable of doing anything perfectly, it's hard to argue that we could do a perfect restoration. One theme that runs through *Jurassic Park* is that these are not real dinosaurs; they aren't identical to the originals. Genetics, especially in the Jurassic Park labs, is a whole lot of guesswork. It would be a similar piece of guesswork to attempt to make a copy of the beach in Robert Elliot's example. In a land ethic, any change like that is a violation; it would be an act that did not preserve the integrity, stability, and beauty of the biotic community. But even if we reject Leopold's land ethic, should we find fake nature less valuable than real nature? Elliot says yes.

Consider the value of a work of art. Doesn't it matter if it's the original? Consider a really excellent copy of the *Mona Lisa*: would it be as valuable as the real *Mona Lisa*? Would coin collectors or stamp collectors still value their collections if the coins and stamps were fakes? Could we blow up the *Mona Lisa*, say "sorry!" and then just replace it with a version that is "just as good"? For that matter, would the *Mona Lisa* still be a great painting if its canvas and paints were made from the remains of murder victims? For some environmentalists, the fake beach is the remains of an atrocity. Wouldn't this be like John Hammond blowing up his park at the end of the movie and then saying, "Heck, let's try it again!" and building the same park, in the same place, on top of the corpses of the old dinosaurs?

Eric Katz believes that the fact that we think we can go destroy a bunch of nature and then happily just "restore it" shows how much disdain we really have for nature. It's nothing but human arrogance to think we can restore nature, like the arrogance it takes to "restore" the dinosaurs. And Katz thinks that the whole restoration argument does violence to the *terms* "nature" and "natural." If these words are to mean anything, they *must* "designate objects and processes" that—as far as humanly possible—are "outside of human influence and control." Human copies of the natural world are not natural in this sense. When humans "restore nature," the result simply is not *natural*. And if we start thinking it is "natural," when it is *faked*, the whole word "natural" makes no sense!

Okay, sure, the dinosaurs in Spielberg's movies are majestic. But so are the Navi in *Avatar*, and so are the aliens in *Star Wars*. Ultimately, there comes the realization that these creatures are not real, and much of their majesty—poof—goes away. The experience of real dinosaurs would be different from a movie featuring fake dinosaurs, especially because we know they're *fake*. We feel reverence for the natural world, especially when this world is untouched by human intervention.

Respectful Restorations

But maybe environmental philosophers have "failed to understand the theoretical and practical importance" of species restoration. Andrew Light takes on both Elliot and Katz directly, arguing for species restoration *and* for moving environmental ethics in a more realistic direction. If Light's arguments are successful, and the science behind Jurassic Park was possible, then the restoration of dinosaurs could be ethically justified.

Light thinks that it may to possible to distinguish between malicious restorations and more positive ones. We could argue that the destruction of the original *Mona Lisa* would be a terrible thing, and replacing it with really a good fake would reduce the loss. But art restoration would only under very unusual circumstances involve destruction of the original. The usual case is that restorers try to help preserve the work from decay and restore it to its original glory. In fact, with works like the *Mona Lisa*, if we don't work to restore them, they will eventually fade, fall apart, and disappear! So we could recognize that some restorations of nature involve showing the same respect for nature that the art restorer shows for works of art.

We should give Elliot and Katz their due, and concede that it is overly arrogant for humans to think we can perfect nature. On the other hand, as Crichton has argued forcefully in *State of Fear*, it's also impossible for humans to not impact the environment, and we have been impacting it for thousands of years. If this is true then the question is not whether we impact the environment, but whether we impact the environment wisely. The real problem with Jurassic Park, then, may not be the decision to restore some dinosaurs, but the heavy handed attempt to restore them for our amusement. *Jurassic Park* is not the story of a failed attempt at species restoration, but the failed attempt to put dangerous wild animals in an amusement park.

Yes, the history of Yellowstone is a disaster. But there have been successful species restorations. It does seem reasonable to say that we could never perfectly reproduce the dinosaurs nor in any meaningful sense their natural ecosystems. But ecosystems, as Crichton has forcefully argued, are not static, and constantly change. Natural creatures adapt and evolve: "life will find a way." It seems that a careful attempt to introduce dinosaurs into an ecosystem could be done with enough respect for that ecosystem. In any case, that ecosystem will evolve with or without our intervention.

We currently lack the knowledge to judge these dinosaur restorations in advance, but then again, we currently lack the knowledge necessary to produce dinosaurs anyway. The fact is, though, that I am bullish enough on science to think that someday we may have the knowledge to restore the dinosaurs, and I believe that we could do so in a way that is consistent with a land ethic. At that time, there will be an overwhelming case that we should do so. And wouldn't it be pretty wonderful?

9
Flea-Market Capitalism

TIMOTHY SEXTON

Discover it. Patent it. Sell it. You can't separate the discovery of knowledge from the ability to make money. Every leap forward in the discovery of the natural world is tied to a leap forward in the world of commerce. This fact of modern life is at the heart of capitalism, the idea that what we make, discover, and shape is ours—ours alone—and *we can do whatever we want with it*. But try telling the *Tyrannosaurus rex* bearing down on you to respect your patent and *back off*! Some things may just not respond well to the whims of our wallets.

What's to criticize about capitalism, you ask? What's wrong with the greatest economic system in the world that has produced more millionaires and billionaires than all the other systems combined? Capitalism created the jobs that turned *Jurassic Park* from an idea in one guy's head into a bestselling novel and then a blockbuster movie! It provided thousands of people with income made from manufacturing and selling the billions of dollars of merchandise based upon the movie.

If anything, this movie that briefly became Hollywood's number one moneymaker and set a new standard for pre-release marketing success should be put on permanent display in the Museum of Capitalism, located not far from the big pile of money its director Steven Spielberg sits on when directing his films. . . . Or so I assume. The Museum of Capitalism can be found beneath the vault where Donald Trump's bankruptcy settlements are stored. (But I don't know for sure.) And doesn't *Jurassic Park* deserve a big, expensive, display in that museum? Actually . . . Nope! As far as teaching us to be good capitalists goes, *Jurassic Park* bites!

Can You See the Fleas?

One of the few quiet moments of introspection in *Jurassic Park* sets the stage for one of the critiques of capitalism. Sitting at a table in the massive park restaurant across from paleobotanist Ellie Sattler, John Hammond reminisces about the first entertainment attraction he ever built: a flea circus. With a motorized trapeze and carousel that apparently had the power to convince those who stopped by for a view that there actually were fleas involved. Of course, there weren't. There couldn't be. You can't train fleas to ride a merry-go-round or fly on a trapeze. It was all illusion made to separate parents' money from their wallets.

Guys at the top of the economic food chain like John Hammond have the means at their disposal to use their great wealth and economic power to make sure we see the fleas they want us to see. The wealthiest control how ideas are transmitted and communicated. They have the ability to influence how we think things just naturally are. For example, almost all news outlets are *owned*. And you'd better believe that they make damn sure nothing is broadcast that they don't want us to hear.

And, so, what they *want* us to believe *becomes* our belief, our "ideology." Metaphorically speaking: if we were to insist that we can't see the fleas, we would be seen as rejecting the ideology. And isn't that true of capitalism? Doesn't even *reading* this chapter make you feel a little guilty? It must be written by some commie trying to destroy our system! Well, not to add fuel to that fire, but here's how Karl Marx (1818–1883) and Frederick Engels (1820–1895) explain capitalist ideology:

> The class which is the ruling material force of society, is at the same time its ruling intellectual force. The class which has the means of material production at its disposal, has control at the same time over the means of mental production, so that thereby, generally speaking, the ideas of those who lack the means of mental production are subject to it.

Here's part of our ideology: we capitalists believe people like Nedry are less important than people like Hammond. Isn't

Hammond the one really in control, the one really with the power? Wasn't it his genius, that *by itself* raised the dead! And doesn't he deserve the right to every hard earned dollar he made from that genius? But Nedry wasn't really less important, was he? He proved that by bringing down the park. . . . Though, on the other hand, he was also a pretty selfish person, willing to risk the lives of others for money. That much he and Hammond had in common.

Our belief that the important people are the ones with the money is pretty messed up. Imagine every hourly worker in a big corporation going on strike for a day. Now imagine the CEO of that company going on strike for a month. Which work stoppage do you think would have the greater negative impact on the company? If we still believe that any CEO is more important than *every* worker, and deserves to make a salary more than thirty times what the average hourly worker of the company makes . . . we might be seeing the fleas. Hammond would have *nothing* without his scientists, computer programmers, and, yes, even his sweaty, smelly, bloodied workers penning those animals. But who do we give our respect, and criticism to? . . . Who makes the *real* money? . . . Just that one man—one man who couldn't have done any of it alone.

Spend a Little Time with Our Target Audience

Target audience. That is the exact phrase that John Hammond, the vulture capitalist . . . er, I mean *venture* capitalist who is the driving force behind Jurassic Park uses to describe his two grandchildren. The term "target" is a reflection on the park's targeting of children. Hammond does view the entire world— even his own grandkids—in terms that boil value down to a monetary transaction. The way Hammond refers to his own grandchildren as a target audience is just one example of how the movie softens the more cartoonish villainy he exhibits in the novel. Hammond is willing to risk his grandchildren's lives just to test his park. Hammond's capitalistic viewpoint allows the children to be transformed into a cash transaction.

When Hammond arrives at Grant and Sattler's dinosaur dig in the Badlands, his private helicopter threatens to wipe away in an instant all the actual hard work done by those who have made his park possible. But their work doesn't produce anything of economic value, so he doesn't worry about his interruption. And just in case Grant and Sattler were to insist on placing the value of their work above the value of his exploitative theme park, Hammond bribes them. How does Hammond convince the two scientists to take part in his effort to get around what little regulatory obstruction stands between him and profiting off the work of others? With a bribe to completely fund their work for the next few years.

For the price of what would likely be a nifty little tax write-off, Hammond exploits the lack of value placed on scientific research that can't be packaged for entertainment, to convince two highly educated people to lend credibility to his capitalist dream. And what exactly is that capitalist dream? An enterprise that appears to be almost entirely free of legal oversight, environmental regulations, and any level of ethical intrusion. Had a gatekeeper not been killed, causing the investors to want evidence that their *money would not be wasted*, the chaos that releases the monstrous predators into a world without regulation or control would have occurred in a park filled with children . . . what a lovely *dream*.

A Question of Vision

Hammond's grandson Tim sits in the electric-powered Jeep stalled right in front of the *T. rex* habitat. Since Donald Gennaro, the lawyer who is their only adult companion, sees no value to be gained from entertaining the kids, boredom eventually leads Tim to the discovery of some night-vision goggles. This behavior finally snaps the high-priced corporate attorney out of his stupor just long enough ask Tim if the headgear is heavy. When Tim says, "Yes," the lawyer replies, "Then they're expensive, . . . put them back."

The Theory of the Leisure Class is a book-length criticism of the effect of capitalist ideology on those who see the fleas driving Hammond's circus, pointing out how people ensure their own ruin. When we're stuck in a poorer economic class, we spend beyond our means in a futile attempt to buy our way into a higher one. Thorstein Veblen (1857–1929) writes at length about this ill-fated attempt to consume one's way into a higher class: "Among objects of use the simple and unadorned article is aesthetically the best. But since the pecuniary canon of reputability rejects the inexpensive in articles appropriated to individual consumption, the satisfaction of our craving for beautiful things must be sought by way of compromise." Basically, we buy crap we don't need (or even *like* much) in order to *appear* part of the class that doesn't want us!

Veblen is suggesting that if the night-vision goggles discovered by Tim had not been heavy—or, indeed, if Tim had lied and said they were not heavy—the lawyer would not have determined them to be valuable. They are not valuable to the lawyer because they are an object of genuinely great use; they're invested with the reputability that comes with being valuable because he has bought into the capitalist ideology that equates worth with expense and expense with weight.

It is certainly worth keeping in mind that the lawyer dies a gruesome death while cowardly hiding on a toilet. That death is almost universally greeted with approval from audiences. Money can't buy you courage. And it's only of value to others who see the fleas. Unfortunately for Gennaro, the *T. rex* saw little of use in the lawyer's pocketbook.

Mosquitoes, Lawyers, and Capitalists

Upon seeing the cloned versions of dinosaurs made possible only as a result of the incessant thirst for blood of mosquitoes dead for millions of years, the scientists are filled with a childlike sense of awe and wonder. After all, they are among the first people in the history of the planet to ever see actual living dinosaurs. The response of the lawyer who represents the investors in Jurassic Park, on the other hand, is an economic forecast.

"We're gonna make a fortune out of this place." Between this prediction and what is one of the most ill-advised bathroom breaks in movie history, Gennaro makes a suggestion aimed at boosting their chance of making money. He suggests an admission charge to enjoy the spectacle inside Jurassic Park somewhere between $2,000 and $10,000 a day. Prices that will limit enjoyment of the park only to the richest people in the world. John Hammond quickly cuts the "bloodsucking lawyer" short by admonishing him that he wants to make the park available to everybody.

The scene has the effect of making John Hammond seem like a friend to the working class stiffs that keeps the highly preferable simulated reality of theme parks profitable. But ask yourself this question: how can he possibly live up to his promise to make Jurassic Park available to any but the wealthiest of tourists? The cost of dinosaur care and maintenance is way too vital to the park's success to be cut. Transportation to an island off the coast of Central America certainly isn't going to get any cheaper. Capitalism makes it difficult even for business owners who really want to help their customers to do so for very long. Think about people like Sam Walton of Wal-Mart, he seemed to really want to help people, but after his death, the policies that he followed, which made Wal-Mart so popular, were abandoned by the investors.

When the owner can no longer suck enough value out of the raw materials necessary for production, the only thing he's got left to cut that won't impact his profit is how much he pays his employees. Marx outlines what he terms the "general law of capitalist accumulation." Basically, it's just the dream of rolling back costs to the point where they don't have to pay anybody to do anything. Hammond can't control the cost of things like transportation, food, insurance, utilities . . . well, the cost of pretty much everything involved in running an enterprise like Jurassic Park is out of his control. But there is one thing he *can* control . . . What he pays his employees.

As long as Hammond can exploit their willingness to work for the lowest possible wages and still do a competent job, he will. *The lower the cost of that competence, the greater the profit.* Needless to say, not having to pay wages at all would be the ideal for profit-making. And our dear John Hammond begins to seem a bit more like the god of capitalism he so resembles . . . "Dear Santa, . . . I want, I want, I want!" But Santa isn't giving away dinosaurs for free, kiddies! We don't take our children to the dear old saint to confess what they are going to *give*! No, they guiltlessly demand what they want. Hammond understands that; he knows what children want, and he's going to give it to them. That isn't exploitation, is it? Just good business. . . .

The Color of Money

One of the things I love most about *Jurassic Park* is that little cartoon that explains the process of cloning dinosaurs. I especially love the way the little string of DNA who serves as the cartoon's star and narrator of the live action part of the video pronounces the word dinosaur: dina-SOUR. I love it so much, in fact, that that's how I'm going to spell the word from here on out.

Notice that in that lovely little video, almost all of the workers are white, but in reality, when we actually see the workers, they have noticeably brown skin. Who is it that gets notice and recognition in the video? Why, again, it's John Hammond! But the poor shmucks getting eaten by raptors . . . well, they don't get any air time. Capitalism has a pretty long history of white industrialists taking advantage of people in the developing world. These people often have fewer rights, and less legal recourse, and so they are ripe for the picking by a corporation that needs to make money regardless of the human cost! They become like the dino-sours of Jurassic Park. . . . *Things* that are useful for making money. This goofy, time-passing little video is clearly sending a message: scientists are the stars, teaching us that *capitalism* is now responsible for man's ability to *literally control the course of evolution*! And all but two of the workers are white.

Spared No Expense . . . Well, Almost

On five different occasions, John Hammond says no expense was spared in creating Jurassic Park. Hammond's obviously quite proud of the money spent on Jurassic Park to ensure its ultimate profitability. But I suspect that Jurassic Park employee Dennis Nedry might disagree with Hammond on the subject of expenses being spared.

When Nedry sits at his computer desk complaining about being overworked and undervalued, Hammond's response is, "Sorry about your financial problems, Dennis, but they are *your* financial problems." It is Nedry and not Hammond who understands that his financial problems actually *are* Hammond's problem, but when he brings his worries to Hammond, his employer cuts him off . . . "I will not get drawn into another financial debate with you, Dennis, I really will not." "You're right, John. You're absolutely right. Everything's my problem." And this answer is right in line with our ideology: poverty is the *poor's* problem, not ours.

A vital part of the mechanics of flea market capitalism is convincing the working class that their failure to become wealthy (in our "classless" system, where *nobody* is excluded from opportunity) must be their fault. If you can't achieve economic success, it must be because you aren't smart enough, aren't ambitious enough, or—our favorite—you just aren't working hard enough. The one thing that is certainly not to be blamed for the financial problems of workers like Dennis Nedry is the capitalist system itself—a system that, according to a 2012 report by the Economic Policy Institute, was responsible for compensation of CEOs like John Hammond rising 725 percent between 1978 and 2011, and a compensation rise for their employees to only 5.7 percent over the same period. And our response to that? "Well, *everyone* can't be rich." But isn't that what we are promised . . . if we're all innovative enough, work hard enough, and *believe* enough, we can all be rich? But we can't all be rich, and it isn't because the *working* class is lazy. I think we are all still seeing the fleas!

See, here's the thing: If Hammond would only pay Nedry what he's worth, Nedry would benefit by having fewer financial problems, and Hammond would benefit by not becoming the victim of corporate sabotage. Nedry's own greed leads him to do something truly horrible. We have to realize, though, that Hammond's own greed played a role in that. And certainly, Hammond's greed is what leads him to cut corners like *having only one man who knows how to control his security system!* The message of *Jurassic Park* could not be clearer: "When everyone is trying to screw everyone else over, everyone gets screwed."

And, Well . . . There It Is

The cloned dinosaurs are in actual economic terms merely raw material. Symbolically, however, they're just as much part of the working class as Nedry or the scientists or the miners digging for amber. Like their human counterparts, the dinosaurs depend on the ruling class for food, shelter, property, and health. The velociraptors, brachiosaurs, *T. rex*, and other species are every bit as exploited by capitalist ideology as human workers. There is, however, one very important distinction.

The forces of capitalist ideology hold no influence over the dinosaurs. So control has to be established by force instead of by subtle manipulation. Rather than taming the revolutionary urge to demand fairness and equality by the working class with numbing entertainment, the dinosaurs are tamed with electric fences. Once that mechanism for domination breaks down, there's nothing to stop the exploited class from seizing power and taking control of what used to be the capitalist dream of Isla Nubar.

See, the difference between us and the dinosaurs is we can be deceived and manipulated by things like a flea circus, but a *T. rex* . . . well, the only thing that will stop him is an electric fence. And when that fence comes down, nothing, not even a large check, will slow him down.

10
Do Dinosaurs Really Scare Us?

Michael J. Muniz

You wake up one morning and see outside your window the bright, shining sun and the beautiful green grass, and hear the birds singing as they fly by. This nice, gentle setting is quite appealing. . . .

Until, that is, you feel a soft rumble on the floor. You see ripples in the cup of water on the night table next to your bed as a result of the intense vibrations. Soon, you realize that it's not an earthquake, but a giant *Tyrannosaurus rex*. But how can this be? You know that they've been extinct for millions of years! But here he is, looking straight at you through your bedroom window. It isn't until his roar wakes you up that you realize that it was all a dream.

It may have all been a dream, but truthfully, it could easily have been a reality. This is where a philosopher comes in and takes into consideration what we know about reality and how we experience it. Here's an extra crunch to your bite: when I say dinosaurs can be "real" you probably think I mean InGen or some other company could recreate them, but no—I mean they are real now. They're real when you watch the movie and read the book. And not just in some cutesy "let's pretend" sense; I mean that in the most important ways you can say, *"real."*

Reel Horror Real Scary

Are the *Jurassic Park* movies horror movies? What about the books? Some have said that these stories are just as "horrific" as *Jaws*. By definition, horror movies attempt to provoke a

negative emotional response from audience members by prey-
ing on their fears. It doesn't necessarily mean that there has to
be some supernatural or gory element to it. Just about any
movie could be horrifying if there's an element of fear. Does
that make them horror movies?

Perhaps *Jurassic Park* may be a horror story because
there's an overwhelming amount of tension between fear and
excitement. In books, we depend on the author's use of words
and plot to tell a story. In movies, we depend on the director's
ability to show us images in a certain order so that a story can
both be told and seen.

We can test the importance of the storyteller by experimenting with a basic fairy tale that almost everybody knows:
The Three Little Pigs. What would happen if Michael Crichton
wrote his own version of the *Three Little Pigs*? We would probably get some horrific tale of three swine-like creatures that
evolved through some unfortunate science experiment and
wreaked havoc on a wolf pen. Although it may technically be
The Three Little Pigs, we wouldn't be getting the same experience from Crichton's version. Obviously, storytellers are a necessary and important component to experiencing a story. To
better understand a story, we should look to how a story is told,
rather than relying only on the story itself.

Unfortunately, with horror on the screen, you can only go so
far. Sure, there may be some tensions, but storytellers (in this
case: the filmmakers) are limited by our understanding of the
human experience and imagination. One of the things that we
tend to agree with is the idea of realism—how to make something appear real. So, we tend to believe "realistic" movies
because they're intentionally made to appear real. In other
words, the more "real" something appears to be, the more we
tend to accept (believe) it as real. With better technology (3D,
CGI, and the rest of it) movie makers attempt to make movies
as "realistic" as possible.

There are two things we need in order to make a realistic
movie: 1. what we know to be real, and 2. what we perceive to
be real. Here's an example of knowledge: I know that the image
drawn below is a circle:

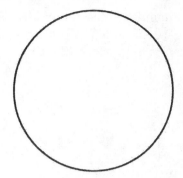

In terms of movies, we know that what we're actually seeing is a bunch of images projected on a screen flashing before our eyes. So we feel pretty comfortable about what we "know," but can we really be so sure? Which brings me to the next requirement: perception.

A perception is the driving force that guides us into knowledge. In other words, without perception, we can't have knowledge. So, ask yourself, am I really looking at a circle? What if I perceive it to be the backside of someone's head, or an eyeball without a pupil? So, what we have here is *shape* versus *definition*. The more I focus on the shape itself, I will always get a circle, but the more I focus on defining the shape, then I can get many possibilities. Ever heard of the old saying: if it looks like a duck, walks like a duck, and sounds like a duck, it must be a duck? Or, in the case of *Jurassic Park*: it looks like a bird, it walks like a bird, therefore, it must be a velociraptor? The point is that we use our perception to determine what we consider "reality." And reality is what we use to determine what we know!

Think about it like this—suppose I draw two more circles, a triangle, and a line in the circle above like this:

Most of us would automatically perceive the arrangement of the shapes as a face. Now, if I add to this arrangement more shapes and figures, it might look like this:

The question then becomes: which of the three figures is more "realistic"? Most of us would say the third one, if we were focusing on the details of a *face*. Which is my point exactly! If we focus on defining reality, then what we are actually doing is perceiving it. We like to think that reality is "out there," but our perceptions are what help us determine reality, and our perceptions are very powerful. Try to look at the circle above and *not* see a face. It's very difficult to do. We *make* that circle into a face, and that becomes reality for us. There is no face there… just lines and circles and triangles. It's our *perception* that makes it a face.

Let's go back to our so-called dinosaur knowledge. Which dinosaur seems more "realistic": Barney the purple dinosaur, or the *Tyrannosaurus rex* from *The Lost World: Jurassic Park 2*, that tromps around the streets of San Diego? That's right—the San Diego *T. rex* probably seems more realistic, even though Barney is actually a guy in a suit interacting with actual children, while the *T. rex* was *never* in San Diego. The more realistic dinosaur is actually the one that is *less real!*

The Aquarium of Reality

John Hammond puts it best when he says, "We've made living biological attractions so astounding that they'll capture the imagination of the entire planet." It seems that he's talking about dinosaurs, but he could be talking about movies themselves. What if the movies that we see in theaters were nothing more than "biological attractions"? What if they're like an aquarium where we are actually seeing people and events that are actually happening right now? Talk about being a peeping Tom, huh? What if we perceive movies as real events?

Perhaps this is the case. Film theorists, philosophers, and psychoanalysts have all contributed to the idea that movies are real in some way. Filmmakers tend to take these theories into consideration and exploit them when making a movie. Think about the idea of danger, or dooming peril, towards children. It seems quite normal to suggest that nobody likes the idea of children in danger. Yet for Steven Spielberg (the director of the first two *Jurassic Park* films), terrorizing children is a great way to elicit fear in a movie theater audience. So, he's done it in just about all of his movies. Going back to our idea of story-tellers, Spielberg's *Jurassic Park* is quite different from Michael Crichton's novel (even though Crichton himself wrote the screenplay). The one element that is guaranteed in all three films, which is mandatory for the stories to work, is danger towards children. To prove it, ask yourself: Would I still be experiencing the same thrill if no children were in danger of being eaten in the films?

Perhaps you can still feel the same gripping fear for the children some other way, but the question then becomes, would you get the same story? Lex and Tim were crucial to the plot in the *Jurassic Park*, especially when Lex hacked into the computer system to turn everything on. Kelly Curtis's gymnastics skills helped in fighting some raptors that were attacking her and Sarah, but it was her very presence on the island that motivated Dr. Malcolm to get off the island faster in *The Lost World: Jurassic Park 2*. Finally, Erik Kirby's disappearance into Isla Sorna was the sole reason why his parents tricked/kidnapped Dr. Grant into coming along, and having the adventure that took place in *Jurassic Park III*. Without these child-in-danger moments the films would not be nearly as thrilling!

The Paradox Rex

Imagine you were undergoing a jury selection survey for a murder trial. The prosecutor asks you whether or not you've ever witnessed a murder before. Now, if you're like me, we've seen a lot of violent movies where murders take place all the time. So, am I telling the truth when I say, "Yes sir, I've seen many murders"? Of course, if you did say that you'd probably be escorted to another courtroom and sentenced to do time at a special facility. Now, going back to the screen, can we say that we've actually seen dinosaurs? If we say no, then why do we get scared, or feel a sense of thrill, when Lex and Tim are being terrorized by the *T. rex* in the Ford Explorer in the first *Jurassic Park*? This problem between knowing what's real and feeling what's real is a type of paradox.

By "paradox" I mean a statement or situation that seems to be logically impossible, or appears to be a contradiction, but is in fact true. Paradoxes have been around for many years. Some would say millions of years, but nobody really knows how long. Paradoxes are used all the time to challenge certain viewpoints about certain issues, like the age or existence of dinosaurs.

One paradox, the Paradox of Fiction, can be stated as three simple sentences:

1. People only respond emotionally to what they believe is real.

2. People don't believe that fiction is real.

3. People respond emotionally to fiction all the time.

The paradox happens after you combine the first two sentences and realize that the third should say that people do *not* respond emotionally to fiction. And yet, the third sentence is also true. Is this a contradiction? We're going to have to dig deeper to get to the bones of the matter and then see how we can escape its inevitable bite. Philosophers, who are determined to show that this paradox can be resolved, attempt to prove that one of these sentences is false. Other philosophers, usually in the minority, have recognized the paradox and settled on the fact that our emotional responses to fiction are basically irrational (i.e. crazy).

There are two major types of emotions: passive and active. Passive emotions are those that occur at the moment without any thought. For example, when you're walking across the street and you hear the sound of loud horn from a big truck that speeds by, you jump back and your heart begins to pound.

You didn't stop and think on what course of action you should perform: your survival instincts triggered brain activity that forced you to jump back and be afraid. Your fear is momentary.

An active emotion is when you dwell on the thought of a situation for quite so much time that you eventually end up with an emotional response. Because your mind is actively engaged in thought, the result is an emotion. The more you dwell on the possible reality of a *T. rex* drinking out of your backyard swimming pool, the more you'll probably be afraid of leaving your dog tied up in the backyard.

Now, this is where the paradox comes in. If I'm actively dwelling on my fears while watching a scary movie, then I will, without a doubt, be afraid during frightening scenes in the movie. So, am I actually afraid of the scene itself, or of my thoughts about the potential situation that could arise if the movie's events were true? Haven't we all at one point or another asked ourselves: What would I do if I were in that situation?

Most people tend to accept that sentence #2, "People don't believe that fiction is real," is true. But, some philosophers have given arguments that would make us think differently. This would mean that fiction (or at least some fiction) is perceived as real. If I see *The Lost World: Jurassic Park 2*, and I know that it's fiction, but I believe that the "Godzilla" sequence (at the end of the film) could occur in my hometown of Hialeah, Florida, then it becomes real to me. Therefore, the fiction has become a sort of reality.

Most philosophers who try to argue against sentence #3 "People respond emotionally to fiction all the time (or at least often)," think that the emotional responses that we produce are in fact not genuine—a sort of make-believe emotion. Some philosophers have gone so far as to say that these are "fictional emotional responses." What the heck is a fictional emotional response? Apparently, while everything else about my emotions is genuine, because the movie (or story) is fictional, I am having a "fictional emotional response." Trying to solve the paradox from this third point leaves us dangling for disaster when it comes to wondering about what is fictional and what is real.

This leaves us with our acceptance or denial of sentence #1 of the paradox, " People only respond emotionally to what they believe is real." Any attempt to deny #1 would mean that you deny that emotions are rooted in beliefs (which is impossible to do because, as I explained earlier, this is the case for active emotions). Now, it seems that we *could* deny sentence #1 by claiming that some part of the brain believes (or perceives) the situation is real. Since perception drives reality, then an explanation could be as simple as: We perceive fiction as real, in some way, while another part of us doesn't. This is the reason we don't run out of the theaters from the dinosaurs in *Jurassic Park* but we're also scared of them. But this might make us just a bit crazy. So, it could be quite satisfying to simply accept the paradox as it is, and not tinker with it. Remember what happened when scientists tinkered with dinosaur DNA found in mosquitos that were fossilized in sap and buried hundreds of feet below? We ended up with a disaster. Don't be afraid of the Paradox Rex (or *P. rex* for short).

Concluding Thoughts for Your Helicopter Ride to Safety

In the end, we all believe that what we're seeing on the screen is either actually happening or not; that the characters and situations are realistic or not. If we accept the paradox of fiction then what we're really saying is that any emotional response to any movie is irrational. So, don't judge me if I'm laughing out loud at Gennaro's death when he was eaten while sitting on the toilet in *Jurassic Park*; or feel sad that the dog was eaten as a snack in The *Lost World: Jurassic Park 2;* or when I feel a sense of awe, wonder, and beauty when I see the carnivorous pterodactyls try to feed their young by dropping Eric Kirby into their den in *Jurassic Park III*. Your feelings are just as irrational as mine.

III

Unnatural Selection

11
What's It Like to Be a *T. rex*?

RICK STOODY

Here's a philosophical question for you. Why would anyone—much less a law school graduate—think that an outhouse is a good place to hide from a *Tyrannosaurus rex*?

Seriously, what was going through that guy's head? He had to be thinking *something*, right? Actually, I'm pretty confident that we are *all* thinking *something*, even if it's "Oh! A *T. rex* is running around eating people! *I'll hide in this bathroom.*" Here's the point: wise or unwise, we are thinking things. We are *conscious*—we have mental *stuff* happening in our heads. And not just thoughts; I bet Gennaro wasn't just thinking, "Well this was a dumb idea," when the *T. rex* bit into him. I bet he was *feeling* a whole lot of pain, fear, and, well, more *pain*.

Okay, so even lawyers are more than just their bodies, they have minds as well. So the next question is, are Hammond's dinosaurs more than the physical stuff they're made of? Are they just collections of matter—bones, blood, brains, DNA? Or is there something else to them? Something non-physical? My gut says that they're entirely physical. A scientist grew them in a lab! But if that's true, it's hard to see where consciousness fits in.

After all, how could something wholly physical be conscious? Islands, jeeps, and electric fences aren't conscious. They aren't thinking, feeling things with their own mental lives. They're simply composed of atoms. And atoms aren't conscious—they don't have thoughts or feelings or desires. But Hammond's dinosaurs are conscious. They do have mental lives. At least, it seems reasonable to think that they do. But if dinosaurs are just collections of atoms, how can that be?

These questions aren't limited to the dinosaurs of Jurassic Park. They also apply to human beings. Are we more than just collections of matter? Are Dr. Malcolm and Dr. Sattler entirely physical? If so, it's hard to see how they could be conscious. And if you and I are just collections of matter, how could we be conscious? The answer, I think, is that we couldn't be. If we were only physical, I don't think we would be conscious. But the fact remains—we *are* conscious. We do have mental lives. So I think there's more to us than just our physical bodies. And since it's reasonable to suppose that Hammond's dinosaurs are also conscious, I think there's something more to them as well.

Mere Flesh and DNA?

A lot of philosophers would disagree. They call themselves physicalists. They reject the notion that there is something more to human beings and dinosaurs than their physical components. Physicalism is the idea that conscious animals are entirely *physical*. According to physicalism, human beings and other animals like dinosaurs are ultimately nothing more than their bodies. There's no immaterial aspect, no mind, or what some call the "soul." They're just physical objects—like tropical islands, jeeps, and electric fences.

Dualism stands in opposition to physicalism, claiming instead that there are *two* aspects to conscious animals—the physical and the nonphysical. According to dualists, there's something more to conscious animals than just the matter they are made of. What exactly is this "something more"? Is it the mind? The soul? Something else? We will look at some different versions of dualism later. But what we need to figure out now is whether physicalism is true or false. Is there more to us— and dinosaurs—than flesh and DNA?

What Does Science Say?

But now science is the belief system that is hundreds of years old. And, like the medieval system before it, science is starting not to fit the world any more. Science has attained so much power that its practical limits begin to be apparent.

—Dr. Ian Malcom, *Jurassic Park*

First, let's see if science has anything to say about physicalism and dualism. The advances and discoveries of the scientific enterprise are remarkable. Although dinosaurs have not really been resurrected through genetic engineering, it certainly seems like it could happen. Science has been a very reliable way of getting at the truth of reality, so if science says that physicalism is true, then we should consider it seriously.

Well then, . . . does science say that physicalism is true? No. Science, by its very nature, can't tell us whether conscious animals are entirely physical or not. The sciences study the observable world. And they are limited to studying that world. So if nonphysical things exist, science is not in a position to tell us about them. That means that the question of whether human beings and dinosaurs are entirely physical is not a scientific question. After all, what sort of scientific experiments could we possibly perform to answer that question? The sciences tell us a lot about the physical part of reality, but we want to know whether there is more to reality than just the physical part, whether there is a nonphysical aspect of conscious animals.

What if science can explain everything about us without having to appeal to anything non-physical? If that were the case, understanding humans would be like understanding television sets, there wouldn't be anything else needed to explain how the TV, or human, or dinosaurs works. But I'm not convinced that's true. Even if we have all of the physical parts of humans put together in the right order, something is missing, and that something can't be observed by science.

What if it turns out that physicalism is false? Would that undermine science? Absolutely not. Science studies observable reality (at least indirectly), in other words the *physical* world. If it turns out that there is also a nonphysical part of reality, that doesn't undermine the fact that there is a physical part of reality that is worth exploring. Neither does it falsify everything that we have already come to know about the physical world. Paleontology is still worth doing even though there is more to reality than fossilized plants and animals.

A Dinosaur's-Eye View of the World

. . . you feel the way the boat moves? That's the sea. That's real. You smell the salt in the air? You feel the sunlight on your skin? That's all real. Life is wonderful. It's a gift to be alive, to see the sun and breathe the air.

—JACK THORNE, *The Lost World*

Imagine walking through the jungle and stumbling upon a velociraptor. She looks up at you and you freeze, hoping she won't notice you if you don't move. No such luck! She has excellent eyesight and she charges you. You run, frantically scrambling over tree roots and rocks. You splash across a shallow stream and start climbing a hill on the opposite side. Then you look back. She's gone. Whew! That was close. You pull yourself over the top of the hill and take a deep breath. But there she is, waiting for you. Before you can think, she slashes at you with her six-inch retractable claw. And then she starts to eat you while you are still alive. Lying there, being eaten by a velociraptor, you would experience a whole range of sensations—fear, surprise, pain, the horrid smell of her breath—none of which could be reduced to a merely physical explanation.

There's a way it feels to have certain experiences. There's a "what-it's-like" aspect of consciousness. When we experience something, there's an insider's view, a first-person perspective, of that thing. So, . . . what's it like to be eaten by a velociraptor? It's like *being eaten by a velociraptor!* It's one of those experiences that you just have to have in order to understand what it's like (and I'm glad to pass on that one!).

Think about your own experiences for a moment. When you listen to the music of composer John Williams, you have certain experiences. When the French horn plays a B-flat, you experience a particular sound, and your experience of that sound is different from the experience you have when you hear the flute play a C. We all have experiences like these. When we look at the deep blue ocean surrounding the island of Isla Nublar, we have a sensory experience of color that is quite different from the sensory experience we have when we see the lush green vegetation of the island. When we chew on salty movie theater popcorn (drizzled with "butter"), we have experiences that are different from when we munch on sweet M&M's.

Having these sorts of experiences is part of what it is to be a conscious being. They are just an ordinary part of our lives. The world appears to *you* in a certain way through *your* senses.

But the world doesn't appear in *any* way to an atom or particle—or to an island off the coast of Costa Rica, for that matter. There is something it is like to be a human being or a *T. rex*. And there is nothing it is like to be a jeep or an electrified fence.

It seems that facts about physical objects can be known from an impersonal third-person perspective. And this is the perspective that the sciences take. Facts about Isla Nublar aren't dependent on any particular perspective. Or, at the very least, we sure as heck don't have the language to express what it's like to be an island. Anyone with access to the island could theoretically come to know everything there is to know about it. In this sense, facts about Isla Nublar are public. Indeed, it seems that all facts about physical objects are public. No special insider's view is required. Everything that can be known about them can be known from the "outside." But our conscious lives don't seem to be like that; our mental lives are private. And this suggests a problem for the idea that human beings and dinosaurs are entirely physical: it can't account for the what-it's-like aspect of consciousness. Let's look at two ways of explaining this problem.

What We Can't Know about the *T. rex*

What would it be like to be a *Tyrannosaurus rex*?[1] Take a moment to think about it. What would its sensory experiences be like? Suppose Hammond's dinosaurs were successfully created and now inhabit Jurassic Park. What would the world look like to a *T. rex*? What would fresh velociraptor taste like? What would the carcass of a triceratops smell like?

Suppose scientists were able to map the entire brain of the *T. rex*. And suppose that they have determined which neural states of the *T. rex* correspond with certain sensory experiences. They might even have a list of these correlations. The taste of velociraptor activates this part of the brain here. Smelling a certain scent activates this other part of the brain over here. And so on. Suppose these scientists have obtained

---

[1] Thinking of the qualitative aspect of consciousness in terms of "what it is like" was made popular by Thomas Nagel in "What Is It Like to Be a Bat?" *Philosophical Review* 83 (1974).

every physical fact there is about *T. rex* psychology. Would knowing all of these facts allow us to know what it is like to be a *T. rex*? Or would there still be some further fact that we are missing?

It is reasonable to think that there are some aspects of what it is like to be a *T. rex* that we can imagine. For instance, paleontologists believe that the *T. rex* had color vision. Additionally, *T. rex* is thought to have had excellent binocular vision, rivaling that of modern hawks. Contrary to claims made in *Jurassic Park* the movie, *T. rex* could see its prey quite well, even if its prey wasn't moving. Human beings also have color vision and binocular vision. So it seems that we can imagine what the world might have looked like to a *T. rex*. And perhaps we share other sensory experiences in common with *T. rex* to some degree. So there might be quite a bit of what it is like to be a *T. rex* that we can imagine.

But there are other aspects of what it is like to be a *T. rex* that are simply beyond our reach. For example, the *T. rex* had an extraordinary sense of smell. Both the *T. rex* and velociraptor are thought to rival bloodhounds in their ability to smell prey. Given that their range of smelling abilities far exceeds our own, it's reasonable to think that they were capable of experiencing smells unlike anything we ever have. So, there are some sensory experiences that they had that we can't have, and without these raw materials, it seems that we're unable to imagine what certain aspects of their mental lives were like. In relation to a *T. rex*, we are like a man trying to imagine the smell of rotten eggs when the only smell he has ever experienced, or is capable of experiencing, is that of a rose. No matter how you describe the smell to him, he just won't be able to smell rotten eggs. Given just how different some *T. rex* mental experiences are from our own, it's hard to see how we could imagine what it is like to be a *T. rex*, even if we knew every physical fact about the brain states of the *T. rex*.

So although we might know every physical fact about the brain of a *T. rex*, we would still be lacking knowledge of something: what it is like to be a *T. rex*. There is a first-person perspective, a what-it's-like aspect, of the *T. rex* that is not really captured by the physical facts. The third-person perspective of neuroscience is missing something. But if all there is to the *T. rex* is the physical stuff it's made up of, then there shouldn't be any facts about the *T. rex* that aren't accounted for by neuro-science. The problem here is that there is a part of conscious-ness that is undeniable—the what-it's-like part—that is not accounted for by the physical facts. This makes it seem as though there is more to a *T. rex* than what the third-person per-spective of neuroscience is able to capture. And this is true of not just the *T. rex*, but any conscious being, anything that has a personal perspective.

What Dr. Sattler Didn't Know

Let's look at this another way. Suppose Dr. Ellie Sattler, before becoming the plucky paleobiologist who has no problem plung-ing her arm into a mountain of dino poo, was a neuroscientist. And suppose that, as a young neuroscientist, she knew every-thing there is to know about the science of color perception. Imagine that she knew all of the physical facts about how human beings perceive color. But suppose that she was raised in a completely black and white environment. She never had any color experience. She had only ever experienced black, white, and shades of gray.[2]

Ensuring that Dr. Sattler never saw color would obviously take quite a bit of effort. She could never look in a mirror at her own face; she could never be allowed to see her own skin or blood. But let us suppose that someone was able to pull it off. (Why would anyone do this? I don't know. Perhaps they read about it in a philosophy book.)

Now, imagine that one day someone shows Dr. Sattler some West Indian Lilac berries. Does she learn something new about color when she sees the berries? Yes. Although she knew every physical fact there is to know about the perception of the color violet in human beings up to this moment, she will learn some-thing new, something she could never have inferred from her knowledge of the physical facts of perception. She will learn what it is like to see the color violet. And this is a new fact about perception. She now knows something that she didn't know before—what the color violet *looks* like. So her knowl-

---

[2] This scenario is from Frank Jackson's famous example about Mary the neurophysiologist, "Epiphenomenal Qualia," *Philosophical Quarterly* 32 (1982).

edge of human perception before she saw the berries must have been incomplete. And this makes it look as though there's more to color perception than what's captured by the physical descriptions. A picture of reality that only includes physical descriptions misses an important part of reality: the what-it's-like aspect of consciousness.

Physicalism Finds a Way

If you thought that dinosaurs and human beings were completely physical, what would you say? One standard response is to point out that these previous arguments focus on what is *known*, which leaves something out: what it's *like* to have the perspectives of a *T. rex* or Dr. Sattler. But a physicalist might point out that it's possible to know something from one description without knowing it from another description. And we shouldn't infer from this simple fact that they are not the same thing. After all, a particular sensory experience and some brain state could be one and the same thing, even if they're described in two different ways. And the fact that we don't realize that they are the same thing is a fact about *us*, not a fact about *that thing*.

We all know that Michael Crichton wrote the novel *Jurassic Park*. But many may not know that he wrote another book under the pen name Michael Douglas when he was younger. Before reading that last sentence, you knew that Michael Crichton wrote *Jurassic Park*, but you probably didn't know that Michael Douglas wrote *Jurassic Park*. Now suppose someone were to argue that Michael Crichton cannot be the same person as Michael Douglas because there was something that you knew about Michael Crichton that you did not know about Michael Douglas: that he wrote *Jurassic Park*. This would be a terrible argument. Just because you knew something about this person from one description and not from another, it does not follow that Michael Crichton and Michael Douglas are two different people. They are the exact same person; you just didn't know it.

In the same way, the physicalist might argue that the same sort of mistaken reasoning is going on here regarding sensory experiences. The sensory experience that a *T. rex* has when it smells the carcass of a triceratops is identical with a certain brain state. Let's call that state the firing of nerve fiber TR2342. So, although our neuroscientists know every physical fact there is about the brain states of the *T. rex*, they don't know that the firing of TR2342 is identical to a specific smell experience. But it would be a mistake to conclude from this lack of knowledge that the firing of TR2342 and a certain smell experience are not identical. "They are the same thing," says the physicalist, "We just didn't know it."

No Escape from Jurassic Park

Does this response work? I don't think so, because it misses the real issue. What's the *real* issue? This: the "what-it's-like" features of consciousness are left out of a description of reality that is entirely physical. By its very nature, the scientific perspective, the objective third-person perspective, simply overlooks them because it does not have access to them. The only way to get at these features is from an insider's view.

The reason that the neuroscientists can't know what it is like to be a *T. rex* or Dr. Sattler is not because they lack information about the physical facts. They have all of those. What they lack are first-person experiences. And it is difficult to see how these experiential or mental events that are accessible from a first-person perspective could ever be identical with physical events that are accessible only from a third-person perspective.

It's true that, so far, we've only argued against physicalism in terms of knowledge. But I think we can rewrite the argument in a way that leaves out all talk of knowledge, like this. Conscious beings have certain experiences (like the experience of a B flat note from a French horn or the shade of violet of West Indian Lilac berries), but a complete third-person description of reality leaves these things out. If all there is to conscious animals is what's physical, then a complete physical description shouldn't leave anything out. But since something is left out, it seems that there is more to conscious animals than merely what is physical.

So . . . Do Dinosaurs Have Souls?

Where does this leave us? Physicalism seems to be unable to account for our daily what-it's-like experiences. There's more to conscious animals than mere flesh and DNA. But what is it? The mind? The soul? Or is it something else?

If you accept dualism—the view that there are both physical and nonphysical aspects to conscious animals—you have two options. The first is to say that human beings are made of two substances: a physical body and a nonphysical mind (or soul). This is known as "substance dualism." On this view, human beings have immaterial souls . . . and perhaps dinosaurs do as well.

The other option open to dualists is to reject the idea that there are dual substances—physical and nonphysical substances—and, instead, say that there are dual *properties*. This view is known as "property dualism." On this view, there is only one type of substance—physical substance—but there are two types of properties: physical properties and nonphysical mental properties. All physical substances have physical properties. Electric fences, for example, have mass, density, and so on. But some physical substances—like brains—also have nonphysical mental properties. Property dualists agree with substance dualists that there is something more to conscious animals than just physical properties. But they reject the idea that there is a nonphysical mind or soul.

Most experts in the fields of philosophy, psychology, and cognitive science are physicalists, not dualists. One reason for this is that dualism has its own share of problems. One of the most puzzling questions is how a physical part could interact with a nonphysical one. In both types of dualism, it seems that there must be some sort of link between the physical and nonphysical parts of reality. But how could this possibly be? How could such different parts of reality interact?

Whether you think that we have souls—and whether you think dinosaurs have souls—depends on whether you accept substance dualism (which, itself, faces some tough challenges). But regardless of whether conscious animals have souls or not, there is definitely good reason to think that there is more to them than just the physical stuff they are made of. This is because physicalism is unable to provide a complete picture of reality. It leaves out what it's like to be a human being. And it leaves out what it's like to be a *T. rex*.[3]

---

[3] For an excellent introduction to these issues, as well as others, I recommend John Searle, *Mind: A Brief Introduction* (Oxford, 2004).

12
Feathering the Truth

BRANDON KEMPNER

As a velociraptor stalks its prey, it calls out to its companions, razor sharp claws clicking on the ground impatiently—it lowers its head in anticipation, locking eyes with the tasty morsel. It's about to tear him into little, bloody bits. The little boy cowers in fear; knowing he has only moments to live, he looks back into the raptor's cold, cruel eyes. The boy's tear-filled gaze shakily slides down to the wide scythe of a smile filled with rows of teeth meant to tear him apart, and then down to its powerfully muscled body, covered in . . . cute, fluffy, *feathers!?*

What the heck? Well, that movie moment hasn't happened yet, but I'll admit, I had a few nightmares about it after I realized that *Jurassic Park IV* might include some real science. Ever since it was announced, *Jurassic Park* fans wondered and argued about whether or not the dinosaurs of *Jurassic Park IV* would have feathers. After all, the most recent science tells us that raptors looked something like fluffy chickens. Would the newest movie follow science (I hoped not), or would it remain true to the frightening vision of the books and the first three films? Because, between you and me, a movie that basically revolves around people running from giant-fluffy-feathered cloned monsters sounds a bit too B-horror flick to me.

But then we heard the good news! Director Colin Trevorrow laid this debate to rest with a simple Tweet: "No feathers. #JP4." Like many fans of *Jurassic Park*, I was both comforted and a bit alarmed by this piece of information. I was glad that the dinosaurs of *Jurassic Park* were going to stay scaly and scary. Still, part of the experience of going to *Jurassic Park* is the promise of seeing "real" dinosaurs (even if in this case it would make them seem a bit more fake). And then I realized the real problem here: the more *real* the dinosaurs are, the more *fake* they seem to us! Like many other things in our lives, the *fake* dinosaurs of *Jurassic Park* are more real to us than *reality*.

When Is a *Fake* More Real than *Reality*?

This question leads us down a philosophical rabbit-hole, where the border between the real and the unreal becomes blurred. We know that the dinosaurs of *Jurassic Park* aren't real; they're based on bad science. They're made of special effects and other movie magic. Still, they feel real, and, even more, we want them to be real. They thrill us with their growls and their jumps, with their violence and their intelligence. As an audience, we end up believing the lie—that fake dinosaurs are more exciting than real fossils—and what we have to wonder is, "What's left of the real world if we are so willing to embrace the *fake* world?" In fact, it might just be that there is no reality left. . . .

Consider the poor brontosaurus, that plant-eating behemoth with the enormously long neck. *It never existed.* Apparently, someone put the wrong skull on the wrong skeleton, and we wound up with a fake dinosaur![1] Still, like many people, I can picture a brontosaurus in my head, and I have a strong attachment to this non-existent beast. This reminds us of what should be obvious: our images of dinosaurs may bear little or no relationship to actual dinosaurs. After all, dinosaurs have been dead for 65 million years, and our scientific understanding is pretty spotty. Trevorrow's "No feathers" exposes the gap between our images of dinosaurs—whether found in novels, movies, toys, or illustrations—and the *reality* of dinosaurs.

This gap between reality and the image is even bigger than whether or not the dinosaurs of *Jurassic Park 4* should have had feathers. Still, that debate certainly riled up dinosaur enthusiasts: "If there is ever a *Jurassic Park 4*, and that movie

---

[1] Brian Switek published a great book on this topic called *My Beloved Brontosaurus* (Scientific American, 2013). There's even an unfortunate picture of a *T. rex* with feathers on p. 154.

has velociraptor reprise its role, the dinosaur should sport some exquisite plumage, Steven Spielberg's sense of taste be damned." (That's also from Switek, p. 152. I told you his book was good.) And, well, that tells us something about *us*, doesn't it? Many of us disagree with the feathers. If someone's going to make a computer-generated image, it had better match my imagination, not reality, dammit!

In every way, the dinosaurs of the *Jurassic Park* franchise are fakes. The characters in the movies know they're nothing more than "genetically engineered theme-park monsters" (*Jurassic Park III*). Even worse, they're based on outdated science, with scales instead of feathers. To top that off, the dinosaurs of *Jurassic Park* are nothing more than a bunch of fancy special effects. Still, those dinosaurs seem real—and there's the rub. When most people think about raptors, they think about those *Jurassic Park* monsters, not the fossils. This brings us to the heart of a crisis of our time: the way that human beings have been treating unreality—computers, video games, Facebook, plastic surgery, cloning—as more real than the real. We prefer our featherless raptors and brontosaurs to the real ones depicted by the fossils. Reality is disappearing at an alarming rate, and it's being replaced by a constantly growing number of *virtual* realities.

The End of Reality

Jean Baudrillard (1929–2007) understands why the fake dinosaurs of *Jurassic Park* seem "more real than real." In *Simulacra and Simulation*, Baudrillard introduces the idea of the "hyperreal." He defines the hyperreal as "a real without origin or reality."[2] While that may sound complex, it's actually quite simple. Think of the flavor "blue raspberry" used in candy, slushies, snow cones, and other delicious treats. Blue raspberries exist nowhere in nature, and yet this artificial flavor is well established in our culture. In fact, it is so well established that back when I was eight, I thought raspberries were actually blue. The real thing came as something of a shock—and a disappointment. "Blue raspberries" are an invention of human-

---

[2] Jean Baudrillard, *Simulation and Simulacra* (University of Michigan Press, 1995), p. 1.

ity without reference to the real world—they are "hyperreal." And Baudrillard argues that we have begun inventing this kind of non-real *real* stuff faster and faster.

Fake fruit might not seem like a very serious issue, so why should we care? Well, Baudrillard claims that hyperreality extends everywhere. Take, for instance, a teenager who plays violent *Jurassic Park* video games. Constantly exposed to that fake reality, he might end up thinking that those video games are *more real than his real life*. Shooting dinosaurs (and maybe the occasional human) becomes fun and certainly not something dangerous. In extreme cases, he might lose touch with the "reality" of violence. His life, or, even worse, the lives of others, might end up seeming like nothing more than a game, and we don't have to imagine the deadly consequences that sometimes results from this hyperreal.

Baudrillard extends his ideas of hyperreality to such vast philosophical ideas as "truth" and the "good." While we won't push things that far, dinosaurs make a great example of the hyperreal. To hammer this point home, let's conduct a little thought experiment. Close your eyes (don't really close them, though, because how could you keep reading?) and imagine a *Tyrannosaurus rex*. Did you imagine a skeleton? Or did you imagine a fully-fleshed tyrant monster, roaring with a green scaly skin? Only one of those things—the skeleton—is real. The other is an image invented by human beings. At best, that image of a *T. rex* is a crude mixture of science and wishful thinking, and yet we think of that image as if it were real.

So what? When this happens over and over again, *we begin to lose contact with reality*. A child mistakes a park for a forest. A young woman thinks that an airbrushed Hollywood image is real and ends up having plastic surgery to look like her favorite celebrity. We might even start to think about our jobs, and the dozens of hours we spend in front of our computers, as being more real than the rest of our lives. The point of having a job, though, is to be able to afford the rest of your life—not the other way around, where you have a life just to do your job. Every day, we're surrounded by things that are "more real than reality," and reality ends up endangered as a result. As Baudrillard says, "more real than the real, that is how the real is abolished" (p. 81). Baudrillard, in fact, argues that *real* reality has disappeared!

Okay, sure, that sounds crazy, but think about it, . . . our own culture is full of the perils of the hyperreal. The mortgage crisis is another good example. Instead of dealing with the realities of the American economy, eager bankers and speculators created a real-estate bubble by focusing on what they wanted homes to be worth, not what they actually were worth. They imagined an economy that could never crash, and then created a hyperreality based on those dreams. Homebuyers were caught up in that fantasy, and took out mortgages they couldn't possibly afford—and we know the sad results. For too many people, it was almost as bad as getting eaten by a *T. rex.*

This is where the plot of Crichton's *Jurassic Park* comes into play. Isn't *Jurassic Park* an interaction with the hyperreal, an attempt to make sense of how the breakdown of reality impacts human life? The raptors of those movies are no more (or less, for that matter) real than Godzilla. They are human simulations created to seem real—and, as Crichton depicts them, they are incredibly dangerous as a result. In his world the hyperreal begins to literally consume the real!

Fake Dinosaurs and the Limits of Science

To boil it down: Baudrillard claims that human beings are constantly constructing images about real things and then mistaking those images for reality. Crichton uses that same idea throughout the *Jurassic Park* series. Here's how he tackles the question in *The Lost World*:

> When you think about it, the fossil record is like a series of photographs; a frozen moment from what is really a moving, ongoing reality. Looking at the fossil record is like thumbing through a family photo album. You know the album isn't complete. You know life happens between the pictures . . . pretty soon, you begin to think of the album not as a series of moments, but as reality itself. And you begin to explain everything in terms of the album, and you forget the underlying reality. (*The Lost World*, Ballantine, 2012, p. 202)

Crichton himself is a victim of the hyperreal. In the years since *Jurassic Park* first debuted, paleontologists have completely revised their view of velociraptors, decking them out in feathers.[3] Despite Crichton's attempts to utilize the best science available—there are numerous references in the *Jurassic Park* books to raptors looking like birds—he got the science wrong. Even worse, the animal depicted as a velociraptor is closer to *Deinonychus*, a similar but larger species of carnivorous dinosaur (*My Beloved Brontosaurus*, p. 121). Finally, many of the behaviors that Crichton shows are pure invention: we don't have any conclusive proof that the animals hunted in packs, were able to vocalize to each other, or were as intelligent as *Jurassic Park* depicts them.

As a result, Crichton gives us animals that never existed. To put this in the terms of Baudrillard: *the scaly raptor is an example of the hyperreal.* It is nothing more than an image, an invention of human beings. Despite Crichton's best intentions, he created something absolutely unreal. What else could he do, though? Short of actually going back 65 million years, we'll have to content ourselves with inventive and inaccurate recreations of dinosaurs.

The crisis, though, lies in how we believe in those images. What do people actually love, dinosaur reality—fossils—or spectacular images? I think the answer's pretty clear: we love the images. Kids don't play with fossilized dinosaur bones. They play with the imagined and reconstructed dinosaurs, and they certainly don't play with feathered dinosaurs! A *Jurassic Park IV* with scientifically accurate velociraptors—animals the size of chickens and covered with feathers—wouldn't have sold a bit! Who would buy toys, T-shirts, hats, and posters with killer-chickens on them? (Well, a few people, . . . but not that many!). We can finally admit what we've known all along: human beings have largely made up our version of dinosaurs to best suit our needs and desires, and they have little connection to "reality." When that *T. rex* in *Jurassic Park* roars—that's pure invention. Dinosaur bones can't tell us what a *T. rex* sounded like. We simply made that sound up, without any reference to science or reality, because we like the idea of a bone-shaking roar coming from such a terrifyingly huge animal.

---

[3] For some great pictures of feathery raptors and a solid introduction to the paleontology surrounding dinosaur feathers, see *Feathered Dinosaurs* (Oxford, 2008) by John Long and Peter Schouten. The raptor picture is on p. 144!

While Crichton and Baudrillard are interested in the same problem—the loss of reality—they are also very different thinkers. While Baudrillard thinks this state of the hyperreal is so advanced that reality itself has been banished, forgotten, and destroyed, Crichton is more concerned with the dangers of mistaking images for the real. Crichton has faith in reality, and *Jurassic Park* is full of dire warnings about what happens when people mistake the hyperreal—their ideas about dinosaurs—for the (semi)-real thing.

Fear the Fake Dinosaurs!

We can begin with the first *Jurassic Park*. We can trace the disaster of *Jurassic Park* to many things: chaos theory or the arrogance of humans, but we can also analyze how this crisis stems from people mistaking their constructions of dinosaurs for real (predictable and understandable) dinosaurs. We learn in the novel that the dinosaurs have been heavily modified. Fortunately for us, and side-stepping the need for any overly-technical mumbo-jumbo, Crichton makes the whole real-hyperreal clash an explicit theme of his work. The head scientist of the Jurassic Park project—Dr. Wu—early on explains that dinosaurs are fake: "'But they're not real now,' Wu said. 'That's what I'm trying to tell you. There isn't any reality here'" (p. 137).

Crichton returns to this point again and again, emphasizing that what's on the island are not actually dinosaurs, but man-made recreations of dinosaurs. The difference between the simulated dinosaurs of *Jurassic Park* and our scientific knowledge of dinosaurs is the central crisis of these novels. The scientists can't predict dinosaur behavior because the dinosaurs aren't real. This is even clearer in *The Lost World*, where scientific misconceptions about dinosaurs (whether *T. rex* can see only motion, whether *T. rex*es have nesting and paternal instincts) leads directly to death. The characters are forced to recognize that "we don't know anything about these animals." The conclusion of *The Lost World* reinforces this ignorance: "We think those beliefs are more scientific and better . . . They're still just fantasies. They're not real" (pp. 295, 415). Throughout his series, Crichton delivers a powerful message about the dangers of mistaking the hyperreal for the real, with the worst of possible consequences: getting eaten by your own fake dinosaurs.

Of course, we're not likely to be chased down by raptors in our real lives (I hope), but Crichton's larger point is still valid. The scientists of *Jurassic Park* have lost contact with reality, and that's something we should all be scared of. As science has advanced, our ability to manipulate the world around us has increased tremendously—but our intelligence hasn't. Unless we're firmly grounded in reality and the consequences of our actions, we can end up treating the world as a game, as something fake that can be easily manipulated. The damage that we could cause—whether through a super-virus, an environmental disaster, or an uncontrolled nuclear explosion—might be overwhelming, and what would happen to reality then?

If we stopped here, *Jurassic Park* seems more like a condemnation of the hyperreal, a warning of what can happen to human beings when we mistake our creations for reality. While Crichton seems to agree with Baudrillard on one level—that the image is replacing the real—he seems to share none of Baudrillard's giddy enthusiasm at that prospect. Instead, we seem to get a sour warning about creating such hyperreality, and the very real dangers that hyperreality presents.

Enjoy the Fake Dinosaurs!

We can't stop with that warning, though, because there's an entire other level to hyperreality in *Jurassic Park*. Those dinosaurs are also hyperreal because they are products of Crichton's imagination and Hollywood movie magic. The dinosaurs of *the movie* never existed and never will exist: they're entirely fictitious. There are even reports that Steven Spielberg rejected paleontological advice when designing his raptors: "Jack Horner, who has been a paleontology consultant for blockbuster dinosaur films, once told me that the director drew a hard line on what the dinosaurs should look like, noting that Spielberg felt he couldn't 'scare people with Technicolor dinosaurs'" (*My Beloved Brontosaurus*, p. 139).

To make the *Jurassic Park* franchise as entertaining as possible, Crichton and Spielberg both modified reality. This teaches us, the audience, a different lesson about hyperreality. Since the fake dinosaurs of *Jurassic Park* are so entertaining, so compelling and so scary, we learn that images are better than reality. While the characters of *Jurassic Park* are in danger from those fake dinosaurs, we never are. The dinosaurs can't get us because they aren't real. Safe in the comfort of our homes or in the theater, we are able to enjoy these hyperreal creations for what they are: pure fantasies.

Like any good author, Crichton himself comments on this process. In *Jurassic Park*, Dr. Wu tells us, "Entertainment has nothing to do with reality. Entertainment is antithetical to reality" (p. 136). Since *Jurassic Park* is, after all, an entertainment franchise—not a scientific endeavor—it needs to be understood as opposed to reality. After all, if the *Jurassic Park* franchise were realistic, it wouldn't make any money! Well, maybe people could trip over fossils and fall into excavation holes, resulting in pretty serious bumps and scrapes, but that wouldn't make for a very exciting movie (. . . and if it does, remember, I said it first!).

As a franchise, *Jurassic Park* teaches us that fantasy dinosaurs are more entertaining, more exciting, and more impressive than reality. We are now deep in Baudrillard's realm, where reality is being abolished by our images. The stakes of this lesson are far bigger than just fake dinosaurs. As we experience the thrills of the *Jurassic Park* franchise, we're learning to accept the hyperreal over the real. What happens if we take that lesson from *Jurassic Park* and begin applying it to the rest of our lives?

Some would say that this is exactly the situation of twenty-first-century America. Many find television and movies more entertaining than their real lives, and more and more people are losing themselves in the virtual realities of cyberspace every day. If you add in plastic surgery, bio-engineered food, the promise of cloning and genetic modification, and ever-more immersive technologies, reality can all of a sudden seem in very short supply. Reality may, in the end, be more extinct than the dinosaurs—at least, in a hyperreal world, we can bring *them* back!

Living after Reality

Crichton himself was well aware of the perils and problems of philosophy. Specifically, he complains about people like

Baudrillard who do "post-modern" philosophy. In the After-word to his novel *Eaters of the Dead,* Crichton comments on these theories, "I mention this because the tendency to blur the boundaries of fact and fiction has become widespread in modern society . . . But the attitude of 'post-modern' scholars represents a more fundamental challenge." Crichton argues against thinkers like Baudrillard, stating, "At best, this attitude evades traditional scholarly discipline; at worst, it is nasty and dangerous" (*Eaters of the Dead*, p. 251). Given how heavily Crichton relies on unreality in his novels, his warning is quite ironic. While Crichton might complain about the breakdown of the real, he never hesitated to use hyperreal situations to make his novels more entertaining.

Just as Crichton was aware of philosophers, Baudrillard was aware of *Jurassic Park*. In one of his books, he even uses the final scene of *Jurassic Park* to demonstrate the crisis of the real: "it's a bit like the last scene of *Jurassic Park*, in which the modern (artificially cloned) dinosaurs burst into the museum and wreak havoc on their fossilized ancestors. . . ." We're caught in a similar place, he thinks, trapped between our "fossils and our clones."[4] For Baudrillard, the crisis is clear. Do we believe in those fossils, the bare trace of reality, or do we believe in our artificial constructs, those cloned dinosaurs? What will win in the final battle—reality or our simulation of reality? As a franchise, *Jurassic Park* places us smack in the middle of this hyperreal debate, and the books and movies force us to consider what exactly is "real" or "true" or "scientific," and how these borders are becoming ever more elastic and confusing.

---

[4] Jean Baudrillard, *The Vital Illusion* (Columbia University Press, 2001), p. 63.

13
Raptor Rights

JOHN V. KARAVITIS

"That doesn't look very scary. More like a . . . six-foot turkey," wisecracked the young boy. Dr. Alan Grant, paleontologist extraordinaire, turned around to see who could have made such a naïve and arrogant comment.

The boy obviously didn't know a thing about velociraptors. So Grant calmly explained how they attacked their prey. "And he slashes at you with this . . . six-inch retractable claw, like a razor . . . across the belly, spilling your intestines. The point is . . . you are alive . . . when they start to eat you. So . . . try to show a little respect." Quite an image—the kind that might just make that young boy pause the next time he finds himself sitting down at Thanksgiving Day dinner.

Humans and dinosaurs, especially velociraptors, find themselves enemies in the *Jurassic Park* movies. But the issue of showing them respect, as Dr. Grant admonished, is always there. What it means to show an animal respect will depend on your point of view.

The first three *Jurassic Park* movies present three philosophical viewpoints on how much moral respect we owe non-human animals:

- **The first movie, *Jurassic Park*, presents the view that animals are property. We don't owe them any respect as far as morality goes, and they don't have any rights—animals are dangerous and need to be under complete control.**

- The second movie, *The Lost World: Jurassic Park*, presents the view that animals are due some moral respect, but only indirectly. Animals still don't have rights.

- The third movie, *Jurassic Park III*, presents the view that animals not only deserve our respect, but that they also have rights—most importantly, the right to be left alone.

Philosophers have thought deeply about this issue, and the discussions have evolved along the arguments presented in these movies. In fact, if you see all three movies, you might just find yourself wondering whether animals do deserve more respect than you give them now.

The *Jurassic Park* movies make us wonder two things: 1. How would *I* escape from a velociraptor? And 2. Do animals deserve rights?

If the second doesn't come to your mind, it probably would while you were being disemboweled by that velociraptor, as the last thought that goes through your mind (other than incoherent screaming) is "Maybe we should have shown them a bit more *respect*."

A Place for Everything, and Dinosaurs All Over the Place

In *Jurassic Park*, the central theme is that dinosaurs—really all animals—are nothing more than objects to be controlled and profited from. That dinosaurs are also dangerous is vigorously, and graphically, emphasized throughout the movie. This is clear from the opening scene where, during transport from a breeding facility, a velociraptor takes a moment to eviscerate a careless employee. If we don't control our property, the scenes warn us, there will be dire consequences.

As dinosaurs are also treated as property with great monetary value, there is little concern for their needs or for letting them live natural lives in the wild. When InGen CEO Hammond meets Grant and paleobotanist Dr. Sattler for the first time, he raves that "our attractions will drive the kids out of their minds." Trapped in the park, the dinosaurs are just attractions—a source of potential ticket sales.

Dennis Nedry, who wants to steal dinosaur embryos to make money, shows no concern for their fate. He's only careful with them because Lewis Dodgson, the representative of a rival company, warns Nedry, "They're no use to us if they don't survive." InGen's lawyer Donald Gennaro best sums up the belief that animals are just property to be used as we want when, seeing *living* dinosaurs for the first time, he exclaims, "We're going to make a fortune with this place!"

Treated as property, the dinosaurs are not even allowed to breed at will. During the tour of the laboratory facilities, Henry Wu, a park lab technician, explains, "There's no unauthorized breeding in Jurassic Park. . . . all the animals in Jurassic Park are female. We've engineered them that way." The animals were also created with a "lysine deficiency" that makes them dependent on the park employees just to stay alive—if they escape, they die. In these ways, the dinosaurs are denied any opportunity to satisfy their own natural tendencies and preferences as animals in the wild, since they are merely property.

The view of animals as property is a long-held belief, and it is a view that the vast majority of people today hold. Animals are seen as lacking important qualities that human beings alone possess. Aristotle (384–322 B.C.E.) argued that, as only man possesses the ability to reason, this alone is sufficient to deny animals any respect or rights. The ability to make rational decisions is seen as the one human quality that is beyond the reach of animals. There is a natural order to the world, and being able to reason places man above the animals.

There are tantalizing clues throughout *Jurassic Park* that Aristotle's view of animals as simply property may not be correct. Game warden Robert Muldoon warns that the velociraptors could be more like us than we would like to believe. "When she looks at you, you can see that she's working things out. They never attack the same place twice—they remember."

At lunch, Dr. Malcolm and Hammond argue about whether the fact that they can resurrect the dinosaurs means that they should. But this conversation implies that the dinosaurs are more than just property. After all, if dinosaurs were just things, it wouldn't make any sense to argue whether it's right to bring them back. Malcolm and Hammond seem to be dancing around the idea of how much *respect* the dinosaurs deserve.

The velociraptors, at the very least, are more than simply dangerous animals. In fact, all of the movies show velociraptors cunningly trying to figure out how to kill humans. If they can outwit humans, then they can't be as dumb as we really, *really* want to think. But if velociraptors do have some level of intelligence, and we can find ourselves arguing about how much respect they deserve, aren't those clues that they are more than just property? Well, the first movie certainly doesn't bring us to that conclusion. At the end of *Jurassic Park*, the survivors are rescued, and the dinosaurs remain trapped on Isla Nublar. The first movie ends with the dinosaurs still under man's control, and Aristotle's view of animals remains secure.

Tally-ho! Forward! The Dino Hunt Begins!

In *The Lost World: Jurassic Park*, the new plan is to build a dinosaur zoo in San Diego, not to resurrect a theme park on an isolated Pacific island off the western coast of Costa Rica. There is no question that InGen's new CEO, Peter Ludlow, thinks that the dinosaurs are just property. "An extinct animal that's brought back to life has no rights. It exists because we made it. We patented it. We own it." And so we begin the second movie where the first left off, with Aristotle's view of animals as property. We don't owe animals any respect or any rights.

But *The Lost World* shifts that perspective and goes beyond Aristotle's thoughts. Even though animals aren't like people, and cannot claim to have rights as we know them, we nevertheless do owe them some measure of respect. This view is based on the ideas of Immanuel Kant (1724–1804). Kant argued that although only beings like humans are due direct moral concern because they're rational, there are indirect reasons why animals should be treated with some care and respect.

It is rationality that determines whether someone matters morally. And animals, lacking rationality, don't really count, says Kant: "Our duties towards animals are merely indirect duties towards humanity."[1] Kant also believed that behaving cruelly to animals could cause people to behave cruelly to each other: "he who is cruel to animals becomes hard also in his

---

[1] Immanuel Kant, "Duties towards Animals and Spirits," in *Lectures on Ethics*, Harper and Row, 1963, p. 239.

dealings with men. We can judge the heart of a man by his treatment of animals" (p. 240). In other words, if you let kids tear the wings off of flies and cut live frogs open, it may not be long before they are adults gleefully slicing each other apart— or willingly shutting off a security system that is *supposed* to keep everyone else alive.

A major plotline in *The Lost World* rests on this more respectful moral stance toward animals. Ludlow hires Roland Tembo, an experienced yet jaded hunter, to lead the InGen expedition to Isla Sorna to obtain specimens to stock the dinosaur zoo. But when Ludlow discusses the hunter's payment, Tembo replies that all he wants is the right to hunt down and capture the most dangerous game—a *Tyrannosaurus rex*.

Hunting for sport appears to be a uniquely human activity, and there are very different behaviors between humans and animals during a hunt. As a sporting activity, hunting has rules, and these rules put limits on the hunter's behavior. A hunter takes pride not only in a successful hunt, but also in the effort that it takes to bring down the prey. The hunter must work for his prize, and this involves skill, risk, and chance. A guaranteed kill is no sport; it is a slaughter. According to the rules of hunting, prey is never to be caused any unnecessary suffering. The hunter also need not kill the prey in order to be successful. An animal can be captured and released, as is done with fishing. Tembo plays by these rules as he tracks down and captures the *T. rex*, so that it and its offspring can be taken to San Diego alive.

Animals don't follow rules when they hunt, and they show no concern for the rights of their prey, but that's because they don't hunt for sport. Animals hunt for food; the goal is to kill and not be killed. Tembo explains to Malcolm, "My point is that predators don't hunt when they're not hungry." There are a number of examples of this lack of moral respect toward humans: the attack on the InGen hunting party by the velociraptors in the field of tall grass; the attack and butchering of Tembo's second-in-command by the swarm of compsognathuses; and the velociraptor attack at the abandoned facility. Here, the human hunters have become the hunted.

Following rules during a hunt gives moral respect to animals, but only indirectly. The rules are followed because, as

Kant claimed, there are direct moral duties the hunter owes people in general. Kant does not think that animals are rational enough for us to give them rights, but he does think that we should not be cruel to them because doing so would create bad habits in us. So, for Kant, it's not that the *T. rex* deserves respect, and that we would be disrespectful to it by caging it in a zoo, depriving it of a chance to live life in the wild. Instead, we owe it to each other to not get into the habit of treating any animal cruelly. Treating animals cruelly could very well lead back to condoning the same callous behavior toward people seen during slavery. The bottom line is that Kant's view recognizes some limited, indirect moral respect owed to animals, but no existence of animal rights. Kant's view does go beyond Aristotle's, but not by much.

Through the theme of hunting for sport, *The Lost World* presents a shift in moral thinking toward animals. We begin to see the human hunter and the prey as more "equal" participants in a hunt, if the animal can be said to be "participating." Although animals do not have rights, they are due some respect. This change in the moral playing field prepares us for the third philosophical view of animals in the third movie. Former InGen CEO Hammond sets forth this view of respect for animals at the very end of *The Lost World* when he proclaims, "These creatures require our absence to survive. We must step aside and trust in nature."

If You Wrong Us, Shall We Not Revenge?

Throughout *Jurassic Park III*, humans and dinosaurs operate on a level playing field, and any distinction between the two is almost non-existent. The velociraptors are depicted as intelligent, creative in hunting, social, and capable of vocal communication with one another—just like humans. When Billy goes to rescue Eric from the pterodactyls, he uses the recovered parasail, in effect becoming like the pterodactyls. To operate in their world, Billy has to become like them. Humans and dinosaurs are now very similar in behavior.

One major plotline that epitomizes this theme involves Billy's theft of a pair of velociraptor eggs, and the velociraptors' efforts at reclaiming them. The velociraptors persistently pursue the humans, and Grant realizes, "Those things know we have the eggs." Here, the velociraptors act a lot like people, and it becomes easy to forget that they are still animals. There's no question that this new view could also affect the way we look at each other.

At the final confrontation between the humans and the velociraptors, any distinction between the two has vanished. The velociraptors have come a long way, and achieve their goal by recovering the two stolen eggs. The deadly creatures look right at our heroes, and we can see them *think* about killing them, but other, more important matters come up, and they *let* the humans live. There is no mistaking this moment. This is no accident. Grant and his friends don't outsmart, outpower, or outmaneuver the velociraptors—the predators *choose* to let the pitiful band of humans go.

We're Just Like You—You're Just Like Us

Tom Regan argues in *The Case for Animal Rights* that animals have "inherent value," and the velociraptors of *Jurassic Part III* best prove that. As living beings who are sentient (they can feel), conscious, and aware of their environment, have preferences, are perhaps even self-aware, and undoubtedly intelligent, the velociraptors are valuable *in* themselves, not *for* human use. Regan tells us they have value because, like humans, they are "subjects-of-a-life." To be a "subject-of-a-life" is to have a life of

> beliefs and desires; perception, memory, and a sense of the future . . . an emotional life . . . with feelings of pleasure and pain; preference- and welfare-interests; the ability to [pursue] their desires and goals; a psychophysical identity over time; and an individual welfare . . . independent of their being the object of anyone else's interests." (*The Case for Animal Rights*, University of California Press, 2004, p. 243)

In other words, a "subject-of-a-life" is capable of living a full and rich life with feelings, desires, and independence. Many mammals meet this criteria, and they are due moral respect; they cannot be treated as objects that exist for another's benefit. Extending Regan's ideas to the dinosaurs of Jurassic Park, it's wrong to capture and exhibit a *T. rex* in a zoo—and it's wrong to treat velociraptors, or even their eggs, as objects for scientific research or for profit.

Regan's argument seems straightforward, but we may have qualms about it. Regan does not expect animals to act morally, and he doesn't need them to act morally for them to have value. He argues that we're being contradictory if we accord moral respect and rights to humans who lack the mental abilities of animals. No one would deny that we owe respect to moral patients such as infants, the senile elderly, or those who are comatose with no chance of recovering consciousness. But if we think those humans who are often less rational than other animals deserve moral treatment, then we cannot deny moral respect to animals.

Some people may suppose that Regan's argument is easily defeated by looking at how non-human animals treat each other in the wild. For non-human animals, there is no rule other than "Eat or be eaten." This is the rule that the dinosaurs live by in Jurassic Park. When the velociraptors and the *T. rex* hunt and kill, they don't show any concern for the rights of humans (or of each other). So, if we show concern for theirs, there'd be a double standard. But according to Regan this reason falls flat—remember, if animals aren't fully rational then *they don't understand morality*. That means it's no more okay to kill or use them than it would be to kill or use a five-year-old because she doesn't understand morality.

Regan's ideas of inherent value and "subject-of-a-life" are vague and seem more like a general description of how human beings face and live life rather than how animals do. But still, Regan's idea of justice demands that all mammals, regardless of species, are owed respect. So, rational humans would need to accommodate the interests of non-rational, non-human animals, even when it's inconvenient. In fact, to fully respect animals, humans would have to become vegetarians. Most of us, for better or for worse, are unlikely to let ourselves be that inconvenienced. . . . Well, unless they forced us to. . . .

The Best Laid Plans of Velociraptors and Men

So, the arguments get dicey: Aristotle saw animals as property, a part of the natural order, with rational man at its head.

Immanuel Kant acknowledged that animals might be owed some moral respect, but only indirectly. Tom Regan believes that all mammals have an inherent value which makes them equally deserving of being treated with respect. For him, animals have rights.

As we see at the end of *Jurassic Park III*, the final showdown between the velociraptors and the humans has the velociraptors being as human as any non-human animal could possibly be. The velociraptors are just like us: intelligent, cunning, creative in problem-solving, able to plan ahead and to execute plans, social, and able to communicate vocally. They're shown as being different only in degree. Any relevant human characteristic can seemingly be found in them: sentience, consciousness, preferences, self-awareness, and intelligence. Seeing the velociraptors as not so different from ourselves, we're left wondering if our casual attitude toward and treatment of animals, in general, may be flawed. One thing does seem to be pretty obvious: had Dr. Grant not been so *respectful*, those very angry velociraptors would not have hesitated to kill the whole group—hungry or not.

You see, it's very easy for us to treat other animals in any way we want *right now*. Humans tend to give rights to others pretty grudgingly. We don't like to give rights to anyone, even humans—just look at the treatment of ethnic and religious minorities and women. And even today children are sold around the world as sex slaves in communities that don't want to give them rights or fair treatment. In other words, we generally don't give others rights *unless they can force us to*. Well, cows and compys may never have that ability, but velociraptors? That's another story indeed. And how we treat them would likely determine how they would treat us.

Animals have always been an important part of our world, and we have always found ways to use them. They act as our companions, protect us, entertain us, work for us, nourish us, and help us increase our medical and scientific knowledge. Our world is richer because of them. But acknowledging that they are more than simply useful tools for our benefit is an idea that has only barely begun to gain ground.

Our rationality has made us masters of the world, but we may one day find ourselves face-to-face with a non-human animal whose behavior is truly equal to—perhaps indistinguishable from—our own. In the not-too-distant past, the Neanderthals, *Homo neanderthalensis*, may very well have been such a species. In the not-too-distant future, an animal may arise naturally in the wild (or be created in a laboratory) that is very, *very* close to humanity. At that moment, it will truly be a new world for all of us. Whether we "try to show a little respect" to this new species, as Dr. Grant would admonish us, or try to enslave it, may well determine whether they will show *us* a little respect in return..

14

If Dinosaurs Were People . . .

Skyler King

> **Dr. Malcolm:** Gee, . . . the lack of humility that's being displayed here before nature . . . staggers me.
>
> **Donald:** Well, thank you, Dr. Malcolm, but I think things are a lot different than you and I feared.
>
> **Dr. Malcolm:** Yeah, . . . What you call "discovery," I call rape of the natural world.

While our clever, smooth-talking, and flirtatious friend Dr. Malcolm thinks he's referring to genetic engineering and scientists gone wrong, I think his fears apply to us daily. The only problem is, we cleverly deceive ourselves into believing that his fears don't exist, that animals aren't as scary or important as they are in *Jurassic Park*. I think it's time for a reality check.

We aren't the only organisms that matter on this planet; we aren't even the greatest thing on this planet. In all honesty, the mighty *Tyrannosaurus rex* and the other dinosaurs would destroy us if they existed today. Yet we waltz around, arrogantly claiming a false superiority. How is such gross self-deception possible? Why do we constantly cling to the incorrect belief that we are unstoppable, that we are the only meaningful creature in existence? Because we *love* living in a delusion. We would rather live in a fantasy than face the truth. Yet, ironically, we all *claim* to be seekers and lovers of Truth.

It's time for these harmful fantasies and delusions to end. The dinosaurs are shouting for retribution, for us to wake up. Can you hear them? Out in the distance, on the very edge of consciousness, their faint voices cry, "Where is this 'liberty and justice for all' of which you speak? We see nothing but death and destruction in your wake!"

Chilling. Challenging. The dinosaurs' ominous choir can be traced throughout the *Jurassic Park* movies. There are several scenes where, even if you aren't too supportive of animal rights or any of the other ethical concerns regarding animal and human interactions, we should pause and think, "Good lord! Did that just happen?! What is *wrong* with these people?!" Those scenes alone should be enough to make us change our approach, to listen to the voices crying from the wilderness of consciousness—but I suspect it will take more of an argument than that to convince most people.

I'll admit it. . . . I, too, have ignored the dinos' devastating and haunting questions for a long time. I, too, counted them insignificant—but then I saw the beauty and simplicity of their reasoning. Those seemingly whacko animal rights activists weren't so far from the truth after all. What if they can prove that animals *aren't* getting "liberty and justice for all," like we constantly preach? What if that proof involves making dinosaurs and other animals *people*? No, not *humans*, like you're probably thinking. Obviously they aren't *human*. But *people*—as in, "someone who *matters*." Is it possible?? I think so.

Dinosaurs Aren't Special Like Us? Why Not?

Assisting the dinosaurs on their quest to becoming people might sound difficult, especially considering the belief of *human exceptionality* (also commonly referred to as "human uniqueness"), but it can be done. You might even be surprised. This first obstacle, human exceptionality, is almost self-explanatory. In simple terms, human exceptionality is the belief that humans are very unique creatures; in its most extreme form, it is nothing more than an extreme bias or prejudice against nonhuman beings that serves to glorify human beings and rob all other creatures of their value. This extreme form of human exceptionality also carries with it the strong belief that humans are inherently better than any animal or nonhuman being—especially nasty dinosaurs!

At first glance, that claim might not seem too unreasonable. After all, humans have traveled to the moon; we're the apex predator, the top of the food chain. Some supporters of human exceptionality even say something similar to, "When monkeys build a skyscraper, then I'll consider changing my beliefs about animals." Most people who subscribe to human exceptionality think that our extreme intelligence sets us apart. However, the velociraptors in *Jurassic Park* were said to show "extreme signs of intelligence." Surely, then, that can't be what makes us so special that we feel we have the right to torture and kill any animal we want on a whim.

Perhaps some of the confusion surrounding human exceptionality is a mistaken belief about evolution. Frans de Waal, a renowned primatologist, says that, for some reason, people believe that we human beings have *always* been *numero uno* on the food chain.[1] But that simply isn't true. Dr. Grant, our dino expert in *Jurassic Park*, shares a similar sentiment when he and the rest of the group are eating lunch with Mr. Hammond. He says, "Dinosaur and man, two creatures that have been separated from each other by some 65 million years of evolution, have suddenly been thrown back into the mix with each other and we have no idea what to expect." In other words, you can bet your next paycheck that if our caveman relatives had lived sooner, they'd have been terrified of dinosaurs—and, just like the banner at the end of *Jurassic Park* says, there is no doubt that "dinosaurs ruled the earth." Not us.

Besides that, rigidly holding onto human exceptionality— though there are undoubtedly some exceptional and unique things about us—is just plain *speciesism*. Speciesism is the fallacy where you only favor your species and you even look down on other species. Basically, it's like racism, only it involves, for example, humans loving *Homo sapiens* and thinking that another species is less valuable. Thankfully dinosaurs aren't guilty of speciesism: they are pretty equal-opportunity in their fighting and killing.

Reasoning with Dinosaurs

If we don't falsely cling to human exceptionality, what do we have left? Are there any other reasons to deny animals at least

---

[1] *The Age of Empathy*, Three Rivers Press, 2009, pp. 18–26.

a *somewhat* more even ranking with us? Essentially, the only reason we can justify treating animals cruelly—like injecting rats with cancer to the point that they have enormous tumors or experimenting on animals to make sure cosmetics aren't poisonous—is by denying them the status of *person*.

What does it mean to be a *person*—not a *human*, but a person? A great philosopher named Immanuel Kant (1724–1804) had an answer to that question: pure reason. Basically, he thought people had the ability to fairly judge facts and scenarios and arrive at the best conclusion possible. He thought people could be "deliberate and unbiased." For Kant, thinking was the biggest and best component of being a person; *anything* that had the ability to think rationally should be respected. (Kant believed that humans possessed distinct capabilities—such as discourse, intellect, reason—and that animals have always lacked such capabilities.)

Can dinosaurs (and animals) reason? If they can, then surely we need to reconsider our current beliefs about animals. Some philosophers, such as René Descartes (1596–1650), adamantly deny that animals possess the ability to reason. Descartes claimed that thinking that the "souls of beasts" were on the same plateau as humans was as bad as not believing in God—and he *really* believed in God. He thought that because animals lacked the ability to speak, they lacked thought; because animals lacked thought, they, obviously, could not reason. Basically, he thought "reason" was something that someone could use in *all* kinds of situations by applying general rules. He might agree that animals *sometimes* show this, but he would say that it is by accident, so it isn't real proof of actual reasoning.

Remember when Dr. Sadler had to go to the shed to manually restore power to the park? She almost lost her life to a vicious velociraptor in there, but she barely managed escape by locking the raptor in the shed. After a while, though, the raptor figured out how to turn the doorknob and free itself. So an animal that has been extinct for a ridiculously long time figured out how to use a twenty-first-century door? That seems like some pretty impressive reasoning to me!

Maybe animals can't use sophisticated language and reason to spell everything out like we do, but they certainly seem to be able to do *some* reasoning. And what about the raptors' systematically testing the electric fences for weaknesses and *never* striking the same place twice?

Furthermore, if animals can't reason, then how do we explain the *T. rex*'s actions during the tropical storm in *Jurassic Park*? Dr. Grant and the little girl were standing in front of the park van while the *T. rex* was trying to find them. Since Dr. Grant is the dino expert, he avoided any initial detection from the ferocious beast. What's interesting though is that the *T. rex* then spun the car around—almost as if something in her brain had said, "Huh, if those two munchy snacks aren't here, then they must be on the other side of this big box thing. How about I check and see?" The *T. rex* spun the car around several times and then she pushed the car off the edge of the dam, almost as if she knew the humans were playing games with her!

Okay, maybe you aren't convinced by that. For the sake of argument, let's just say that Descartes is right and animals *can't* reason. Let's go back to Kant's qualifications for persons. If we do that, what we're left with is this: we are denying animals the status of persons because they can't reason at all and, even if they could, they couldn't reason *as effectively* as humans. But what humans are we talking about? Are we talking about only philosophers or people like Einstein? Who gets to be the norm, here?

For the sake of simplicity, let's settle for a definition like this: "Effective reasoning" is something an average human being can accomplish. That's still quite vague, but it highlights an interesting paradox buried in what we've been saying thus far. If you are committed to human exceptionality and the belief that reasoning makes us infinitely better than animals, then you are also committed to the view that some *humans aren't actually people*. According to the belief that reasoning is what makes humans exceptional, humans who have fallen into a vegetative state and maybe all humans with any sort of mental disorder or mental disability would *not* qualify as a people because they cannot "reason as effectively as an average human being." If we look at recent data from the National Institute of Mental Health, we find that 26.2 percent of Americans suffer from some sort of mental handicap. [2] Is it really fair to say that 26.2

---

[2] <www.nimh.nih.gov/health/publications/the-numbers-count-mental-disorders-in-america/index.shtml>.

percent of Americans really *aren't* people because they can't reason like an "average human being"?

Dinosaurs Apply for Personhood

Perhaps you say that Kant's qualifications for being a person are simply not good enough. If we find a new system, you might say, then we will easily see that our dino friends are not, in *any way*, close to being people. Fair enough. Maybe we do need to find a more rigorous system.

We can start with Mary Anne Warren's system. She claimed that if we weigh the situation fairly, much like Kant wanted us to do, then we could agree to five criteria that must be met for someone to be considered a person:

1. **consciousness**

2. **reasoning**

3. **self-driven activity**

4. **the ability to communicate**

5. **the ability to form self-concepts.**[3]

Additionally, she thought that any entity that met most of these requirements should be treated respectfully. So, let's start going through our "Dino Personhood Checklist"!

Do our *Jurassic Park* friends have consciousness? Well, the dinosaurs are definitely aware that they are alive; they feel desires such as the need to eat and drink; when a *T. rex* munches on the other dinosaurs, they definitely feel pain; and the dinosaurs know how to move their limbs and respond to various sights and smells in order to distinguish foe from friend. However, I think Warren meant "consciousness" the way Descartes asserted—meaning, they need to express thoughts to meet this first criterion. So, no.

Since we've already discussed reasoning and decided it *could* be inconclusive, let's just skip criterion #2.

The next item on our checklist is self-driven activity. "Self-driven activity" basically means that the dinosaurs have to con-

---

[3] "On the Moral and Legal Status of Abortion," *The Monist* 57:1 (1973).

sistently be able to distinguish between their natural, instinctual roles encoded in their DNA and choices of their own willing. Recall our earlier discussion of the *T. rex* manipulating the car when she wanted to eat Dr. Grant and the little girl. That kind of behavior certainly wasn't encoded into the *T. rex*'s DNA. Therefore, the only conclusion we can draw from that behavior is that the *T. rex* acted in accordance with this third criterion! Remember, though: Warren argued that *most* of the requirements had to be met, not all of them. So, even though the dinos are 1-for-3 so far, they haven't lost yet.

Next is the ability to communicate. The velociraptors showed signs of communication. They made weird screeching and squawking noises to each other and, depending on the pitch of the call, the others knew that either prey had been cornered or their pal needed some help. Another example of the dinosaurs communicating is when Dr. Grant and the kids slept in a tree and woke up to a brachiosaurus looming over them. Dr. Grant, being a dino expert, was excited and attempted to pet the dino—but it quickly drew its head back and grunted at Dr. Grant. In fact, later, when the girl tried to pet the brachiosaurus, it blew snot all over her, as if to say, "Hey, get your hands off me, you crazy creature!" The brachiosaurus eventually allowed the humans to pet it though and, thus, we see a fascinating form of communication that *did not use words*. So, score another point for the dinos' chances at personhood!

Finally, the toughest criterion for our dinosaurs to meet is "the ability to form self-concepts." Unfortunately, given the fact that we have an outsider's perspective for all three movies, we can't really tell if the dinosaurs are able to form any self-concepts. We can't tell if they can think inside their heads—even though all the dinos were said to be impressively intelligent—which prevents us from being able to properly evaluate two or more of Warren's criteria. That kind of puts us in a bind. But what if I told you I had an ace up my sleeve that would make it impossible for you to refute my argument, while also allowing all five of Warren's criteria to be met?

Dinosaurs Play Language Games

My trump card comes from an Austrian philosopher named Ludwig Wittgenstein (1889–1951). In his work *Philosophical*

Investigations, he made a very interesting claim that even if animals *could* talk, even if they had a language similar to ours, we *still* would not be able to understand them. Why? Because animals adapted and experienced an entirely different world than we have for the past several centuries. The worldviews that animals would create in their worlds would be so different from ours that they would seem bizarre to us.

Perhaps you're unwilling to accept such a bold claim at face value. Perhaps you think it's a cop-out. Then think about this: Wittgenstein said, "It is sometimes said: animals do not talk because they lack the mental abilities. And this means: 'They do not think, and that is why they do not talk.' But—they simply do not talk. Or better: they do not use language—if we disregard the most primitive forms of language."[4] Essentially, Wittgenstein thought we impose unfair and harsh standards when judging animals; in fact, claiming that animals are unintelligent or worthless because of their lack of language actually reveals a great and foolish pride in our views about the world. As Wittgenstein argued, animals are *not* deficient *human* life-forms; they are *different* life-forms. And, if we are to properly understand their languages, then those languages must be viewed in their contexts. Wittgenstein also urged us to view language as part of our natural history, developing as we do, not as some special mental ability we humans magically have.

So, what this tells us is that we were wrong to reject Warren's criteria. If the dinosaurs are not required to have language like ours, then it would be unfair to say they don't have some kind of consciousness (#1). If the dino "language" doesn't need to be like ours, then we can definitely say they have reason (#2)—again, maybe not *human*-like reasoning, but they have their own "primitive" type of reasoning. Even Descartes's objection would become irrelevant: he would have to alter his definitions of "thought" and "reason," which would make him agree to this claim—even if he really didn't like the idea of agreeing to it.

For the third criterion, self-driven activity, we could assume by the various behaviors exhibited by the dinos that they were having some sort of thought—again, maybe not a complex, word-oriented thought like humans have—and were acting from some sort of self-driven activity.

---

[4] *Philosophical Investigations*, Wiley-Blackwell, 2009, p. 16

Continuing on, we see that the dinos definitely have the ability to communicate (#4). It doesn't matter if we *know* what they're saying; that doesn't mean they aren't *people*. After all, if you don't speak Japanese and you traveled to Tokyo, do you think you could speak to Japanese people? Probably not. Does that mean, then, that *you* are not *actually* a person? Not at all!

Additionally, you can't deny that the velociraptors possessed communication in *Jurassic Park*. The complexity of their communication system is quite extraordinary, really. The velociraptors' calls not only indicated that some predator or prey had been spotted, but also *expressed* a particular velociraptor's *internal* attitude, which is something both Descartes and Kant overlooked in their rejections of animal reasoning and intelligence! In simple and clear terms, a velociraptor's calling for help expresses that a velociraptor is afraid or worried *because* of *some*thing external to itself; the act of calling means that a velociraptor understands that another creature could *hear* its call, *interpret* that call, and *respond* to that call appropriately. That, in itself, is a rather sophisticated form of communication—and the raptors don't even have to use words!

Finally, if our kind of language isn't required for consciousness and the dinosaurs can think and reason in ways specific to their life-forms, then that means that they *might* also be able to form self-concepts (#5). Again, maybe Wittgenstein is right and the animal "language" is radically different than ours. Maybe the dinosaurs don't refer to themselves as "I." The concept of "I" is definitely how *humans* express self-concepts, but it is wrong to assume that, if animals had language similar to ours, their expression would be the same as ours. And even if the dinos *lack* the ability to form self-concepts, we have still accepted four of the other criteria, which, according to Warren, means that the dinosaurs succeed in qualifying as people!

Well, look at that! With Wittgenstein's theory, the dinosaurs of *Jurassic Park* meet Warren's requirements—and even Descartes's requirements too!

Rape of the Natural World

Hopefully you can agree now that we need to change our approach and our beliefs concerning animal ethics. As philosopher Tom Regan has said, "We are each . . . a conscious creature having an individual welfare that has importance to us whatever our usefulness to others."[5] We have established that animals, too, are conscious creatures. What kind of changes should we make, then? That, my friends, is best answered by referring to Tom Regan's system. He calls his approach the *rights view*, and he says that all individuals and *all creatures* have inherent value—value that is acquired by nothing more than *living*—and that "usefulness" or "rankings in society" mean nothing. He *also* says that it is unquestionably immoral to treat *any* individual in a way that disrespects his or her or its value and to violate any creature's individual rights.

Even if you still aren't entirely convinced that we should change our ways, there are at least two scenes in *Jurassic Park* that should seem abhorrent—absolutely terrible—to you. One scene is when Dr. Grant and Dr. Sattler first arrive on the island. Dr. Grant spots a cow tied in a harness and he asks, "What is happening to that cow?" He is told that the cow is lunch for the velociraptors that are trapped in a cage-like structure. The cow is then hoisted down into the cage, mooing the entire time, and we hear its screams as the raptors rip it to shreds. That cow never even had the chance to run—it was strapped down and offered as a sacrifice to its predators.

The second such scene is when Dr. Grant, Dr. Sattler, Dr. Malcolm, Donald, and Mr. Hammond's grandkids begin the tour. Their cars stop at the *T. rex* cage and we see a goat transported in via an elevator. This goat, just like the cow, is bound, chained to a post. At first, the *T. rex* doesn't eat the goat; we have to listen to its nervous bleating. The goat is safe—until the tropical storm hits. That's when the *T. rex* mercilessly devours the poor, defenseless little animal.

Doesn't it say something about us, as a species, that we even need such extensive arguments like this one to remind us that we aren't as great as we think we are? Why is it so difficult for us to believe that other living creatures deserve respect? Certainly, the fact that we regularly dominate and destroy nature is evidence that we believe we're better than everything else. And it isn't just animals that we destroy. It took Europeans a few centuries to realize that Native

---

[5] "The Case for Animal Rights," in *Ethics: The Essential Writings*, edited by Gordon Marino, Modern Library, 2010.

Americans weren't "soulless" creatures but actual *persons*; it took several more centuries to "discover" the same about other non-White and female humans, too. Isn't it about time we learned from our past mistakes?

"Where is this 'liberty and justice for all' of which you speak?" the shadowy, eerie voices of the dinos cry, their chorus radiating from the dark, distant forest of consciousness. "We see nothing but death and destruction in your wake. We see the rape of the natural world."[6]

---

[6] I am indebted to the following people for this chapter: Jim Sheppard, for pushing me to think about many multi-faceted ethical problems and discussions in ways that I had never considered before; Andrew Graham, for extensive discussion on Wittgenstein's complex and difficult views on language and animals; and Charissa Motley, for always offering invaluable advice and comments on my writings.

15
Who Gets a Second Chance?

LISA KADONAGA

Let's say there are two sealed vials on my desk, marked *"Tyrannosaurus rex"* and *"Gila crassicauda."* Each contains the complete genetic code for a different extinct species. All I have to do is pick one of the vials and pop it through the delivery hatch into the laboratory next door, where a team of specialists will start cloning the species I've selected. So which one should I choose? Which species deserves a second chance?

Tyrannosaurus rex was a six-meter-tall carnivorous dinosaur that lived *sixty-five million years ago* in what later became North America. The thicktail chub, *Gila crassicauda*, was a small fish that used to live in Central California until *the middle of the twentieth century*.

This would appear to be an easy choice. Certainly the large spectacular dinosaur, world-famous because of movies like *Jurassic Park*, would trump the mundane little minnow! Reversing extinction has been a longstanding dream of conservation biology—the branch of the life sciences that focuses on trying to protect species and environments from destruction. And surely in this situation, might it not be fitting to "go big or go home"?

What Is Its Purpose?

I can't help thinking about the story of Pister's Bucket. Edwin Pister, a biologist for the state of California, had an experience on August 18th 1969 that turned from near-disaster into triumph, involving a different species of tiny fish. He saved the last Owens pupfish from extinction. He described a profound sense of relief that he'd managed to fetch a couple of buckets in time and rescue the very last Owens pupfish in the world from a rapidly-shrinking pond.[1] Well, imagine how giddy people would feel at bringing such a magnificent creature as the *T. rex* back from oblivion!

But isn't there more to a decision to raise the dead than awe and wonder? Isn't there the question of purpose and usefulness? But what is the purpose of a wild creature? What are our intentions for these wild creatures? So what kinds of purposes might endangered—or resurrected—species be serving? Putting the species on display for a fee, and licensing the merchandising rights, are obvious possibilities for making money. There's also the possibility of further material profit from valuable or life-saving discoveries, especially now that genes can be patented.

If the *Dilophosaurus* venom that paralyzed Dennis Nedry as he was trying to flee to the mainland with his stolen embryos turned out to have pharmaceutical applications, InGen would be able to cash in. There are also some other more symbolic types of reasons for bringing an extinct species back to life: education, prestige, human responsibility, and ecosystem function. All of these factors could help us decide whether a *T. rex* or a fish should get a second chance. So let's throw down then! *Tyrannosaurus rex* versus *Gila crassicauda* in the ultimate battle for continuing existence! Who will come out on top?

T. rex versus *G. crassicauda*: Best for Education?

One reason for restoring endangered or extinct species and ecosystems is to get people enthusiastic about the vital importance of biological diversity. It would also encourage support for scientific research—biotechnology in particular. News about the cloning of a dinosaur or a woolly mammoth could create the kind of excitement similar to the launch of Sputnik or the Apollo moon landings, which got a generation of young people involved in science.

---

[1] Edwin Philip Pister, "Species in a Bucket," *Natural History* 102 (January 1993).

But most of the time a few photogenic species get most of the media attention and financial resources. They're selected as symbols for countries and sports teams, or appear on T-shirts or coffee-table books. In 1986, Bil Gilbert noted that the majority of the funds for US endangered species recovery efforts were going to a handful of high-profile mammals and birds, rather than being doled out based on the likelihood of success.

As one London Zoo expert observed while his workplace was preparing to receive a pair of giant pandas, it would be possible to maintain multiple species of endangered insects for a fraction of the cost. And for plants, it's much easier to conserve habitat and guarantee a viable population on relatively small amounts of land, compared with what's required by top-level carnivores, especially a *T. rex*.

If it's press coverage you're looking for, a tyrannosaur would undoubtedly create more of a stir than a boring freshwater fish. The sad thing is, there are plenty of examples of still-living species as spectacular as the *T. rex*, and if they aren't enough to motivate us to protect the environment, a dinosaur probably wouldn't work either.

But, as far as which animal is the best poster child for fundraising—decision: ***T. rex.***

T. rex versus *G. crassicauda*: Best for Prestige?

The coolness factor for cloning a dinosaur of any species is undeniable. In terms of the sheer technical challenge, trying to find genetic material would be far more difficult than for the thicktail chub. A project like the one in the *Jurassic Park* franchise, where the dinosaur DNA is extracted from prehistoric amber, would offer tremendous bragging rights.

It's this very challenge that would make the tyrannosaur so attractive for any sponsor and team willing to take on the project. Thorstein Veblen (1857–1929) would have been thrilled by such a great example of *conspicuous consumption*, a term that he coined while observing rich people in the era before World War I. The goal is to be seen spending your money on something that is not of immediate practical value, like the amber handle on John Hammond's favorite cane. It could be a visible display, like an extensive collection and facilities to house it, or it could be more subtle, like a university degree in a discipline that requires dedicated study of obscure topics like art history . . . or paleontology.

So for anyone aspiring to be seen like John Hammond, again, decision: *T. rex.*

T. rex versus *G. crassicauda*: For Which Are We Responsible?

It's ironic that Hammond tries to impress his guests at the park with a gourmet lunch of Chilean sea bass. It's been called a poster species for overfishing. Organizations like the Monterey Bay Aquarium and David Suzuki Foundation have issued warnings about it to consumers.

This is just one of the ways in which the theme of human responsibility runs though the movie. Hammond argues that his critics would not be objecting if he had created California condors instead of dinosaurs. Malcolm retorts that, of *course* not—condors are being threatened by human actions! And the mathematician's got a point; not all extinctions are considered equal.

One of the key principles expressed by the Society for Conservation Biology is that human-caused extinctions are unacceptable. If we're going to apply that viewpoint to restoring extinct species, the ones that were driven out of existence by humans would surely be first in line.

The tyrannosaurs went extinct long before humans appeared, but the main factor that seems to have wiped out the thicktail chub was the destruction of its habitat: California's wetlands drained for farms and subdivisions, or to divert the water to thirsty Los Angeles. Bringing back the species that we endangered or eradicated would be a way to make amends, and give humans hope that we'll get a second chance too. To be sure, there's one way in which these intentions could backfire: by undermining the certainty that "extinction is forever," people may be less inclined to see endangerment and extinction as a big deal if they think that species can be brought back. Could this send the wrong kind of educational message? Even so, Pister described how that day in the desert saving the Owens pupfish had given his life meaning—and how humbled he felt, "standing between life and extinction" (p. 19).

Decision: *G. crassicauda.*

T. rex versus *G. crassicauda*: Ecosystem Function

Would losing certain species make a big difference to ecosystem functioning? Many endangered species tend to have relatively restricted ranges and small populations. Bil Gilbert argued that California condors haven't played a crucial role in the ecosystem for a long time, and their populations were already decreasing due to environmental changes even before white settlers arrived.

Jeremy Bentham (1748–1832) advocated trying to create the greatest good for the greatest number, an idea that became known as utilitarianism. For the thicktail chub, this could include other species as well as the human inhabitants of the area. Because of its role as both predator and prey, the chub is likely more important to California than the condor—and both of those species would still be a better fit for the ecosystem than the *T. rex.*

If the purpose of resurrecting an extinct species is to allow it to resume its former niche in the environment, *G. crassicauda* has a much better chance than any dinosaur does. As top carnivores, tyrannosaurs would have been relatively rare even in their heyday. In contrast, the thicktail chub was an important food source for the native Indians and also supported a commercial fishery. Bringing it back in significant numbers raises the possibility of also restoring populations of other species that rely on it, along with economic and cultural benefits.

But even the chub runs into the problem of impacts on present-day ecosystems. Could any existing species be displaced? What if they're also rare or valuable? From Bentham's utilitarian perspective, if many species are harmed this could outweigh the possible benefits to others. True, the negative repercussions likely wouldn't be as obvious as for reintroducing the California grizzly. Abruptly releasing large bears into an unprepared coastal California could be as disruptive as the *T. rex* lumbering through suburbs in the Lost World sequel.

Decision: ***G. crassicauda.*** The two species are tied, 2–2.

You Can't Go Home Again

Dinosaurs may not be compatible with present-day ecosystems. If they were brought back, they would have to be kept in artificial conditions, not present-day landscapes. Ellie Sattler pointed out in the first movie that many post-Cretaceous plants are not compatible with dino digestive systems. She suspected that West Indian lilac or some other flowering species might have been responsible for poisoning the ailing triceratops.

When species that may not even have lived in the same time period or geographical area are suddenly thrown together, ecological chaos could result. We're seeing this today with invasive exotic species. In Australia, indigenous predators like the kookaburra die after eating poisonous cane toads. In Guam, the brown tree snake that arrived with shipments of military equipment gobbled down thousands of unsuspecting local birds.

We could always hope for the best, and that with the efforts of scientists and the cooperation of local residents, even a large predator like a tyrannosaur could have a quiet, uneventful life in semi-captivity. No. 56, a radiocollared black bear living in Minnesota, roamed free through inhabited areas although she was tracked and observed constantly by researchers for decades. As of mid-2013 she had lived past age thirty-nine, making her the oldest known wild bear in the world. It would be much more difficult for a *T. rex*, with its specialized carnivorous diet, though. Conflicts with humans and livestock would be a constant concern.

The *Jurassic Park* dinosaurs are meant to be restricted to a couple of protected areas, conveniently placed on isolated islands. But these may not be large enough to support a healthy population, especially of the larger carnivorous species like *T. rex* and the Spinosaurus. In fact, by the end of *Jurassic Park III*, the more mobile Pteranodon species are winging it away from Isla Sorna, looking for new habitat.

Even if it could succeed, John Hammond's original dream also creates an ethical dilemma. Peter Ludlow, Hammond's nephew, argues in the second movie that an extinct animal that's been re-created has no rights: it only exists because we made it. He seems to be implying that this also means that we can decide what kind of life it will lead. Does engineering a formerly-extinct species so it can't breed—or will die without human intervention, like the "lysine contingency" used by the *Jurassic Park* geneticists—interfere with the basic rights of the species to exist? Real-world biotech companies have been criticized for implanting a "terminator gene" that should prevent a GMO crop from replicating.

So which species requires less effort on our part to keep it alive? It seems that the *T. rex* would require extensive effort to create artificial conditions. And in the case of Jurassic Park, tremendous effort would be taken to change them genetically in order to control them. There is a worry here that all of these changes, especially ones to the species, directly violate their own right to exist as themselves. A *T. rex* isn't a toy, and given the opportunity, she will *prove* to us how seriously we should take her when she decides to eat us.

As the debate currently raging over domestic cats shows, the legal rights of non-human organisms are still controversial. There is a wide range of opinions: some activists have argued that because cats can hunt and kill rare species, people should not own them unless they are isolated indoors and are unable to breed. Others maintain that cats have an intrinsic right to as natural an existence as their wild ancestors would have had, including hunting, mating, and reproducing; and that trying to impose human expectations on them is wrong. There are passionate arguments over where to draw the line: sterilization, declawing, or attempting to feed them vegetarian diets.

So which species requires less environmental and genetic modification, and avoids the ethical worries of messing around with their DNA so that we can turn them into marketable objects for our amusement? Well, not *T. rex*.

Decision: **G. crassicauda.**

Final Decision: Pister's Bucket

"But wait!" The world would likely say before our judges come to the decision to bring back *G. crassicauda* instead of *T. rex* . . . "But think of the wonder, the majesty, the money!" Bringing *T. rex* back would not only be *financially* amazing, it would just be *amazing*. An act of human creative will! Think of the awe and power we would experience when being able to look at a massive *T. rex* from the safety of a park or a zoo. Wouldn't that be profound? Sure, maybe we owe *G. crassicauda* and it would be far better for the environment, but the thing we *want*, the thing that will enthrall us, would be *T. rex*. Shouldn't we take that into account?

Think about it like this, . . . even at the moment of his success, Edwin Pister, the guy who saved the last Owns pupfish, wasn't triumphant, but subdued: "I could not help but ponder the ultimate fate not only of the Owens pupfish but also of all southwestern fishes and species in general." He knew that if habitat kept disappearing, he was only postponing the inevitable. The remaining pupfish would end up in ever more precarious situations, until eventually someone dropped the bucket. A captive breeding and relocation program requires a lot of effort and resources, and is not guaranteed to work. Especially when the number of survivors is very small, as in the case of the California condor, where there are risks of inbreeding and infertility.

In order to conserve maximum genetic diversity in captive populations, zoo animals are now managed like racehorses: detailed records are kept in studbooks, and matings arranged to minimize inbreeding and reduce the spread of harmful genes. Captive species may require this care for a very long time. Some may spend many generations in captivity before enough habitat can be protected for them to create a strong population. This may even result in a slow transition to becoming a somewhat domesticated species, as the individuals that are too wild to stand constant human contact die due to stress-related illnesses. The sick triceratops in the original *Jurassic Park* movie seems to be accustomed to people and allows strangers to touch and examine her, but many of the patients at the wild animal clinic where I used to work were far less calm and trusting. Their reactions would serve them well if they were to be released into today's world, but not so much if they and their offspring needed to survive decades—even centuries—of forced cohabitation with humans.

In the first movie, a wonderstruck John Hammond helps the velociraptor hatchling out of its egg. Whether or not the filmmakers were aware of this, it's a very appropriate metaphor. For birds, which have many similarities to dinosaurs and likely evolved from them, well-intentioned help could actually be bad for the hatchling. It's crucial that the blood has enough time to move from the egg membrane into the hatchling. Trying to force it to hatch too early could result in severe blood loss or internal injuries.

Just as a hatchling that's started cracking the eggshell may not be ready to be pulled out just yet, the way things are heading right now it would be very difficult to guarantee a secure future for either the *T. rex* or the thicktail chub. —Especially if the goal is to reintroduce them back into the environment. Around the world there have been unprecedented changes to ecosystems and the climate itself, along with increasing demands from a growing human population with a rapidly-rising standard of living.

If we can make it through this next century, we'll have a much better idea of what is actually possible. If these projects are worth doing, it's also worth waiting until they have a much better chance of succeeding, and not only the resources and technology, but also the habitat are available. If we rush in now there's a strong possibility that we'd have to watch the resurrected species go extinct again.

Think of the tragedy of that. . . . We bring back *T. rex* or another majestic dinosaur to amaze us, only to have it die off a second time. I'm not sure what is worse, causing a species to go extinct due to ignorance and selfishness, or bringing one back to amuse us as our plaything, only to let it die off again because we were too arrogant to realize we lack the ability to really give them the care they would need to survive. I can't help but imagine humanity gleefully clapping its ignorant hands as *T. rex* is born again into the world, only to pout when it goes extinct a *second time*, and then, of course, shrug its shoulders and move on to our next plaything.

So, I think, it's Pister's Bucket that wins out. Maybe for the moment, while we're still pretty damn ignorant, we should spend our time trying to save the species that *we* are currently killing off. Just changing that would be a difficult and *wondrous* task. Maybe bringing species back from the dead should take a back seat to stopping the damage that we are doing *right now*.

It's okay to admit that we don't know what could happen if we bring back extinct species. It's also okay to defer any decision about which species get to experience de-extinction. For now, put the vials away and keep them safe. As Alan Grant observed in *Jurassic Park III*, the great thing about studying bones is that they will never run away. We'll always know where to find them.

IV

Staying Alive

16
Superiority Is Our Weakness?

CHRISTOPHER KETCHAM

Imagine this . . .

March 17th

DR. ALAN GRANT: Damn, they've escaped the island!

DR. IAN MALCOLM: Um, wait, what escaped the island?

GRANT: The raptors. They're on Nava, an inhabited island about a hundred and ten clicks from here.

MALCOLM: [*Mumbles to himself*] What can go wrong . . .? [*To Grant*] How?

GRANT: Supply ships, I suppose. The raptors are apparently very resourceful.

MALCOLM: How many. How many are missing?

GRANT: A whole pod of them from the southeast quadrant. Remember the eggs you saw? They're breeding . . . a lot. Natives on Nava have reported seeing hupia [raptors] and they are killing wild game.

MALCOLM: Game, not livestock or domestic animals?

GRANT: Yes, just game. That is rather odd. They appear intelligent enough to go after the easier prey. I wonder . . .

MALCOLM: Smart, perhaps too smart. Maybe they already know that we know. Maybe they know that if they attack livestock we will attack them.

GRANT: Extraordinary thought. How smart are they?

Where is intelligence? Is it in our genes? Animal behaviorist Richard Dawkins, in his book *The Selfish Gene*, tells us that our genes are selfish, aimed at our survival, and that survival strategies vary. What's really weird is that that even altruistic behavior (behavior that seems self-sacrificial), such as caring for offspring, can be explained through selfishness.[1] So our genes are always selfish (even though at times, they make us altruistic). In the end, the question for the genes is, "What's in it for me?" Certainly, intelligence must be a survival strategy and the nature of intelligence—whether raptor or human—is a mystery. Is intelligence just selfish genes, or could it be something else, some kind of consciousness?

By "selfish," Dawkins meant that we (anything with genes) are the creatures whose job is to make sure our genes survive. They have programmed us to do their bidding by breeding survivors who choose to live in a way that preserves them. The selfish gene pushes you to work hard for the good life and encourages beautiful people to hook up with other beautiful people. These ancient genes also push raptors of *Jurassic Park* into packs to hunt prey and altruistically care for their young. Really, our genes seem to determine everything we do!

There is further news . . .

March 23rd

The Costa Rican News: Initial reports of dinosaurs from Jurassic Park escaping to the island of Nava have been confirmed by Park scientists. So far, they have not attacked humans but the South American Nature Conservancy reports that these are meat-eating dinosaurs from another age that may irretrievably disrupt the fragile ecosystem of this small island and are calling for an investigation and analysis of their impact on the island. The Costa Rican Coast Guard is on the alert because Nava is only two miles from the mainland. Every vessel venturing within a hundred-mile radius of Nava is being searched. Jurassic Park has been closed indefinitely, pending further investigation. Park officials, however, have stated that these raptors cannot swim for any distance. The United States is discussing whether to increase its naval presence in the area.

[1] Richard Dawkins, *The Selfish Gene*, third edition, Oxford University Press, 2006, p. 2.

April 27th

The island of Nava, Dr. Ian Malcolm's diary: Their evidence is all around the island in the jungles farthest from this small fishing village where I'm staying. Raptor footprints, crushed underbrush, perhaps a nesting site, scat and bones of local animals and birds. But all evidence stops at the edge of the jungle. Even in the fields of cattle and pigs there's no evidence they have been there. The raptors seem to be avoiding people. They did not in the park. What's the reason for this change in behavior? Haven't seen a single raptor yet and there have been no reports of sightings for three days now. A tracking party of seventeen came back yesterday . . . not a single sighting in a virtual sweep of the island. They didn't seem so stealthy in the park. Curious!

What if raptors are smart enough not to eat humans? Consider the wolf. Some think that because humans are messy and create garbage dumps wherever they go, some wolves long ago profited at humanity's dumps and stuck around. Then their pups were even less fearful, and *voilà!*—in just a few generations they were tame enough to co-exist with humanity in a new kind of pack of dogs and humans, each providing the other companionship and protection. But, most wolves remain wild (I guess our dumps weren't too exciting to them!). So, even if some raptors are like wolves, we still have the problem of wild and perhaps unpredictable pack—scary, hunting raptors.

April 30th

The Island of Nava, Dr. Ian Malcolm's diary: They have *all* left the island. I am sure of it. Fish tales. Fish tales. Too hard to believe. A shaken fisherman, Manuel, was found by the Costa Rican Coast Guard mumbling incoherently in his boat not far from the mainland. When sailors approached Manuel's boat he shouted about demons and dragons. He claimed that the hupia rushed from out of nowhere as he loaded his boat on Nava to go night fishing and they crowded him onto the boat, snapping their jaws. The hupia boarded after him and pushed him towards the controls. Remarkable. Remarkable. But believable? I don't know. The Costa Rican Coast Guard has him and they let me see him this morning. He looked like he was in shock, his eyes wild and rocking back and forth and rambling on and on about the hupia snapping at him if he deviated from a course aimed straight at the mainland. But he was otherwise unharmed—not a scratch or a bite mark. Somehow they avoided the scrutiny of the coast guard and other boats on this journey. When he arrived at the shore he said the raptors quickly leapt out of the boat and disappeared into the jungle.

Too fantastic, just too fantastic. But where are the raptors? They aren't here. There are no bodies. God help us if there's any truth in this.

Fearsome Friend or Foe?

So, what would our intelligent raptors become in this brave new world of theirs? Perhaps the stuff of nightmares, their genes programing them to survive at any cost. Would those genes scream selfishness? Or, would raptors be like the wolf—fearsome, but the ancestor of the domestic dog, "man's best friend"? *Jurassic Park* hints at both scenarios. Isn't co-operation a selfish survival strategy, as well?

We'll soon find out.

March 17th, Ten Years After the Escape from Jurassic Park

New York Times: It has been ten years since the first reports that a species of ancient dinosaur escaped the now shuttered Jurassic Park on Isla Nublar, off the coast of Costa Rica. Since then all remaining park animals have been euthanized and the stock of embryos and reproduction paraphernalia from the colossal genetic experiment gone wrong have been confiscated. Yet the single escaped species called velociraptor has thrived outside of captivity and now has been reported on all continents except Antarctica. Efforts to restrain their migration (which some have called infestation) have proven fruitless and many countries have acceded to a kind of truce—a "peaceful coexistence," some have called—it for humans and raptors. A United Nations subcommittee on the Reintroduction of the Dinosaur has produced a controversial but inconclusive report as to what this means for Earth, humanity, and the global ecosystem. Animal rights groups and conservationists cannot agree whether this introduction is harmful, neutral or helpful to the environment and to the world at large. Epidemiologists from the World Health Organization report no evidence of the introduction of mutating viruses or other harmful biologic effects in areas where raptors now have become part of the ecosystem. Nor do biologists agree as to whether this ancient species is harmful to present-day animal populations. They are carnivores but do not limit their hunting to any one local species. They seem to keep their reproduction in check and maintain small but co-ordinated and widely-spaced groups. They have always, until now, avoided humans, going out of their way sometimes to skirt human habitation. However, there are now reports in some areas of Venezuela and Ecuador that raptors are venturing into towns at night to scavenge at garbage dumps and restaurant trash bins. Few of these reports have been verified. Wildlife cameras have revealed no pictures, but those devices placed in the path where raptor sightings have occurred have been clawed and bitten into pieces.

Fifteen Years After the Escape from the Island

The Journal Nature, *September 6th*. Abstract for Raptor and Human, an Investigation into Inter-Species Communication: While investigating raptor population growth in the Congo we began hearing reports of a remote tribe that seemed to be peacefully co-existing with a pod of raptors. Our subsequent investigation has revealed that the raptors do have a closer relationship with the humans of this tribe than anywhere else in Africa. While humans and raptors do not live together, per se, sometimes they hunt together and share the kill. More importantly, this relationship includes a kind of rudimentary communication. While we have not conclusively established that this is anything more than what might occur between a dog and its master, both humans and raptors use the same grunts and clicks to identify different objects and to suggest different activities such as turning left or right. In addition to describing these grunts and clicks as we recorded them in the wild, we have outlined a rudimentary lexicon of the language and its purported meaning as explained by the tribespersons.

What's It Like to Be a Raptor?

The report in *Science* was only the beginning. Humans and certain pods of raptors developed a quite sophisticated common language in the decades that followed. The raptors became less wary of humans, but humans were still wary of these creatures, because how could we begin to understand how they think?

Thomas Nagel once famously asked, "What is it like to be a bat?"[2] How can we ever crack into someone's skull and peer

---

[2] Thomas Nagel, "What Is It Like to Be a Bat?," *Philosophical Review* (1974).

into his or her consciousness to understand what they're think-ing? If we can't do this with each other, how can we even begin to understand another species—a radically different species—whose countenance screams, "*I want to eat you . . . and I can, you know!*" Even within our own species we are great at find-ing ways to brand races and ethnicities as being inferior, slovenly, violent, . . . anything that separates them from our "superior" selves. Without even peering into the consciousness of these people we treat so poorly, we know what they are by the brand we have given them.

Wouldn't we brand the raptor as being a dangerous enemy—even if we had IQ tests that told us that it is *at least* equal to us in intelligence. What if they could converse with us? Or if they could find a way to write? But they are so dif-ferent, their anatomy is almost nothing like ours! Would we still think them inferior? My guess is that we would be very unwilling to grant them rights, or treat them as anything more than "damn dirty raptors!" But if we inspect the genes of different species—even one as different from humans as velociraptors—we find that their genes are mostly the same as our own. In fact, we share a scary amount of genetic sim-ilarity with fruit flies, and even bananas—some say as much as fifty percent! So why are we so sure our intelligence is automatically superior? Just because it's human, rather than raptor?

I think our feeling of superiority is a selfish gene trait—It's a way of convincing ourselves that we're above all in order to justify our taming and exploiting the world. Some humans believe God tells them they are the chosen beings, and believe that when God punished us for our sinfulness, he let Noah and his family on the ark so that we could survive. God didn't spare the raptor and other dinosaurs. . . . But wait. The mosquito supped from dinosaur veins and in the end, raptor DNA was preserved in amber, so it could thrive again. God? Selfish Genes? What?

Fast Forward a Hundred Years

Let's say raptor intelligence rivals our own. They harness their need for prodigious amounts of meat into animal husbandry businesses that they run and hire humans to maintain. And they employ their brain power to consider the mysteries of the universe. "This year's Nobel Prize for Physics goes to . . ." What if humans even learned to speak and write Raptorian and they, human languages? Yet, we would be *uneasy*. This being is so unlike ourselves. Our psychology, our motivations, our . . . very *being* seem so different, so alien from each other. We're still wrestling with whether they're intelligent by our standards: are they conscious, like humans?

Certainly, raptor brains need to be large for there to be intelligence. But what *is* intelligence, and how can we differentiate the intelligence of a very smart animal from a human-like intelligence? Well, let's start here. Humans go through many stages of development. Jean Piaget theorized six stages from the very youngest infant through to the pre-adult adolescent who still does not do well in abstract thinking, and then to the adult. But Piaget only gets us to adult, where abstract thinking is possible. We know that there's more to thinking and being than just becoming an adult or thinking abstractly; some people . . . well, seem to go through life differently than others.

Susanne Cook-Greuter has categorized psychological growth at higher levels than just abstraction and reasoning.

- **In the first stage, or "autonomous stage," she says we're comfortable being who we are: I can deal with most psychological challenges using my own personal resources. Translated: "I can handle life." Many humans may never even reach this stage.**

- **In the second stage, called construct awareness, I am aware that I have a past, I know it has influenced me, and I realize that I will change and evolve even more over time. But I question, "Will I ever be fully aware of myself; will I ever really know who I am?"**

- **In the third and highest, or "unity stage," I let life come into me and I flow with it in the moment. I become deeply conscious of what is and what is not and it . . . is as if I am acting in my own play.**

Cook-Greuter thought of the "unity stage" as being in the state of *"perpetual peak experience."* [3]

Why is all of this stuff about psychological stages important to our relationship with our raptors? It's what we may need to understand in order to co-exist with a highly intelligent velociraptor. There are few humans who exist in a state of perpetual peak experience, but what about the raptors? They're built for speed, stealth, and quick thinking. Like ninjas, they see and capitalize on weakness. Perhaps that's why they're so frightening to us; when around them, we feel like actors in *their* plays, not our own. They seem to make opportunity appear out of thin air and this sends us back down into a more primordial state of being. It might only be what raptors are genetically programmed to do. But what if the raptors *can* make their own decisions beyond the gene? Humans and raptors both have superior intelligence that can be measured. But as we have seen, humans and raptors would approach existence and co-existence in the world in different ways. What if our stages of development (humans and raptors) were not in synch? What would that mean?

It would mean trouble. Human and raptor social and physical requirements are so different that there is good reason to believe we could not co-exist.

Association for the Preservation and Evolution of Raptors (APE–OR)

Senate hearing on the wild raptor population and its danger to humans. Chairman Pampous called the committee to order. Leonard Hupia, raptor representative for APE-OR is the first witness. The following is an English translation from Raptorian.

MR. HUPIA: Mr. Chairman, APE–OR has commissioned three independent studies of our wild velociraptor kin, and there is no indication that any wild raptor has ever harmed a human—intentionally harmed.

SENATOR FINEWINE (ALABAMA): What about the school bus in Ecuador that went off the cliff? Dozens of kids

---

[3] In Allan Coombs, *Consciousness Explained Better* (Paragon House, 2010).

killed. And the carnage in this country from raptor-car accidents.

MR. HUPIA: If you recall, senator: in that instance the driver had been drinking and the raptor was holding her ground against an injured companion. The car accident problem can be easily resolved by using the highway deer bridges like they have in New Jersey. Senator, we have incontrovertible evidence that the nomadic raptors prefer these bridges in the garden state.

SENATOR BIGGUTS (NEW JERSEY): Mr. Hupia, I don't know about my other learned colleagues but I find it so very disconcerting to have those beady eyes, no disrespect sir, staring at me through hedges and fences. Scares the hell out of my kids, too. It's just disgusting seeing them tear at a carcass of some poor animal at the side of the road. They are a menace that needs to be eradicated—or caged, at the least.

SENATOR AMORPHIOUS (MISSISSIPPI): And my esteemed friend from New Jersey only has to deal with this menace in the summer months. In Mississippi, we have them all year long.

SENATOR FINEWINE: I agree with the Senator from Mississippi. Just the other day I found a whole pod of them in my garage. What a mess! —And I had to put in one of those raptor-proof doors, at considerable expense, I might add.

SENATOR WIGGNINS (NORTH DAKOTA): And what about the population studies, Mr. Hupia? I understand that your wild kin are breeding like rabbits.

MR. HUPIA: Senator, wild raptor populations level off with the availability of prey like most other animals, . . . unlike humans, who do not.

[*Crowd roar*] Gavel! Gavel! Gavel!

CHAIRMAN PAMPOUS: There will be no more outbursts in this hearing.

SENATOR FINEWINE: That is what I am worried about, Mr. Hupia. All you bleeding-heart liberals out there don't seem to understand that they will come for us when there are no more deer!

MR. HUPIA: Senator, we have no evidence of . . .

Because we and raptors are so different, we would have trouble co-existing. This may have happened before. Why are there no more Neanderthals? Did Neanderthals become extinct by disease, or were they unable to survive climate change? Did humans cause their extinction by forcing them from productive land, or did we just simply kill them? Do humans have a superiority gene that says we would try do the same to raptors? Before you answer, consider what we have done to others of our own species.

Humanness as Property

Justice Henry Billings Brown of the US Supreme Court wrote in the decision *Plessy v. Ferguson*, 163 U.S. 537 (1896) of legalized segregation:

> If he be a white man and assigned to a colored coach, he may have his action for damages against the company for being deprived of his so-called property. Upon the other hand, if he be a colored man and be so assigned, he has been deprived of no property, since he is not lawfully entitled to the reputation of being a white man.

If humans can make whiteness property, why couldn't we also make humanness property—which of course would exclude raptors and, for that matter, all other animals? While there are too few genetic differences in human "races" to make any case for exclusion (which hasn't stopped us, of course!), humanity could more easily make a genetic-difference case between raptors and humans. One hundred years in the future, it's not hard to imagine that in some countries people will have relegated these intelligent beings to the status of animal, which they mistreat without care.

However, John Stuart Mill reminds us that mistreatment of animals belongs in the same category as racial discrimination.[4]

---

[4] Cass R. Sunstein, *Animal Rights: Current Debates and New Directions* (Oxford University Press, 2004), p. 1.

Some of us are left with the sinking feeling that mistreating these intelligent beings is wrong. We don't have a successful track record of living with *ourselves*, let alone with other species. But we brought back to life an alien intelligent species.

What if raptors used their brand of intelligence to become part of the world again, but this time in a world inhabited by humans, not other dinosaurs? Selfish gene or otherwise, the raptors have become part of the fabric of this hypothetical world because of their ability to survive and thrive in a world where humans require superiority.

But in this new world, which intelligence is superior?— raptor or human?

17

You Monkeywrenching Bastard!

SETH M. WALKER

Bastard!? That's a bit harsh, don't you think? Then again, wouldn't you call someone who destroys other people's equipment a bit of a jerk? Wouldn't you be especially annoyed if that person was messing around with dangerous animals, putting lives at risk, and bypassing safety measures? I guess you'd say anyone who would do this might certainly be a bastard. But, what if that person is doing it for the *right* reasons? Is it okay to be a bastard to save the Earth? Let's see.

InGen arrived on Isla Sorna ("Site B") in *The Lost World: Jurassic Park* with a pretty basic goal: to track, trap, and relocate specimens to the United States mainland. John Hammond's personal team had also been sent there, but for a much different purpose: to document a "living fossil record" in an effort to protect the island from any interference and intruders. After witnessing the abuse of the captured dinosaurs, Hammond's video documentarian and field photographer, Nick Van Owen, confessed to the others: "Uh, I think I should tell you guys: Hammond told me these people might show up. I thought we'd be finished by the time they got started, but in case they weren't, he did send a backup plan . . . me." Nick also happened to be a member of Earth First! (EF!)—one of the largest, real-world "radical" environmentalist groups—so sabotaging InGen's camp and freeing the caged dinosaurs wasn't too far outside his comfort zone. But, did it make him a bastard?

The good guy–bad guy clash between Hammond's team and InGen BioEngineering—now controlled by Hammond's nephew—was set up fairly early in the movie. But, what are we supposed to think of these acts of sabotage and liberation? Although they *appear* to be "right," the justification of Nick's actions—his so-called "monkeywrenching"—is not as straight-forward as we might assume.

Despite what you might be thinking, "monkeywrenching" does not refer to the latest pop-dance craze. Made popular by Edward Abbey's *The Monkeywrench Gang*, the term is actually used to describe "direct political action undertaken for environmental protection."[1] Abbey's novel also inspired Dave Foreman—the founder of EF!—and Bill Haywood's *Ecodefense: A Field Guide to Monkeywrenching*, which outlines a number of different ways to successfully "monkeywrench" in the field (not on the dance floor). Some of these methods include cutting power lines, road and tree spiking, disabling vehicles, removing or rearranging development markers, and liberating captive animals.[2]

The Earth Liberation Front (ELF) and Animal Liberation Front (ALF) take these practices to much more extreme levels; they avoid the more common "civil disobedient" forms of protest. The ELF is notorious for large-scale acts of arson, and the ALF is famous for breaking into various facilities to rescue non-human animals being mistreated and tortured. Their goal is to cause as much economic damage as possible to industries and organizations that are destroying the environment and harming its creatures. They exist entirely because people are frustrated by how ineffective it can be to picket and write letters to government agencies. The fact that Nick Van Owen is explicitly connected with these groups forces us to think more deeply not only about his actions in *Jurassic Park*, but also about events we read about in news reports, too.

I Know You. You're That Earth First! Bastard, Aren't You?

Let's look at Nick's actions (and possible bastardliness) in terms of the "ecodefense argument." This is based on the

---

[1] Thomas C. Shevory, "Monkeywrenching: Practice in Search of a Theory," in *Environmental Crime and Criminality: Theoretical and Practical Issues*, edited by Sally M. Edwards, Terry D. Edwards, and Charles B. Fields, Garland, 1996, p. 185; Edward Abbey, *The Monkeywrench Gang* (Lippincott, 1975).

[2] See Dave Foreman and Bill Haywood, *Ecodefense: A Field Guide to Monkeywrenching* (Ned Ludd Books, 1985).

assumption that destroying the trees in a neighboring forest is the same as an attack on our homes, so we can fairly act in self-defense. But, this certainly isn't the only perspective we could explore while looking at dino-liberation and Jurassic "monkey-wrenching." The "consequentialist argument" analyzes the costs and benefits of our actions so we can decide if we can justify their consequences.

The consequentialist argument requires us to weigh all of the potential positive and negative effects of acts of sabotage. Did the release of the dinosaurs spare them unnecessary and undeserved suffering? When the tyrannosaurs were brought to the United States mainland, they killed the entire crew on the cargo ship, not to mention how many lives were also lost as the adult made its way through San Diego looking for its baby. So, maybe Nick is even a hero for humans—when he foiled InGen's plans to bring back even more dinosaurs, did he end up saving many other human lives in California as a result?

Most of us probably feel there are obvious answers to these types of questions, but what about the possible negative effects of Nick's actions? Hammond's team may have been wise to ask themselves how their actions would affect the wellbeing of everyone involved. Would the dinosaurs safely get away? Would the team risk getting the dinosaurs killed by scared InGen members confronted with a loose herd of dangerous animals? Would those occupying the InGen camp be put in harm's way by such a sudden and mass release? After Hammond's team's RV was destroyed by two tyrannosaurs (which was a direct result of the team's involvement in sabotaging the InGen camp and rescuing the injured baby *Tyrannosaurus rex*) they were left without functioning radio equipment to call for help. The released dinosaurs also destroyed most of the equipment in the InGen camp, which made everyone's rescue from the island practically impossible! So maybe Nick really is a bastard, since he didn't think about these types of consequences beforehand.

They're Just Protecting Their Baby!

These concerns are obviously important if we're calculating a cost-benefit analysis of Nick's actions, but the ecodefense argument provides us with a much more fascinating perspective. Nick was ardently *defending* these animals, wasn't he? He didn't seem to be interested in a calculated sequence of actions based on a careful analysis of their ramifications. That even *sounds* boring—especially for someone who had previously shot footage for *Nightline* in Rwanda, Chechnya, and Bosnia, and had worked alongside Greenpeace (even if it was only for "the women"). Most ecosaboteurs are not even motivated by thoughts of the consequences of their actions: the ecodefense argument is based on an appeal to a higher moral law—not on grounds like those above.[3] So, the basic structure of the ecodefense argument, as it applies to the scenario in the movie, would look something like this:

1. We're entitled to defend ourselves and our homes against invasion or attack.

2. InGen is attacking innocent beings on Isla Sorna.

3. Isla Sorna is our home—that is, it's home to those of us who live on this planet. The island is just as much our home as are the structures in which we live.

4. Therefore, we're entitled to take measures to defend the beings on Isla Sorna against InGen.

Although this logic is central to the ecodefense argument, we can easily stumble upon some issues when we think about the way the word "home" is being used.

In the narrow sense of the word, "home" might refer to personal property, but the broader sense of the word is the only way the argument can work: our environment is our "home." This draws on ideas associated with "deep ecology." Coined by Arne Naess in 1973, "deep ecology" contrasts a *shallow* approach to ecological activism, which simply revolves around pollution and the depletion of natural resources. A *deep* ecology goes much further, expanding our sense of "self" to include the non-human world. This is biocentric equality—the equality of all things, dinosaur and human, living in the ecosphere. Following this biocentric perspective, all dinosaurs "have an equal right to live and blossom and to reach their own individual forms of unfolding

---

[3] See Derek D. Turner, "Monkeywrenching, Perverse Incentives, and Ecodefence," *Environmental Values* 15 (2006).

and self-realization within the larger Self-realization."[4] In other words, the velociraptors and Hammond's scared nephew are both part of an interrelated whole and are inherently equal.

So, following these concepts, how should we interpret Nick's actions? Should they be considered acts of vandalism, or expressions of self-defense on behalf of him-*Self*? From the perspective of deep ecology, Nick seems to have been obligated to defend and rescue the injured *T. rex* calling out in pain. Roland Tembo (the InGen team's guide) broke the baby's leg to lure its parents into a trap. Biocentric equality tells us that the baby was not only equal in worth to Nick and Sarah Harding—it had its own "equal right to live and blossom" as part of the interconnected reality it shared with Nick, Sarah, Roland, and the others. Nick and Sarah were not simply helping a seemingly defenseless animal; they were responding, as moral agents, to distress within the ecosphere. So, really, Roland breaking the baby's leg was actually *Self*-destructive. Freeing the captives from their cages was not merely a courageous act of liberation, but Nick's expression of a *deep* concern for the welfare of his fellow beings. Biocentric equality suggests that those "who can do so are entitled to come to the aid of other living creatures whose right to live and blossom has been violated, when those other creatures are unable to defend themselves."[5] The deep ecological perspective requires this type of action and encourages this sort of concern.

Earlier in the movie, Hammond's team is briefly separated from Sarah when she is trying to take photographs of a baby stegosaurus. When its parents notice how close she is, and are drawn closer by the baby's frightened howls after a camera malfunction, the team's paleontologist is left struggling to escape their protective wrath. "Shoot her!" Ian Malcolm, Sarah's boyfriend and charming chaotician, commands Eddie Carr, the team's field equipment expert. "They're just protecting their baby!" Eddie yells back, hesitant to take aim and pull the trigger. "So am I!" Ian responds. We can't help but notice that the relative worth of other beings is still a noticeable feature in this sort of framework, but "mutual predation is a

---

[4] Bill Devall and George Sessions, *Deep Ecology: Living as if Nature Mattered*, Gibbs Smith, 1985, p. 67.

[5] "Monkeywrenching, Perverse Incentives, and Ecodefence," p. 224.

biological fact of life."[6] Rescuing and attempting to heal the baby *T. rex*, even at the risk of losing their own lives (our thoughts go out to your friends and family, Eddie), recalls this earlier scene in the film. Indeed, perhaps Nick and Sarah were, in a sense, also "protecting their baby," as were its biological parents.

An Extinct Animal that's Brought Back to Life Has No Rights.

How could Hammond's nephew be so cruel to say such a thing? Why shouldn't they have any rights, given the way we've been examining them? Well, that's just it: all of this might sound great to those who already accept the idea of deep ecology, but why would anyone else accept a biocentric perspective and save the lives of cute little velociraptors and baby tyrannosaurs? British ethicist Peter Singer's "principle of equality" might help us figure this out. For Singer, and countless other ethicists who speak for "those other creatures" who cannot adequately "defend themselves," non-human animal life should be given equal moral consideration.

This doesn't mean that we should be treating groups of certain non-human animals exactly the same way we treat other groups of human animals. We don't usually even do that among humans because we are so different and have such different abilities. But, for Singer, "The basic principle of equality does not require equal or identical *treatment*; it requires equal consideration."[7] In other words, it would be absurd for Nick to hold a baby *T. rex* to the same level of expectations as he would Ian's daughter Kelly. Her abilities are very different: should the baby *T. rex*'s inability to climb through a maze of scaffolding and perform an Olympic-style bar routine in an old shed while evading a velociraptor make it less worthy of good treatment? Likewise, is Kelly less worthy because she lacks a bone-crushing jaw and the ability to safely consume raw flesh? For Singer, "There is no logically compelling reason for assuming that a factual difference in ability between two people justifies any difference in the amount of consideration we give to their needs and inter-

---

[6] *Deep Ecology*, p. 67.
[7] Peter Singer, *Animal Liberation*, HarperCollins, 2009, p. 2.

ests" (p. 5). In other words—our differences don't mean that one is more deserving than the other.

According to Singer, the kicker here is a being's interests—and more specifically, a being's interest in experiencing enjoyment or pleasure and not experiencing any pain or suffering. Simply put, if something can suffer, then it has an interest to not suffer, which makes it worthy of equal consideration: "If a being suffers there can be no moral justification for refusing to take that suffering into consideration. No matter what the nature of the being, the principle of equality requires that its suffering be counted equally with the like suffering—insofar as rough comparisons can be made—of any other being" (p. 8). So, thinking back to that injured baby *T. rex* calling out in pain, we can assume that Nick and Sarah guessed, based on physical and psychological similarities between their species, that it was experiencing discomfort and wanted to be released from the straps tying it down.

Were There Any Alternatives that Could Have Been Considered?

Although Nick's actions quickly produced effective results (the dinosaurs successfully escaped their broken cages and the baby *T. rex* left the RV with a stunning new leg brace), was there another—perhaps better—option to secretly breaking open the cages with a gigantic pair of bolt cutters (too bad it wasn't an actual monkey wrench, right?) that we haven't really considered yet? Nick could have marched down to the InGen camp and made his case in front of everyone. He could have emphasized the greater importance of his own group's goals over their own, and explained that if they didn't listen to him, then he would be forced to take matters into his own hands and release the captured animals. Sure, he could have done all that. But, the odds of this working would have probably been slim, given the determination of InGen to save itself from another monetary disaster. With time not on their side, Hammond's team did what they thought best to spare the suffering of innocent non-human animals—and who's going to argue with the guy carrying the gigantic bolt cutters?

A common criticism of such sneaky behavior is that these private acts escape accountability and display a lack of respect for the social system in place. But, don't you remember how secretive movements like the Underground Railroad were? The acts needed to remain hidden if they were to be continuously—and successfully—performed.[8] If we entertain the possibility of Nick approaching the InGen camp before releasing the captive dinosaurs, and telling them what he was about to do, they would have probably tried to stop him from doing so (if not detaining him in the process, confiscating that impressive pair of bolt cutters), and he would have most likely failed in his quest to save the innocent creatures. Regardless of whether or not Nick's particular acts can be considered morally justified, covert behavior was clearly necessary for them to remain swift and effective in the context of the movie.

What if InGen Returned the Favor?

But what if the tables were turned? Moral consistency could quickly become a serious issue. Without a clear distinction between acts of sabotage geared towards protecting the environment and those motivated by other goals, the ecosaboteur is left with a potentially unsettling realization: all other, non-ecological acts of sabotage must also be accepted as morally justifiable if they are based on something that is also highly valued.

Judging actions by beliefs and values can get incredibly messy. So, without an objective distinction that separates ecological sabotage from other types of sabotage, Nick would need to be okay with InGen destroying his own camp, just as long as the act was based on highly valued beliefs and circumstances; for example, he would have to accept it if they wanted to remove the dinosaurs from the island just as much as Hammond's team didn't want them to. It's also worth noting that the InGen team rescued Nick, Sarah, and Ian from falling to their deaths after the two tyrannosaurs pushed their RV off the edge of a cliff. Would the team have done the same thing for InGen? That's certainly a question at least worth thinking about.

Life, uhh . . . Finds a Way

A major problem with trying to base a justification of ecological sabotage on something like a cost-benefit analysis is that it is

---

[8] See Michael Martin, "Ecosabotage and Civil Disobedience," *Environmental Ethics* 12 (1990).

unlikely to succeed in the modern world.[9] There are too many people "who prefer economic growth, jobs, and development over preservation and restoration" (p. 392). InGen is much more interested in rebuilding itself after John Hammond's big muck-up than it is in documenting his living fossil record. The only green movement they're interested in is the inflow of money from a dino-zoological spectacle in California: "Jurassic Park: San Diego." It's as simple as that—and a catchy name, too!

But, the ecodefense argument also has its own problems. Aside from issues surrounding traditional ideas of "property rights," the biocentric outlook also cannot be proven in a way that other—observable—aspects of reality can. As an "ultimate norm" being *deeply* grounded in a particular worldview, it is impossible to objectively and universally appeal to those with differing values and opinions.[10] If we don't all agree on what matters, it's impossible to claim that connections between life forms definitely matter! But, taking into consideration the interests of other beings, such as the dinosaurs wanting to roam the beautiful landscape of Isla Sorna instead of being cooped up in cages where they can hardly move or lie down, might solve this problem.

Regardless of how we dino-lovers might try to frame things, "monkeywrenching" remains a controversial form of environmental activism. But can we really call Nick a bastard for his actions? His motivation was his belief in his, and our, inseparable connection to our home, and our responsibility to it.

At the very least, considering the broader implications of his actions—and noting his Earth First! affiliation—might encourage us to think more critically about similar types of actions we witness in real life; the media often cast such acts by "radical" environmentalist groups in a negative light by focusing on the destruction and economic damage that has resulted. But we don't really hear much about why they do what they do.

So, the next time you find yourself outside on a beautiful day, perhaps you'll more deeply consider your surroundings and the creatures occupying our shared home.

---

[9] See Thomas Young, "The Morality of Ecosabotage," *Environmental Values* 10 (2001).

[10] See Paul Taylor, *Respect for Nature: A Theory of Environmental Ethics* (New Jersey: Princeton University Press, 1986), p. 167.

And, if you happen to spot a baby *T. rex* in the distance, remember, you may not think of yourself as "one" with nature, but if it eats you, we won't be able to separate you from it. . . .

18
What We Leave Behind

Tim Jones

Ragged and exhausted, the men and women run screaming from the titanic predator hunting them. Snapping its reeking jaws shut, it feasts on the few humans left who haven't learned how and where to hide. What's left of humankind has learned to rarely leave shelter, stay well armed, and never, ever, try to steal velociraptor eggs. While this new breed of human huddles around their meager meals, terrified of the howls, roars, and shrieks that echo in the dark, they sometimes ask each other, "What kind of people chose to create this world?"

It's not a difficult scene to imagine once the dinosaurs escape their island prison, is it? Right this second, we have technology that is both awe-inspiring and terrifying. The world is truly ours to shape or to break. But the people most dramatically affected by the progress of our own time are not any of us, but the people of the future—the future people who are inevitably forced to live in the world created by our actions right now. Barring complete global destruction, these people are definitely going to be born at some point, and yet have no say whatsoever in the things that we do today that will make their lives better or worse. Is this fair? And are there even any alternatives?

It's all too easy for us not to worry about these questions, since we'll be dead by the time that the worst consequences of our actions actually take effect. But this doesn't mean that the state of the future is any less our own fault. And if an independent genius like John Hammond causes the rebirth of the dinosaurs, and these dinosaurs break free and evolve beyond our ability to contain them, then the consequences for future people could make the consequences even for the residents of San Diego at the end of *The Lost World* look pretty small in comparison.

We can see the early potential for some frightening developments in the craftiness of the raptors in *Jurassic Park III*. Rather than simply taking the route that would bring them the quickest satisfaction and eating the hapless mercenary Udeski, they use him as a trap to bring more prey to the table. The end result of this intelligent approach to gathering and harvesting their food could well resemble our own factory-farming practices, with humans crammed into cages and grown in unnatural and torturous ways purely for the dinosaurs' convenience. The most middle-class amongst their number might even argue that free-range humans taste better, while also happily being more ethical and better for the environment.

Either way, life for future people would be pretty bleak. Enough to make them look back to a time *before* the dinosaurs were resurrected by Hammond and wonder why on Earth no one stopped him. Contemporary philosopher Rupert Read has come up with a potential solution for all this that he calls the "Guardians of the Future." The more we're able to affect the experience of the generations that follow us in massive and potentially catastrophic ways, Read argues, the more pressing it becomes to have a kind of super jury that will look over the laws our governments are passing with a watchful eye on the effects these laws might have on future people.

One of the Guardians' chief duties would be throwing out any proposed legislation that negatively impacts future people's "basic needs and fundamental interests."[1] So if an independent genius like Hammond were to dream up a project involving the creation of dinosaurs and the exhibition of them in a theme park, he wouldn't have a choice in whether or not the legality of his plans and the tech they need would be checked against their effects upon future people. And the thought that one day dinosaurs might break free and rule tyrannically over humankind would, we hope, be enough to stop Hammond's idea from becoming reality. The technology he

---

[1] *Guardians of the Future*: <http://www.greenhousethinktank.org/files/greenhouse/home/Guardians_inside_final.pdf>

requires might be banned outright. And the future people could breathe a sigh of relief.

But is such a heavy-handed (some might say dictatorial!) approach really necessary? Aren't even the most independent of scientific geniuses capable of thinking consequences through for themselves and learning from their mistakes? By the close of the first movie, Hammond has realized the potential wrongs that can result from his creations and graciously decides not to take his project any further. Perhaps there's no need for the Guardians after all. The family of the poor man killed at the beginning might think otherwise, but at least it now seems *much* less likely that Hammond's project will be allowed to take things any further.

A look at what happens in *The Lost World* and *Jurassic Park III* should make us think again. Caution is no use at all once the dinosaur has already bolted.

Hypocrisy and Kant

German philosopher Immanuel Kant (1724–1804) would probably scoff at a body like the Guardians of the Future and its potential for interfering with independent genius like Hammond's.

Kant praises a quality that he calls Enlightenment. The opening sentences from Kant's helpfully titled essay "What Is Enlightenment?" give a handy definition of this key philosophical concept. Enlightenment is an "emergence" from a state of "immaturity"—and, for Kant, this immaturity is "the inability to use one's own understanding without the guidance of another." What counts is individuals listening to and following their *own* judgment. Kant pours scorn upon the very idea of asking for advice and valuing the views of other people over your own.

Enlightenment isn't so much a matter of being hugely clever as it is one of using whatever intelligence you have with a confident independence. Kant also describes being enlightened as a matter of *courage*, which makes it sound pretty much like a moral virtue. This sounds fair enough, really, considering how hard it is to follow your own motivations and go your own way when the powerful people and leading institutions around you are insisting that you think how *they* would have you think, and behave how *they* would have you behave. To link Enlightenment with courage makes sense.

Kant doesn't really touch on the subject of scientific achievement. His most common complaints relate to the lack of free-thinking in religion. This is probably, more than anything else, down to the time when Kant was writing. But we can perhaps see from the vast differences between his period and our own precisely why it is that, judging from our position in the twenty-first century, Kant's ideas about Enlightenment might seem very easy for him to hold, but increasingly dangerous for us to follow. For the keenest thinkers of his day to throw caution to the wind might well have caused religious controversy that got them imprisoned or occasionally executed or upset the nobility. It was highly unlikely that Kantian Enlightenment would lead any of its eighteenth-century followers to cause a catastrophe on the scale of resurrecting and letting loose the velociraptors. Consequences of their actions would be personally, not globally disastrous, and so a proposal like the Guardians of the Future just wouldn't have been all that necessary.

However, we can now destroy the world all too easily. Or, at the very least, we can act today in ways that leave the world all but uninhabitable for the future people who will follow us, a fact that might lead us to reconsider whether or not it's still so great for people to act according to their own thinking without asking for second opinions and following the advice of others. Even when a trail-blazing genius like Hammond moves for himself towards preferring a cautious approach, is this enough to make the Guardians of the Future unnecessary? The first three *Jurassic Park* films ultimately suggest not, for the consequences of other people's actions pretty much demolish the positive effects of Hammond's own move at the end of the first film from Enlightenment to caution.

A Cautionary Tale

Hammond might at first seem like exactly the sort of enlightened individual with whom Kant would love to go for a beer, but the Guardians of the Future might need to keep him in check. Following his own ideas (and with the financial backing of InGen) Hammond has managed to bring not just one extinct species, but a whole *series* of extinct species back from the dead. In the words of InGen's Peter Ludlow in *The Lost World*, Hammond's 'dream' is indeed 'Grand. Outsized. Bold.'

And when Grant, Sattler, and Malcolm arrive at the Park, they are astonished at what they see there. Their reactions make it clear that no word of what was happening on Isla Nublar leaked out into the public domain. Hammond and his team have clearly been working alone. The isolated island location of the Park symbolically confirms the sheer independence of Hammond's vision. Spielberg's epic camerawork as the team approach in their helicopter portrays this independence as beautiful. Majestic, even.

So far, so Kantian.

By the end of the first movie, however, we have seen the value of the caution that Kant ridicules. The entire film is actually generated by a moment of extreme caution. The death of an InGen employee in the opening moments leads to the company being scared about the Park's safety and, therefore, demanding that Hammond get the Park checked by a team of experts. True, the requirement comes from his financial backers' concerns that the family of the dead employee will sue them rather than through sheer altruism, but the effect is the same. Hammond's independence as a scientist and as a businessman is immediately limited by the demand for a rigorous review of his ideas.

Hammond begins the movie convinced that the Park will pass the test with flying colors, and the reactions of Grant and Sattler to their first sight of a brachiosaurus only confirms his confidence in his vision. Again, Spielberg's direction ensures that the results of Hammond's vision appear as spectacular to us as they do to the characters themselves. So even though Hammond did not himself invite this review of his work, the initial results don't worry him. Malcolm soon warns Hammond that the Park is dangerous, but he is teased and ignored. So here we can see the resistance that a truly independent, enlightened mind might have accepting the negative feedback that he might get from a review of his work. At this point, Hammond still adheres pretty solidly to Kant's ideals, showing contempt for the feedback that contradicts his own view of his work. *He* knows his research is great and this is enough. The feedback that confirms his own view, he is happy to accept; the feedback that challenges him, he ignores. Nothing will shake his own confidence in the project.

By the end of the movie, Hammond's position has done a complete U-turn. As the survivors flee towards the waiting helicopter, Grant informs him that he will *not* be endorsing the Park. Hammond doesn't argue with him. Considering the chaos that has led up to this moment, his acceptance of Grant's conclusion isn't perhaps all that surprising. But given the strength of his self-belief at the start of the movie, we could well imagine him arguing for trying again, for increasing the Park security, for building in additional fail-safes to prevent the dinosaurs from leaving their own environments. On the contrary: he accepts the results of Grant's survey without the slightest resistance. His experiences have led him towards a belief that maybe Kant was wrong about the worth of having new ideas checked by outsiders and following the advice those outsiders give.

When a genius as independent and grand as Hammond can change so dramatically, perhaps the Guardians of the Future don't really have much to worry about.

The Lost World

And look at how well Hammond's move towards caution sticks. In his brief appearance at the start of *The Lost World*, Hammond tells Malcolm, without hesitation, that Malcolm 'was right' and that he, himself, 'was wrong'. Hammond even hopes that public opinion will be enough to prevent InGen's new board of executives from exploiting the dinosaurs currently living on Isla Sorna, his original test site. He has learned from his own experiences about the power the opinion of others can have in checking wayward ambitions, even seeking to use it as a weapon to stop others going down the path that he was once on himself.

This lasting personal development might still imply that there is no need for the Guardians of the Future. A scientific genius can, through listening to the advice of others, realize the dangerous nature of his own work and, so, limit it rather than take it any further. But look at what happens during the movie's final sequences. The *Tyrannosaurus rex* is let loose from Isla Sorna and manages to trash much of San Diego. This sequence would prove wrong anyone who might point out that Kant describes enlightenment mainly in terms of *thinking*—and not so much in terms of actions.

Like the path the *T. rex* takes from the island to the mainland, thoughts can escape and lead to devastating real-world
consequences, even *after* that very clever man has turned away
from scientific independence and embraced caution. This situation could only have been avoided if wide-ranging legal
restrictions had been implemented, from above, on the tech
Hammond needed to get his project off the ground, well before
he even got started.

The ultimate irony rests with Peter Ludlow, who tells the
game hunter Roland Tembo, once he has caught the *T. rex* that
is to be taken back to San Diego, that "Everyone on the planet
is going to line up to appreciate everything you've done for us."
Once the damage has been assessed and repaired, this will
clearly not be the case. The citizens of San Diego are highly
unlikely to thank either of them. Ludlow's stance is opposite to
the one Hammond has matured into by the end of the first
movie. It's an assumption of people's opinions that has no
actual evidence behind it. You never know with the general
public, but it's not impossible to imagine that, when asked
whether or not they wanted a *T. rex* brought to the middle of a
packed city, their response might have been along the lines of,
"That sounds rather dangerous."

This result *could* have destroyed Ludlow's certainty that it
was such a good idea. But even if he had bothered to check, we
don't know whether or not he would have been as humble in
the face of public refusal to support his ideas as Hammond is
in the face of Grant's refusal at the end of the first movie. It
seems unlikely. Hammond's own caution doesn't mean much
when other people exist whose use of Hammond's creations will
still lead to mass devastation. Once the tech has been created,
its creator can't control the uses it will be put to and the consequences of these uses. It doesn't matter whether or not he's a
nice man who ultimately regrets what he's started. He needed
to be prevented from starting it in the first place.

Once the dinosaur menace has been stopped, *The Lost
World* continues to remind us about the importance of personal
goals and individual motivations being checked. Hammond's
televised warning that Isla Sorna be left alone is delivered not
only to a relaxed Malcolm and Harding, but also directly to the
viewers in the cinema or at home. Its breaking down of the
fourth wall between fictional characters and viewers is the

clearest sign that *we* are supposed to take away a message in favor of caution. And now we've seen a bustling urban area itself threatened by the consequences of an enlightened individual acting separate from public opinion. Hammond now couldn't care less about controlling personal motivations through using public opinion, as he was doing at the movie's start. *Now* he insists that it is 'imperative' to 'work with the Costa Rican Department of Biological Preserves to establish a set of rules for the preservation and isolation of that island.'

So we return to an apparent need for larger institutions like the churches and other organizations that Kant criticizes for seeking to contain individual thinking. It's no longer a case of people soliciting advice from others, rather than following their own motivation. The word 'rules' implies an active prevention of certain behaviors, through policing and even punishment. The fear is that people can't be trusted to behave responsibly, or to work out for themselves what is right or wrong, so the decision needs to be made for them.

Back to the Future People

Notice that none of the restrictions that Hammond argues for actually stop the Dino-Soars paragliding operation from getting Eric Kirby stuck on Isla Sorna in *Jurassic Park III*. If they want their isolation of the island to ever be successful, then the UN and Costa Rican authorities will have to keep on fighting the fact that entrepreneurs will always find a way. Hammond's own move towards a cautious approach by the end of the first film is again pretty irrelevant, since people will continue to take advantage of what he has created. It would only be effective if everyone were to follow him into caution, which the two sequels suggest is never going to happen. He might as well not have bothered.

The final scene of this movie shows three pteranodons soaring into the distance—a lasting image that again stresses the impossibility of any rules or regulations containing this new life once it's already created, or of knowing how it will affect the people of the future. As a final image, it reminds us that we don't know anything about where they're going, or what they'll get up to once they're there. Perhaps they're already intent on world domination—we just don't know. If so, future people will definitely lament that Hammond's project wasn't stopped before it even got off the ground, since his own caution came far too late to prevent its long-term consequences. "Where," they might ask, "were the Guardians of the Future when we needed them?"

Future people's answers to this question aren't likely to leave the technologically-driven ancestors who got them in such a mess looking so good.

19

It's Only Natural to Blame Technology

Daniel Kokotz

The plan was great. Real dinosaurs in a park—how awesome is that? Being able to watch them in their natural surroundings, to watch them eat, sleep, move around in herds (and they *do* move in herds!) is something most grown-ups and probably all children are excited about.

And thanks to John Hammond, it's finally possible to bring those awe-inspiring creatures back to life. Their extinction is overcome by his scientists, a victory of technology over nature. Finally, humanity has taken the biggest step in its pursuit to control nature so far: The creation of life itself. The plan was really great. But it wasn't meant to be.

We all know what happens. We, the audience, watch this science fiction from our safe seats at home, glad that it wasn't us on the island there, and marvel at the horror that the technology of cloning dinosaurs has brought upon the people on the island—the horror which they have brought down on them themselves. Humanity alone is to blame for the unreasonable handling of dinosaurs. Science is responsible for everything that has happened! . . . Or so it would seem.

But is it really science's fault? The dinosaurs are, after all, living beings, originally formed by evolution and elements of the natural world. Isn't *Jurassic Park* really a story of survival? Mankind fighting against primal natural forces in the form of dinosaurs?

Then again, the dinosaurs were bred by humans in a lab and kept in compounds for the amusement of visiting tourists. So if they come from the lab, they're still products of technology, right? And so Hammond and his scientists *are* responsible for their existence and the results of their behavior. But humans can hardly be responsible for an animal's natural behavior, right? So what are Jurassic Park's dinosaurs? Elements of nature, or products of technology? And what does it say about us and the world we live in if we suddenly fail to distinguish between the two?

The answer to these questions will not only reveal something about the dinosaurs, but also about ourselves. The dinosaurs even teach us an important lesson this way. They show us that we are not as different from nature as we would like to think.

How to Make a Dinosaur

We all know that in order to create his dinosaurs, Hammond's scientists creatively repurpose amphibian DNA to fill in the holes in their available dino-DNA. As a result, they get technologically altered and bred dinosaurs, which are still based on naturally evolved genes from both dinosaurs and frogs.

So from the genetic point of view we can't even call the dinosaurs "true" dinosaurs. They do not share the same genes as their ancient siblings—at least not entirely—and are therefore just dinosaur-like dinosaur-frog-hybrids. These animals, in their modern forms, didn't evolve naturally; their existence is rather the result of technology and human involvement. And still, they are living beings who appear to be as much a part of their natural surroundings as any animal would be. Hammond mixes the dinosaurs' natural elements with modern technology—and, so, we can't decide on whether they are one or the other.

Natural Philosophy . . . but with Dinosaurs

We usually think of the natural and the technological as opposites, leading us to believe that a thing is either a part of nature or created by a human being on purpose, but not both. A tree, for example, is free from human interference. It has grown by itself, survives by itself, and if it happens to be the perfect resting place for hunted humans until they are woken by a sneezing brachiosaurus, this is purely coincidental. A fully equipped kitchen, on the other hand, is made to serve a certain purpose for us, and so it is clearly a technological construct. Even if raptors are choosing it as their hunting ground, it does not change the fact that the kitchen is part of and the result of technology. There seems to be something that clearly divides those things that are human-made from those that do not owe their existence to mankind.

This contrast between nature and technology, though I admit not as old as the original dinosaurs, has still kept humanity company for over two thousand years. It goes back to the Greek philosopher Aristotle, who distinguished natural things and human-made things and drew a strict border between them in order to get a clearer understanding of the world.

According to Aristotle, natural things are the elements, plants, and of course all animals and their parts. Although he didn't specifically think and talk about dinosaurs back then, it's safe to say that he would have agreed to fit them (as animals) into this list, as well. Aristotle thinks these things are natural because they are motivated by so-called "inner final causes"— basically they are driven to function *by* themselves, but also *for* themselves. They change without someone or something making them change, they move on their own, grow and reproduce, all just because their inner final causes allow them to do so. They are not subject to any control or force from the outside that makes them behave in the way they do—they are not machines for others, but live and function for their own good.

So far, this description suits *Jurassic Park*'s dinosaurs perfectly. They're living beings, belong to the animal kingdom, move around the island, hunt their own food, produce big piles of . . . well, you know how Dr. Malcom puts it, and finally reproduce after some of the only-female population start changing their sex against the rules. They are as much animal as every other animal: they do not behave any differently simply because they come from a lab and are genetically manipulated. When they eventually reproduce they even break the limits set upon them by the scientists in order to follow their natural inner final causes even more obviously than before.

It's this thought that Dr. Malcom emphasizes when he says that "life finds a way," and it makes Jurassic Park's dinosaurs so much more awe-inspiring than mere robotic imitations in museums. They're as natural as they can be and there is no reason to deny them their inner final causes. Therefore, according to Aristotle, Jurassic Park's dinosaurs must be natural beings. Case closed.

—Except it's not. Sure, we could now leave it at that and once and for all define Jurassic Park's dinosaurs as natural beings. If we did, technology would play only a minor, negligible and insignificant role in their existence and the dinosaurs are more of a natural disaster than an actual technological threat. Mankind's position as apart from nature is still intact, then. But let's have a look at the technological side of Aristotle's distinction. We wouldn't want to jump to rash conclusions, after all, would we?

For Aristotle, technological artifacts come into being only by outward causes, meaning that people design and construct them intentionally. So they have a purpose which is imprinted upon them by those who produce and use them. They cannot grow, change, or reproduce without someone making them do so from the outside. If neglected, they will lose their artificial form and decompose back into the elements they were made of. The whole Jurassic Park complex shows this remarkably in the later movies: once built for visitors and staff alike, the buildings eventually fall apart and are overgrown by the forest after they've lost their purpose.

So far, this description suits Jurassic Park's dinosaurs perfectly. . . . *Again.* They only exist because John Hammond paid a couple of scientists to clone them, simply to have them in his park and to have visitors enjoy them (and pay for this extraordinary enjoyment, of course). They would not have come into being all by themselves (especially not with the additional frog-DNA in their cells) and exist only for the human purpose of having them around as amazing entertainment. As far as the plan goes, they are originally even dependent on the park's staff to reproduce and would have died out quickly without proper care. Therefore, Jurassic Park's dinosaurs must be technological artifacts. I guess it's case open again!

Chewing on the Problem

Now we're facing a serious problem. Aristotle's famous distinction does not work anymore, so we can't explain the existence of the modern dinosaurs as natural or technological.

Although this doesn't seem too important when you're being hunted through a field by hungry, razor-toothed carnivores, the distinction between the natural and the technological is crucial for our basic understanding of the world.

We have a different view of things, depending on whether they're natural or technological—it's one of the most fundamental distinctions we learn as children: we are separate from nature because we can change it technologically. And we continue to apply this view throughout our whole lives, more or less aware of it. We are able to create our environment ourselves and do not have to live in natural surroundings anymore—our technological understanding is what makes us feel so special to be human, and not "mere" animals. The difference between our own technological world and the natural world "out there" is *so* important for us that we think differently about certain things, depending on whether they come from the one or the other.

For example, imagine yourself in Dr. Grant's position. He's shown around the labs and eventually witnesses the birth of a raptor in its nest. The nest, of course, is part of an incubator designed by scientists to mimic the process of breeding, and he's shocked to find out that dangerous dinosaurs are bred by the scientists. But when he later stumbles on a natural nest left behind by a dinosaur, his reaction is quite a different one: he is astonished and awestruck about the wonder of the naturally-breeding dinosaurs, regardless of the fact that the eggshells could even have been left behind by a happily expanding raptor family with hungry baby carnivores. We accept the natural much more easily than the scientific, although Dr. Grant had no influence on either nest. Still, the technological nest is part of a questionable scientific enterprise, while the natural nest doesn't bother him much, although both serve the same purpose.

This shows that events that happen naturally are much easier to cope with than the same events if they are caused by humans. If it is our fault that something terrible happens, we know who's responsible and who's to blame, leaving us with the responsibility of learning from our mistakes and knowing what to do in similar future experiments. But if the same terrible events are caused without us humans screwing things up, and instead have a natural basis, we have to live with it; it's just some form of bad luck if you're eaten by a natural predator, for example. What's more, we only say that we are "playing God" when we produce something by technological means that turns out to be bad, but not if we let (negative) natural events happen although we could stop them through technology. A natural catastrophe is apparently to our minds less awful than a technological one.

Digesting the Problem

So how is it possible that the dinosaurs are both natural and technological beings? Aristotle's distinction seems legit in its core. We might not agree in the details, but the idea that humans and their creations are different from natural things is still widely accepted and unquestioned. How do Jurassic Park's dinosaurs fit into this pattern, then?

Let's have a look at the nest and the incubator again. According to Aristotle the nest would be an element of nature. It's part of the animal world and comes into being as a part of the dinosaur's reproduction cycle. On the other hand, it was built by someone (although not by someone human), and will decompose if not tended by the parent dinosaurs. Is it therefore truly natural, or does it already have technological features, since it was *built*?

And what about the incubator? It runs on electricity, is constructed by scientists for the purpose of breeding dinosaurs, and shows all the other signs of a technological device. But the form of the nest, the material the eggs are laid on, and even the imitated process of brooding are imitations of nature. So the incubator cannot be seen as purely technological; it still contains elements of the natural process it mimics.

Apparently, we need to be more careful with our understanding of nature and technology. The incubator is a problem because it's created specifically to imitate a natural process— the seemingly clear border between nature and technology is already breached in its very design. Obviously, then, things can belong to the area of technology and to the area of nature at the same time.

The same can be said about the dinosaurs in the park. They are created by scientists with a purpose in mind but they are essentially still natural beings with their own lives. —So they're part of a new kind of technology—biotechnology—which uses natural elements and processes for technical purposes. Cloning, genetic manipulation, and the possibility to choose the sex of the dinosaurs all belong to this special field of technology, and as a result the dinosaurs do, too. That does not mean that they are purely elements of technology, but neither are they entirely natural. Just as they tear apart the useless fences that are supposed to hold them, they destroy the once clear but now weak boundary between what we used to call nature and what we used to call technology.

How does that leave us with Aristotle's work on the difference between the natural and the technological? Aristotle's distinction is famous for its simplicity, but not the ultimate answer on questions concerning this topic. Even before Hammond bred dinosaurs for his park, humanity has changed nature by technological means (think about urban forests) and crafted technical devices by imitating nature (artificial flowers, for example). The rise of biotechnology and the reappearance of the dinosaurs just make the problem so much more obvious.

Where Do We Run from Here?

The problem can be solved when we move away from the question what constitutes the natural and the technological and how the dinosaurs fit into those categories—because that's what they are. Both the natural and the technological are categories which are constructed by people in order to classify our surroundings and make our thinking so much easier.

So when Aristotle says that natural things are driven by inner causes and technological artifacts by outside causes, it's wrong to assume that those categories are clearly defined. All this statement can do is serve as a rule of thumb for our handy differentiation between the two. Jurassic Park's dinosaurs blend them, since they are neither pure natural beings nor are they solely technological, but somewhere in between. Cloning, genetic manipulation and modern dinosaurs meet in the grey area between our understanding of nature and our concept of technology because our world cannot be strictly divided into two parts.

So we can't answer the question of whether Jurassic Park's dinosaurs are natural or technological beings with a simple "yes" or a "no." They belong to both categories at the same time. Still, there seems to be something different between an incubator and a dinosaur, even though they belong in part to both categories. We tend to see the incubator still more as a technological device while the dinosaurs are (as living beings) probably still more natural. To put both in the same grey area between nature and technology seems wrong.

And that's because it is. The area between the natural and the technological must not be seen as a third, distinct option. In fact, this view is as wrong as Aristotle's strict separation. Instead, we need to think of the natural and the technological as extremes of a large spectrum of possibilities. So if we have to find an answer to the question if Jurassic Park's dinosaurs are natural or technological beings, we'll have to answer with "more" or "less"—more natural maybe than the incubator they come from, less natural than their ancestors, whose DNA was free from human interference. They are subject to both inner and outside causes alike, and while their hunger belongs to their natural side, their modern origin as genetically manipulated hybrid beings will always be part of their technological one.

Leaving a Bitter Taste

So what does that show us about ourselves and the world we live in? Aristotle's famous distinction comes to a sudden end when we try to figure out if we are responsible for the dinosaur's mayhem or if it's just another natural disaster. Appealing as it might be on first glance, the strict border between the natural and the technological just doesn't fit reality in our modern world, and is certainly not enough to make decisions concerning guilt and responsibility.

But if the dinosaurs don't fit, what about us? According to Aristotle, humans and what they produce belong to the technological world. Since there is no such thing as a pure technological world, we can't view ourselves as completely distinct from nature. Our ability to change our natural surroundings by means of technology is great but doesn't exclude us from what happens naturally.

We tend to think that we are different from nature and that we are not affected by it, even if we change it. But we can't do what we want to nature and expect it to have no influence on us. This is one of the main lessons *Jurassic Park* can teach us: In spite of all the technology we have, we're still dependent on and affected by those things that are natural—there's no reason why we and our technological products would be different from nature.

Yes, our technology—or at least, Hammond's technology—can influence nature and create dinosaurs, but if they follow their natural hunting instincts, we're still nothing more than prey.

20
Decline of the Meatosaurus

KENN FISHER

I had just turned nine years old. The theater was dark. For the first time in my life, sounds of the movie came from behind me. *How did they do that?*

About twenty minutes in, the man who doesn't want kids saw the really big dinosaur with the long neck. His delight, surprise, and awe—all captured exactly how I was feeling. A half-hour later when things got really scary, my mom whispered to me: "Do you want to leave?" I shook my head. This was the most amazing thing I had ever seen!

Something that left me puzzled that day, and for years after, was why Dr. Grant would later be in the group speaking out against the park. Surely (my matured mind would later think), there are human-eating animals in zoos all over the world. Why would this be any different? For many years, I argued that without the selfish and stupid actions of Nedry, the park would have been a success. At the very least, why didn't they try to start the park again with herbivores only?

What I now realize, though, is that creating dinosaurs and putting them in a park for tourists to observe would be a failure without carnivores. It would be an admission of defeat and a recognition that we may be at the top of the food chain now, but we would not be compared to those awesome extinct predators of the past. If we didn't raise the meat-eating dinosaurs from the dead too, we would be admitting that we were not as superior as we like to think—we would be admitting that we're basically just their helpless prey.

For millennia, human beings have needed to believe that they are superior to all other animals. *Jurassic Park* seriously challenges this belief. We share the middle of the food chain with many other animals, with predators above us and herbivores below us—this is something we like to forget, but a massive *Tyrannosaurus rex* would serve to remind us very quickly. *Jurassic Park* reminds us that being a hunted and weak animal is not fun. What we don't want to admit is that if we can't force *T. rex* and all extinct predators to bow to us, we'll have no choice but to remember that being prey sucks. So now there are suddenly serious ethical repercussions to that realization. How can we justify doing the same to other animals that are similar in size, behavior, and intelligence as ourselves as we all cower together in the middle level of the food chain?

This dilemma presented in *Jurassic Park* is a very old ethical debate. Ever since Darwin, the understanding that humans are in fact just a small part of the animal kingdom—and in many cases, barely more intelligent than many of our fellow beasts—has become increasingly acknowledged. This has, understandably, prompted questions about eating meat and how we treat animals. After all, humans do not need meat to survive, and we have the ability to make the ethical choice not to eat meat. These two facts combined with the realization that we would prefer not to be eaten if we were in the same situation, means that a vegetarian lifestyle is actually a pretty reasonable concept.

Through the actions of John Hammond and his employees, *Jurassic Park* captures a fading idea that human beings are above animals, and are closer to God. Hammond tries his best to prove this by playing God as often and as recklessly as he can. But when it's clear that humans are no closer to God than any other creature on Earth (now, or in prehistoric times), the concept of equality between animals becomes more and more logical.

The (Extinct) Great Chain of Being

DR. MALCOLM: God creates man. Man destroys God. Man creates dinosaurs.

Since Plato (around 428–348 B.C.), there has been a misconception in the Western world that humans are objectively greater than other animals. Plato, who believed in different "realms" of being with a hierarchical structure, put humans in the exact middle between Gods and Earth.

The concept of humans residing above nature and below the divine arose through Judaism and Christianity. In these religions, humans are given full control over all other animals, simply because it is thought that we are above all of them. In Genesis 1:28, God commands men to "have dominion over the fish of the sea, and over the fowl of the air, and over every living thing that moveth upon the earth." Eventually the understanding of what is now referred to as *The Great Chain of Being* would look like this:

God

Angelic Beings

Humanity

Animals

Plants

Minerals

often with subdivisions. For example, kings would reside at the top of the "humanity" category, while snakes would rest at the bottom of the hierarchy of animals.

As the Great Chain of Being evolved over the centuries, it became increasingly important for religious teachers to separate everything about man away from Mother Nature. *Instinct*, and *natural tendencies* were evil, they were trying to corrupt humans, and it was our responsibility to fight against any of these *urges*. When a comparison was made between humans and animals, this was negative (or, *evil*), but when a human was compared to an angel or a God, this was positive (*good*). Humans were supposed to strive to be above everything else on Earth, in every conceivable way. René Descartes, who has been called the Father of Modern Philosophy, maintained that animals were indistinguishable from inanimate objects in that animals were not conscious.

In *Jurassic Park*, Grant observes a similarity between the dinosaurs and human feelings towards God (in a paternal, Old-

Testament sense of the word): ". . . children liked dinosaurs because these giant creatures personified the uncontrollable force of looming authority. They were symbolic parents. Fascinating and frightening, like parents. And kids loved them, as they loved their parents."

For millennia, the love of children for their parents, or of adults for their Gods, has indeed been a comforting one. God is flawless, and by mimicking him, we are flawless too—even when this means that we have to do things that are *very* flawed. Wars and genocide, invasions and forced relocations, murder and cruelty towards our fellow man (and our fellow animals) have all been committed in the name of God.

The rise of the Scientific Method, combined with Darwin's Theory of Evolution, as well as the decline of religious belief and influence in the nineteenth and twentieth centuries, changed Western culture's relationship to The Great Chain of Being. Malcolm paraphrases a quotation from Friedrich Nietzsche that has had a substantial impact on modern philosophy: "God is dead. God remains dead. And we have killed him." This quote is not to be taken literally, but rather that the concept of God and the importance of this figure in our culture has dramatically declined in recent generations. God has lost a great deal of what was once his territory—in the state, in the family, even in ethics. This decline in the traditional belief in God has challenged the traditional belief in humans. If there is no God and no angels for us to be below, are we still above the animals, plants, and minerals?

However, modern Western culture has now continued the belief in some form of hierarchy by replacing God with something a bit more practical: the computer. The great Polish philosopher and filmmaker, Krzysztof Kieślowski (1941–1996), made this connection in his 1989 work, *The Decalogue*. He presents a computer as the "other gods" that the first commandment warns not to put ahead of the God of the Old Testament. Movies like *Ghost in the Shell* and *The Matrix* have made similar comparisons between computers and God. Humans now have a tendency to think of themselves as closer to computers than to animals. The Internet has many God-like qualities. After all, what is more all-knowing than Wikipedia, more all-powerful than Google, or more all-judgmental than Facebook?

Hammond (who looks like every pre–Morgan Freeman Hollywood interpretation of God) spends most of *Jurassic Park* in a room full of computers, trying to control the events on the rest of the island. The computers are accorded God-like abilities throughout the *Jurassic Park* franchise.

Living at the Bottom of the Great Chain

Many people do still believe in God, and even amongst people who don't, there are many arguments still being made that humans are separate from other animals. Very few would argue that a fruit fly and a human are completely equal. I am not suggesting this, but rather that it is now easier to understand that an animal can feel pain—or that we have an ethical responsibility to the animals that we choose to consume.

In *Animals as Persons*, a popular text on animal rights, Gary L. Francione describes the change in our relationship with animals:

> Before the nineteenth century, we generally regarded animals as things both in moral theory and under the law . . . The animal welfare position, which became popular in the nineteenth century . . . separates use and treatment and holds that it is acceptable to use animals for our purposes. We do, however, have a moral and legal obligation to treat them 'humanely' and to avoid inflicting 'unnecessary' suffering on them.

Laws started to appear in the early twentieth century to protect against animal cruelty. However, most of these laws revolved around the idea of animals being property. In other words, animals that belonged to human beings were more protected than other animals, and what was considered "cruel" treatment of them was relative to their use as property.

For example, if an animal was a "farm animal," then any "necessary" farming activities that were imposed on it, no matter how cruel, were considered justified. There were some extreme limits, but these have been equated to smashing your own car with a hammer. A rational person would not do this to their own property—not because of a concern about cruelty, but rather to protect the economic value of the property. Francione points out that "courts have held consistently that animals used for food may be mutilated in ways that unquestionably cause severe pain and suffering and that would normally be regarded as cruel or even as torture."

To demonstrate Francione's point, compare the use of electric cattle prods and electric fences used in the *Jurassic Park* movies. In the middle of *The Lost World*, when Dieter Stark tasers one of the compsognathuses, he's seen by the audience as a cruel human picking on a small, defenseless animal. This is mostly because the animal did not belong to him. He's later punished by being killed by a school of the "compys." However, the electric fences that are placed throughout the park in the first movie are not deemed cruel (although the voltage is a lot higher) because they keep these "zoo animals" in their cages.

Playing God

MRS. KIRBY: This is how you make dinosaurs?

DR. GRANT: No, this is how you play God.

When having to deal with the choices of humans being closer to animals or to God, the psyche of the egomaniac always prefers to be close to God. But this frame of mind can lead to dangerous places, and the *Jurassic Park* franchise proves that this effort is futile, and shows its failures through man's main inadequacy compared to God: control.

In the *Jurassic Park* novel, there are more chapters with the word "Control" in the title than any other. These chapters take place in the "Control Room," where the inhabitants have no control at all throughout the book. The irony is that they are constantly defending their ability to control, with the illusion that they are always one step away from having the park completely within their grasp.

In the first book, Hammond describes focusing his investments on computers, saying that he automated wherever he could. This includes digitizing the animals. By the time of the events of the book, the scientists are on version 4.4 of the dinosaurs. As Arnold says, "It is like software, in a way. As we discover the glitches in the DNA, Dr. Wu's lab has to make a new version." The computers also have an all-seeing quality;

above the animals, the computers have a variety of technologies to count the number of animals on the island. It's only through a human error that the computers are not instructed to look for more animals than expected. The computers also have an all-knowing quality; the databases are designed to be able to hold enough information for three billion records—enough to track DNA strains.

This attempt at controlling a power that is impossible for humans to control fails almost immediately. Malcolm warns of the dangers of humans ignoring their place in the world, "But you decide you won't be at the mercy of nature. You decide you'll control nature, and from that moment on you're in deep trouble, because you can't do it." He continues, suggesting that power and knowledge are not the only things that one needs to play God, but rather a use for these tools: "Science can make a nuclear reactor, but it cannot tell us not to build it. Science can make pesticide, but cannot tell us not to use it."

As the park begins to lose this sense of control, the people who falsely convinced themselves that they could have such a power refuse to admit that it's gone. In the movie, Hammond argues to Dr. Sattler that he would be able to recreate the park with a few minor changes to fix the obvious flaws. Sattler is not impressed, and tells Hammond that he never had control, comparing that illusion to someone thinking that he or she saw fleas in a flea circus. In the book, Arnold refuses to admit, until the very end, that they have lost control. To him, the problems that occur are just temporary anomalies.

Even the park's design shows obvious failures of control. Several times, we learn that the creators of the park are trying to mimic as realistic an environment as possible. Wu claims, "We want Jurassic Park to be as real an environment as possible—as authentic as possible." However, the scientists failed to even get the numbers of animals even remotely correct. The book describes the island as having 238 (official) animals ranging over 15 species. According to the manifest, there are 65 carnivores to 173 herbivores. The book describes most predator-prey populations as having one predatory carnivore for every four *hundred* herbivores. This inconsistency tells not only of the park's failure to be realistic (which it's aiming to be), but also of the creators' preoccupation with having power over the carnivores.

The Rise of the Herbivore

In the movie, *The Lost World: Jurassic Park*, Peter Ludlow describes the dinosaurs as having "no rights" and claims complete ownership over them due to his company's patent. In the book, the character Dodgson explains the old school of thought on the subject:

> . . . every year, we get more pressure not to use animals for testing and research. Every year, more demonstrations, more break-ins, more bad press. First it was just simple-minded zealots and Hollywood celebrities. But now it's a bandwagon.

Francione says:

> In a sense, we already accept that animals are persons; we claim to reject the view that animals are things and to recognize that, at the very least, animals have a morally significant interest in not suffering. Their status as property, however, has prevented their person-hood from being realized. . . . The notion that we can be "kind," "compassionate," or "humane" to the animals whom we bring to slaughter and eat is one of the most profoundly perverse and delusional ideas in the history of human thought.

The idea of animal rights is gaining momentum in our society. Ask yourself how many vegetarian restaurants you see in a given day, compared to fifteen or twenty years ago. Or, more tellingly, how many vegetarians you know or are in your family.

As the idea of separating humans from animals in the collective psyche of our society deteriorated, "radical" ideas like that of the utilitarian Jeremy Bentham now attract more of a following:

> The day may come when the rest of the animal creation may acquire those rights which never could have been withholden from them but by the hand of tyranny . . . But a full-grown horse or dog is beyond comparison a more rational, as well as a more conversable animal, than an infant of a day or week or even a month, old. But suppose they were otherwise, what would it avail? The question is not, Can they reason? nor Can they talk? but, Can they suffer?

Utilitarianism is a theory of ethics which maintains that the moral course of action is the one that maximizes utility, usually defined as maximizing happiness and reducing suffering. This line of reasoning, which has proven fruitful for humanity for the better part of two centuries, is easily transferable to animals once the artificial border between humans and animals is eliminated in human minds. If there is going to be a moral or ethical principle that centers around the idea of pain (or the lack thereof), should we not include anything that feels pain? Modern science has shown that animals feel pain. Should their pain not be taken into consideration?

It makes perfect sense to try to limit pain and to increase happiness—and it's just as easy to do this for our animal counterparts once they are considered to be our equals. Peter Singer describes this potential equality in humans: "The principle of the equality of human beings is not a description of an alleged actual equality among humans: it is a prescription of how we should treat them." Could we not just as easily describe animals as deserving to be treated as how they *should* be treated?

For centuries, Western belief would deny that animals deserve such consideration, so what logical argument defines animals as needing to be treated as equal to humans? Singer responds that

> Equality is a moral idea, not an assertion of fact. There is no logically compelling reason for assuming that a factual difference in ability between two people justifies any difference in the amount of consideration we give to their needs and interests.

We Can Discuss Sexism in Survival Situations When I Get Back

DR. SATTLER: Dinosaurs eat man. Women inherits the earth.

Meat eating has a long history of being associated with maleness. In *The Sexual Politics of Meat*, Carol J. Adams describes the trends that have followed human culture for millennia. Meat is associated with patriarchy. The meat of the meal will almost always go to the father first, a portion that is much greater than necessary, while the female and the children will, in the case of an insufficient amount of meat, take any cuts.

In response, feminists have often taken vegetarianism on as a part of their ideology. As far back as the seventeenth century, early modern feminists such as Mary Astell become concerned with animal rights or became vegetarians long before the diet became mainstream. Early opponents of the rights of women actually parodied the case for women's rights by comparing them to the rights of animals. Thomas Taylor anonymously published a piece called, "A Vindication of the Rights of Brutes" in response to early feminist Mary Wolstonecraft's "Vindication of the Rights of Women" in 1792. The idea that women had what we now call human rights was as ridiculous as giving those rights to animals.

Jurassic Park is a feminist masterpiece. Sattler was a pioneer for female characters in monster/action/adventure blockbusters. She handles herself in the face of the dinosaurs better than most of the male characters, and does so as a brilliant, strong and confident super-woman. What's more, the dinosaurs (at least, the adults) are all female. It is unusual for the antagonists, especially ones so associated with strength and domination, to be female. Throughout the books and movies, the carnivores are usually referred to as "he," showing how strongly we associate meat-eating with maleness.

In *The Lost World: Jurassic Park*, Roland Tembo shows his interest in male-dominating carnivores by demanding to take down what he sees as the ultimate predator, "My fee: You can keep it. All I want in exchange for my services is the right to hunt one of the tyrannosaurs. Male. A buck, only. How and why are my business." His desire to dominate over animals in this manner is telling of the human desire to be, once again, on top. This man, who has spent a career dominating predators across the world, sees the male of this meat-eating species as the ultimate prize—the measure by which to compare himself, and raise himself above all of the animal kingdom.

The one (outed) vegetarian in *Jurassic Park* is Lex Murphy, who also happens to be the youngest female in the series. Demographically, this is accurate. Murphy never uses computers to dominate the animals, and this quality ends up making her the hero for saving everyone still alive on the island when she is able to get her hands on a computer. Perhaps this suggests that humanity can be saved. The next generation and the generation after that could very likely become more concerned with the rights of our co-inhabitants on this small planet.

Lex gives us hope that perhaps the Chain of Being is actually more like a *Circle* of Being; the closer we get to godliness (or technological advance), the closer we get to ethically treating the animals who share the planet with us.

I noticed in the news today that, for humane reasons, all of the elephants from my hometown zoo have moved to a sanctuary in California. Yeah. There might be hope for us yet.

21

How Ethics Can Save You from Being Eaten

ROGER HUNT

What should you do when encountering dinosaurs: find a good place to hide, cover your scent, maybe try climbing a tree? If these fail, try covering yourself in a smell disgusting to the dinosaur (I imagine the teenie-bopper perfume "Daisy" by Marc Jacobs would work really well!). If this still fails, maybe spend your last few seconds trying to empathize with them. But perhaps the best strategy, as it is with all beings, is try not to encounter them without first considering how to treat them. Hopefully, if you treat dinosaurs right, they will not want to eat you in the first place! With some like *Tyrannosaurus rex* it will be best just to avoid the situation in the first place, but what about some of the smarter ones, . . . might there be a way to treat a velociraptor, that prevents your untimely (but tasty) death?

I guess being ethical in our treatment of dinosaurs is also important since we like to think we're kind, caring people. We should treat the world with some shred of consistency in our actions. For example, if intelligence matters, then shouldn't we give serious thought to how we treat a velociraptor? They seem to be almost as smart as us! But most of all we may want to consider how we treat other beings that are way bigger than us and could kill us relatively easily (or at the very least cost us lots of money in terms of developing a National Dinosaur Defense Department).

God Creates Dinosaurs. God Kills Dinosaurs. God Creates Man. Man Kills God. Man Brings Back Dinosaurs

We humans, who also happen to be animals (warm-blooded, hairy mammals, in fact), have developed a method to understand concerns like how to treat one another with respect and dignity. We call it ethics. If we ever hope to revive an ancient species of being, like dinosaurs, we'd better be prepared to do them justice and bring them into a world worthy of their existence, however frightening they may be.

The *Jurassic Park* series is a phenomenal example of how to do ethics improperly! There are two things we need to question when creating or recreating new life. First, we must question the intuition that we're superior by default. This *may* be the case, for instance, if we can prove that we have divine souls and the animals and dinosaurs do not, but this has been notoriously difficult to do without relying solely on faith—which, while powerful, is not convincing from a scientific perspective.

Dieter Stark brilliantly shows the pitfalls of the belief that we're superior by default. His first encounter with dinosaurs shows him zapping a pack of what seem like miniature *T. rexes*, the compsognathuses. He is hunted down and devoured by about twenty of them later in the movie. He certainly thought he was superior. He was wrong.

Second, we must question the intuition that we have ownership of the dinosaurs as property simply because we created them. This time, Peter Ludlow teaches us this lesson when he leads the expedition to reclaim InGen's "property" (a baby *T. rex*) to make a profit by creating a park in San Diego, but is caught by mama *T. rex* and used to teach baby *T. rex* how to hunt. The stories of *Jurassic Park* make perfectly clear that characters who hold those "I'm-just-better-than-you" perspectives are ultimately eaten, which is precisely the fate many hope to avoid.

We need to consider the consequences of lording over a particular species, as Hammond intends with his original plan to create a zoo-like theme park. The problem with holding this view of other species is that it seems possible that if we deny them some kind of moral value, then we obviously have what it takes to deny other living things—including humans—moral value. It's clear from human history that such devaluation of human life is not only possible but dangerously likely under the right conditions. Not only should we treat dinosaurs with respect just because they're living things, but also because we may even earn the added benefit of not being eaten.

So, what is the moral status of dinosaurs? Dinosaurs share many characteristics with others in the animal kingdom (including humans), but there seem to be some differences between humans and other animals. Non-human animals lack complex language, a heightened sense of self-awareness, and the capacity for abstract thought. We have thought for millennia that lacking these characteristics implies that animals are somehow beneath us humans in the moral order of things.

We often feel justified in enslaving and harvesting animals for a variety of purposes including food, medical testing, and companionship, all of which have certainly contributed to the development and progress of human existence. But it seems strange to simply accept these things without thinking about what we're doing, especially if it ends up being necessary to extend the same ethical standards to dinosaurs, in order to escape becoming dinner.

They Don't See the Consequences

There are at least three arguments expressed by the characters interested in the dinosaurs of *Jurassic Park*. First, there are the opportunists (who are, of course, eventually eaten) who argue along the traditional lines already mentioned: humans are superior and justified in using dinosaurs for whatever purposes we deem necessary, including entertainment and genetic experimentation.

Next, there are the preservationists who argue that reviving dinosaurs promises to make the world a more interesting place through the progress of scientific knowledge and our interaction with them, whether in terms of creating dinosaur zoos or having them live an isolated existence in peace.

Finally, there is Ian Malcolm who presents the Pandora's Box scenario, arguing that we should not genetically engineer dinosaurs because with so many moving parts and potential dangers, cosmic randomness (or chaos) will cause all hell to break loose, as it obviously does in the movies.

These arguments are certainly in line with what most people seem to think: we can treat dinosaurs this way because of what we can get from them. However, some people have serious reservations. In the films, Dr. Grant is appalled at this project. He's both emotionally upset and unable to accept the value of creating such life. He argues that while observing dinosaurs in real life could probably lead to a better understanding of their lifestyle and habitat, we could learn much of it from doing traditional paleontology. And although it may take longer, at least we aren't breaching any moral rules.

So, either we gain unparalleled scientific and entertainment value from these genetic experiments, cross serious moral boundaries, or destroy the world!

> "They are paleontologists. They dig up dinosaurs." And then he began to laugh, as if he found the idea very funny.

Two popular arguments criticize this kind of treatment of animals (and, by extension, dinosaurs). The first claims that the potential value created in terms of knowledge and entertainment does not outweigh the harm caused to the dinosaurs. The second insists that non-human animals, including dinosaurs, have rights.

To make the first argument work—let's call it the argument for the value of all living things—we need to separate the dinosaurs' usefulness—what they contribute in terms of knowledge and entertainment—from their value as living things. Try thinking of the subjugation of dinosaurs being like the way we used to reject the equality of the sexes and races. In this sense, our treatment of other animals and future dinosaurs could be considered speciesism, and this argument says that we shouldn't be speciesists—exactly like we shouldn't be racist or sexist.

To someone like Dr. Grant, the knowledge we gain from having live dinosaurs is reached through normal paleontology, while the knowledge we can gain from genetic experimentation is probably not going to contribute to how much we value other species, since their genetic code is so different from our own. We accept that it's morally wrong to conduct experiments on apes, even though it could certainly contribute to an understanding of our own bodies. But they are so genetically similar to us that our speciesism kicks in and we won't let it happen. So it becomes easier to accept experimenting on species farther away from ourselves (genetically speaking), even though that knowledge doesn't much help us, so it doesn't outweigh the harm they're caused by it. As one philosopher puts it: if you are unwilling to experiment on someone with extreme brain damage or a newborn baby because of the damage to their value as living things, you should not feel comfortable experimenting on other animals or dinosaurs.

Dr. Sattler, Dr. Harding, and a variety of philosophers disagree with the argument for the value of living things. They argue (before being mercilessly attacked by a *T. rex*, of course) that we gain so much knowledge from these kinds of genetic experiments and behavioral observation that we are able to save thousands, if not millions, of lives. If we increase the value of life by saving more sentient beings than we sacrifice, then we are justified in using the animals and dinosaurs. In fact, Harding outlines the advances in understanding of the parental behavior of dinosaurs which could potentially reinvent the field of paleontology and animal studies in general! If this is the case, as the movies at least seem to demonstrate, then to increase the value of life, or the happiness of sentient beings, not only is it *ethically okay* to raise dinosaurs within an experimental setting, but we are *obligated* to do so.

I think the scientists win the argument on that score. As Tom Regan puts it, anything that can feel, has a nervous system, or is at least partially conscious has basic rights which need to be respected. This means that treating any such creature differently based on the quality of that life is unethical, and to treat animals as any different than humans is speciesist.

The power of the argument for ethical treatment of dinosaurs lies not in the "value of life" view (which makes it okay to treat animals and dinosaurs as slaves and experiments if it helps others more than it hurts them), but the "rights view" (which focuses on *unconditional* individual value). They have their own rights because they exist, not because they serve some purpose for someone else. The problem, however, is determining exactly what rights they have.

But let's take a step back. The "rights" view is great, but it can work for both sides: those in favor of subjecting animals *to* human desires and those in favor of protecting them *from* human desires. If we want to argue that we (humans) should be able to use animals, then we need to determine what makes us so special. Let's assume for the sake of argument that there are no such things as souls, all beings have some level of consciousness, and that language, thought, and society exist in all species in one form or another.

So what's left? Well, since rights protect the most fundamental aspects of life—like being alive, being healthy, or being fed, it makes sense that rights come from the ones who do the protecting. Our government, for example, grants us certain rights and denies us others. History has shown that the protectors have denied such protections to other animals—so they can eat them, put them in to work, and enjoy them for entertainment— but the protectors *could* give those protections to animals, allowing them to live free, happy, and healthy lives. They could *also* choose to extend some protections to some animals, but not others, and in limited forms (perhaps we let them roam free, but only until it is time for dinner, or we allow them a luxurious lifestyle until it is time for the bull fights). So, if we are to revive an ancient species and want to justify our treatment of them on moral grounds, we will have to determine which approach we would like to take: no rights, some rights, or all rights.

They Are Not Free at All. They Are Essentially Our Prisoners

The first *Jurassic Park* movie offended our moral sense by using dinosaurs for experimentation and entertainment.

The second film reinforced this offense, when a clearly evil man was hell bent on opening another zoo in San Diego (thankfully, he was properly eaten). At least the second movie also introduced us to Hammond's insight that perhaps there's more to dinosaurs than meets the eye, and that they should be allowed to live full lives.

The third movie gives us the sense of what else dinosaurs have to offer in terms of intelligence, and perhaps frightens us into thinking that if we are to live with dinosaurs, we should protect ourselves, but by making dinosaurs prisoners, like in the aviary or in San Diego, where we might argue that they are denied their ability to live a full life!

It seems like we're getting nowhere, so if we want to make it all as simple as possible, we can stop worrying about whether all life has value, or who should get rights and who shouldn't. Those things get messy and really tend to depend on what we believe.

There's a different way of looking at the whole picture. We realize rights are given, but the *capability* to live a life? That isn't something someone else gives. Humans and dinosaurs (all animals, in fact) have lots of capabilities—like life, health, play, and social involvement. When we aren't allowed to fulfill those capabilities, we don't *flourish*. Maybe you'd survive, but you wouldn't live a full, robust, happy life while in prison, being beaten, or hiding from crazed dinosaurs.

Martha Nussbaum points those capabilities out. And she thinks that those capabilities make a much better guide for morality and ethics than rights. We *all* want to flourish— including dinosaurs—so maybe we shouldn't prevent others' flourishing. If putting dinosaurs in an aviary prevents them from living full and fulfilled lives, maybe we shouldn't cage them like that. It's hard to imagine that a *T. rex* penned up in a San Diego zoo would really be able to roam, hunt, and play in a way that fulfills its capabilities. So just like you don't want others interfering with your capabilities, perhaps we shouldn't interfere with their capabilities. That wouldn't so much be a matter of giving rights, as recognizing that *we don't have the right* to get in the way of other flourishing lives (especially *just for* fun)!

Ms. Sattler, I Refuse to Believe You're Not Familiar with the Concept of Attraction

I get the sense that the movies ask us to consider dinosaurs not simply as other animals, but as rivals to the human species. That makes sense—both our species and their species have ruled the planet by being the most widely-effective species. And as rulers of the planet, we really just took from the dinosaurs the job of instituting the rights of all the creatures on the planet after the mass extinctions. So maybe we should consider that dinosaurs are moral equals to us humans.

But—we probably won't. We'd probably reanimate the dinosaurs and force them into servitude, violating their rights.

It would be fair for them to punish us in their way: eating us.
. . . So, how not to be eaten? Not reviving dinosaurs would be a
good start. But if we must revive them, we must be prepared to
extend to them the moral rights they expect as a species that
also wants to flourish.

V

Death Is My Destination

22
When You Go Extinct, *You* Don't Get to Come Back

NICOLAS MICHAUD

Okay, let's be honest. We're gonna die. And if we're *really* honest, we know we don't just mean you and me. We mean *everyone* . . . the whole species.

Poof! Someday, no more human race . . . just like the dinosaurs. Gone. Whether it's when the sun explodes, a meteor hits us, or that mega-volcano in Yellowstone blows, we won't survive it. The volcano in Yellowstone is so large it will take out most of the US. It's about forty thousand years overdue, by the way. . . .

You might think that we'll get ourselves off the planet before anything like that happens, colonize space, make it to other solar systems, but I doubt it. Seriously—how do we spend our time and resources? Building better iPhones. My intuition is that the day the sun explodes we will all be happily playing "Candy Crush," blissfully unaware. You'd think we'd learn from the dinosaurs, but the fact is, even if our species makes it, you and I won't.

"Ha!" You might reply. "You haven't thought this through! Obviously, cloning and science can save us. Like the dinosaurs of *Jurassic Park*, we can return!" And maybe you're right. All it takes is a greedy businessperson, some unethical scientists, and, well, your average lawyer. And *boom!* baby! I'm back! *Tyrannosaurus rex* isn't the only one who can do that magic trick; we all are potentially revivable, right?

Nope. That's my point. We. Are. Doomed. No cloning, no science, no afterlife, no *Jurassic Park*–like return from extinction, nada. I don't mean to be pessimistic here, but I can prove it!

Our three best hopes for living forever—souls, cloning, and the essential self—all aren't enough to keep out of the abyss of inescapable extinction!

How Much Does Being Eaten Hurt?

My guess is that you might already be thinking to yourself, "Silly philosopher! I don't need to be cloned or worry about the sun exploding because I have an *after*life!" So let's start there. If I try to prove the afterlife "false," I will fail, because it is beyond our understanding . . . beyond science, beyond logic. But it's a fascinating idea. It's interesting that we call it the *after*-life, when really it would be just *more* life. If *you* go off to heaven after your body dies, then *you* are in heaven. So, then, you aren't really dead, are you? Problem solved: we do get to live forever! So the next time we are about to be eaten by a velociraptor, we don't have to worry too much, because after the pain is over, we get to live on.

But think about this. . . . We agree that if I go to the after-life, I probably leave my body behind. If I do that, I leave all of the stuff that belongs to my body behind as well. So we can pretty comfortably say that my body isn't *me*, right? I'm in Heaven, and my body is on Earth. So, if I clone a dead *T. rex* I'm not bringing back the *same T. rex,* am I? No. I've made a new *T. rex*—who we will just call "Rex"—unless Rex's soul comes back from dino Heaven. But either way, there is only one of each of them, and one of me. Rex and I have our own separate and *personal* identities.

Now, when you think about that personal identity, it is very much *you*, right? Whatever you think and feel is your own experience. In fact, you know that many of those experiences aren't the same thing as your *body*. Imagine a velociraptor is gutting you, the way Dr. Grant describes, cutting you across the middle, and then eating your innards. You'd still be alive when this started to happen. And it would be *painful—very, VERY* painful. But where is that pain located? We might think, "Well, obviously in my stomach," but if you investigate, you won't find "pain" there. You will just find mutilated tissue.

So where is pain? For that matter, where are color, smell, love, and all of our other experiences? When Dr. Sattler is looking at those giant, prehistoric leaves, she's experiencing *something*. And she would probably call her experience of that leaf "green," but you can't find "green" in the brain, can you? So, "Ha!" You might say, "There is more to us than our bodies; we have *experiences* that are our own. I feel the pain and see the color *in* my body, but the pain and color aren't the *same thing* as my body!" So the original *T. rex* would not be the same *T. rex* as her clone, Rex. They would be two different beings, with different individual perspectives, two *souls*.

Where Is the Smell "Brachiosaurus"?

Well, here's the problem. Let's say I accept *all* of that; there's more to our experiences than physical stuff. In fact, let's even say that I agree that this "personal experience" idea is evidence that Rex really does have a soul, since her personal experiences (like pain and color) have to be *non-physical*. True, when we experience pain a specific part of the brain fires, but your *experience* of pain when velociraptors eat you isn't *just* part of your brain firing, is it? Any more than Ellie seeing green is the same thing as certain fibers in her brain firing! But here's the problem. We know that when Ellie experiences green, part of her brain does fire. If it doesn't fire, she doesn't see green. In fact, we also know that if we remove the part of her brain that fires when she claims to see green *she won't see green anymore*. She'd still have working eyes and brain, but without those fibers firing, not only will she not report seeing green, but she won't be able to *imagine* or even *remember* green!

So even if there's more to you than the physical, we know that this "more" isn't necessarily soul-like: it's dependent on your body, specifically your brain. If we remove those parts of the brain, you stop having those experiences. When damage happens to the brain, you can lose memories, which explains Alzheimer's. Alzheimer's isn't a disease of the *soul*; it's a breakdown in the *brain*. So even if our memories aren't physical, they *depend* on the physical to *cause* them. Ideally, if that velociraptor were eating you, if you could remove the part of your brain that creates pain, your experiences would be a good deal less . . . well, painful!

The Spirit of Jurassic Park

But . . . let's make the problem worse. Let's imagine that dinosaurs do have souls. And when we clone a dinosaur, that individual soul moves in to that new body. Well, we've already agreed that science can't interact with the non-physical, right? In other words, you can't clone souls. You can't find them with X-rays, CAT scans or MRI's. In fact, that's part of the appeal of the soul: you can't prove it wrong! It's so non-physical, there is no test for it, *ever.*

But if nothing can touch the soul, how does the world interact with the dino's soul? How does its *physical* body interact with its soul? Didn't we just say nothing can touch the soul? Then how does the dino's body write its memories on the soul? And how does its soul move its body around, *if it can't interact with the physical world?* It sounds like we're cheating. We want to say we can't prove the soul false with science, but then we want it to do something very physical.

Let's put one more nail in the dinosaur's coffin. Let's start with an analogy: At the end of the first *Jurassic Park* movie, the park is a mess. In fact, it's pretty dead. When Hammond admits he won't endorse his own park, Jurassic Park is destroyed. Maybe there can be a different Jurassic Park (in San Diego), but that original park, Hammond's Park, is dead. . . . But aren't the buildings still there? Aren't the dinosaurs still there? So doesn't that mean the "body" of Jurassic Park still exists? So, then . . . if I say Jurassic Park is dead, does that mean it has a soul that has gone somewhere?

We would probably say, "No." Jurassic Park is closed. Its buildings exist, and so do the dinosaurs—heck, even the workers can still be there—but something is missing, and it probably isn't the "soul" of Jurassic Park. It's all of those things working together in a particular way. In other words, Jurassic Park exists as long as there are humans, dinosaurs, and equipment working together in the way that *makes Jurassic Park.* Imagine that Jurassic Park was a success, and over many, many years they replaced each and every building. In fact, it got so old that it outlived Hammond, his scientists, and all of the original dinosaurs, but it would still be the *same* Jurassic Park. And it isn't because it's on that particular island; couldn't we (if we had a *lot of money)* move the whole park to a new island?

What we realize is that Jurassic Park exists because there are physical things that work together in physical ways to produce something that really isn't physical, something really hard to define. The same thing happens with sports teams, countries, schools, corporations, and anything that isn't the "stuff" but is instead the result of "stuff" itself, working together. Couldn't the same be said for dinosaur souls and our own souls? If our experiences are dependent on our brains, maybe *we* are just the result of our brains working in a particular way. The "pain" of the velociraptor eating you isn't just one neuron firing; it's a neuron firing, and being responded to by other neurons in the context of your whole brain. And even when *that* neuron dies, as long as another neuron plays the same role, you will still feel pain. In the same way, even if Dr. Malcolm died in Jurassic Park, the department of mathematics he teaches for wouldn't disappear, because as long as *someone* can play his role or a similar role, the department can continue to function and *exist*.

So couldn't it be that when we are talking about souls and minds, we just mean *a mind is what happens when a brain functions in a particular way*? That's what Gilbert Ryle (1900–1976) thought: Our whole way of describing the soul was a language mistake. We keep treating souls like "things" that can go places and hold memories and personalities. But, really, the soul, to Ryle, is just what happens when you have the parts working together, just like Jurassic Park exists when you have buildings, fences, dinosaurs, humans, and money all working together. And if the park closes, even if all of the people, buildings, and dinosaurs are still there, Jurassic Park ceases to exist. And when our brains stop functioning, our mind doesn't *go* somewhere, it simply ceases to exist, like closing the park.

If It Looks Like a *T. rex*, and Eats Like a *T. rex* . . .

So with that in mind, let's go back to our cloned dinosaur. Here we have a couple of choices: 1. It has no soul, never did, and the dinosaur that now exists is completely different from the new one, or 2. The dinosaur's soul has been recalled to the new body. Well, if that soul was hanging out in dinosaur heaven, and it had no brain to create the sensations that we think of when we think of life (all the stuff that caused Rex to feel pain, remember things, see color, and smell meat rotted away in the ground long ago), what similarity does that soul have with Rex? And that problem becomes even more annoying if we make Rex 2. After all, if we have a clone of *past* dinosaurs (Rex 1), why not make a clone of Rex 1? We'll call her Rex 2. Do they share a soul? Are they the same dinosaur? What if it was you: if we cloned you right now, would you say your clone was you? Probably not.

So, then, we know for sure that our DNA isn't us. Our DNA helps make us, but it isn't the same thing as us. But as Ryle points out, that doesn't mean we're a magical spiritual thing; it means that when our DNA is used to arrange cells in a particular way, then you get *me*. It makes sense to ask, "If that's all there is to being me, then wouldn't my clone, or Rex's clone be the same exact thing as the original?" But that's impossible, right? Because you can't be in two places at the same time *having two different experiences*.

So here's our hope: even if the soul doesn't exist, I am *more than my physical self*. I have personal experiences—maybe those personal experiences are caused by my body, but there is something else that is *me*, and *essence* of me, right? It's beyond physical, and dammit, there might actually be hope that I could live forever through cloning. But when we say that something is "Rex" or "me," what do we mean? To be "Rex," there has to be something fundamental that makes her, herself. I mean, if we *define* Rex as "a dinosaur with two legs" and then we remove a leg, then she, by our own definition, isn't Rex anymore. Of course, we know this can't be right; she's just Rex missing a leg, so we know her leg isn't *essential* to her. It's part of Rex, but it *isn't Rex*.

So then—what makes Rex, Rex? There has to be something, essential to her, that makes her who she is. Something that, if you remove it, she ceases to exist. Of course, we have to be careful, because if we remove her heart, or something, she'll die. . . . But, if you think about it, isn't it possible to make an artificial dinosaur heart that can replace her original one? If that's true, then Rex's heart isn't *her*. It isn't essential to her. In fact, we also know her DNA isn't her either, because her DNA can change over her lifetime. This happens to all of us. Our DNA does change a bit through our lives, but that doesn't mean we cease to exist, right? And we've already said that the clone isn't me, though it shares my DNA—it's something very similar, but it's not *me*.

Who Is John Hammond?

Well, now we realize the problem: everything that seems essential to us is actually something that changes, so it can't really be considered essential. Imagine, for example, that Hammond gets Alzheimer's in his old age. He begins forgetting things; in fact, his personality changes dramatically (as often happens with Alzheimer's), so we now have someone who looks like Hammond, but with different memories and a different personality. So how is it still John Hammond?

Let's take that step even further. Compare that John Hammond with ten-year-old John Hammond. What if Old John Hammond as we know him is afflicted with more than Alzheimer's—let's say that due to severe trauma to his head from a helicopter crash on the island, he forgets who he is and everything about his past. What does he have left in common with his ten-year-old self?

You might say they have the same body, but they really don't. Every day we are taking in new atoms (as we breathe and eat) and getting rid of old ones. As you read this, you are losing parts of yourself and bringing in new parts to replace them. So the difference between ten-year-old Hammond and today's Hammond is that they have *completely different atoms*. After all of those years, there is a good chance that John doesn't have a single shared atom with his ten-year-old self. So he has none of the shared memories (due to his blow to the head), he has a different personality (due to his Alzheimer's) and his body not only is unrecognizably different in appearance, but every atom is different! How can we say Hammond is the same person over time?

I guess we could say that Hammond is the same guy over time in the same way we could say Jurassic Park is the same park over time even if we replace all of the buildings. As long as it keeps running pretty much the same way, it's basically the same park. But there isn't an "essence" to Jurassic Park, and there may be no essence to us either. Companies change philosophies after their founders die all the time, and even if

Hammond does have a soul, his personality and memories belong to his brain (which is why he can lose them when something happens to his brain) so his soul has little of worth in common with him. His body isn't the same, his personality isn't the same, his memories aren't the same, so how can he be said to have an essence?

You Crazy Son of a Bitch!

You've probably realized that what I've just said is obviously insane. Not only have we attacked the idea of the soul, but we seem to be attacking the idea that any of us have a "personal identity." We think we have personal identity, and *essence* to our very selves. We're really quite confident about it—so confident, in fact, that people report that their personality has always been the same and will always be the same, even though those around them can see profound differences. Daniel Gilbert recently did research showing that we think our personality won't change over time, but it does.

But Hammond, for example, doesn't experience the change of himself, *because he doesn't experience his past self.* Even if Hammond got his memories back, he wouldn't experience them as a ten-year-old. How often do we remember thoughts or feelings we had, and laugh at them? That's because we don't experience our memories as who we were, we experience them as *who we are!*

In other words, whoever you were is gone. In fact, whoever picked up this chapter and made it to the end is gone. You have different memories, thoughts, feelings, and atoms than the ones you had before. "What's wrong with changing?" you might ask. Remember, if you can change a thing and yet it remains the same thing, then whatever you changed isn't the essence of the thing.

Well maybe what I'm saying here isn't so insane! When Hammond dies in the novel, that's it: He's done. In fact, he never really existed over time in the first place. It's just that the thing that replaces Hammond every day is so similar to yesterday's "John Hammond" that we might as well keep calling him John. Just like when we replace the buildings of Jurassic Park—it really isn't the *same* Jurassic Park, but it's so similar that we might as well just keep calling it "Jurassic

Park." But if we change it too much, then we can't recognize it as the same thing. If we burn it to the ground, even if some buildings survive and some dinosaurs, some people, and the island are still there, it's just too different, too quickly to still be "Jurassic Park."

And it's like that for us and our extinction, too. Death is a sudden radical change. Your change from your one-year-old self to now has been significant, but seems slow to us, so slow we don't notice from day to day. So we think of you as the same person, even though you're different *in every way that matters*: memories, personality, and body. Death, though, changes all of that very radically, especially our ability to interact with others. Perhaps we could clone you, but it still wouldn't be you, for the same reason you aren't the same person as one-year old you, . . . because the clone is made of different matter, has different thoughts, feelings, and has some different memories, and it exists in a different place in time.

So, well, there it is. When we die, we go extinct. No coming back *as yourself* in any way. But here's the good news: if this idea is right, we die *all the time*, and we never notice because we're too busy being here. That past self with different personality, memories, and body is gone, and, to be honest, I've never noticed my past self complaining about the lack of his existence. So maybe we don't really need to be cloned by Hammond and his team; perhaps extinction isn't so bad, after all.

23
Playing God in Jurassic Park

JEFF EWING

The desire to create reality in your own image is the essence of Jurassic Park. But playing God requires more than will; it requires *mastery*. If Hammond and his scientists had mastery over themselves *before* they tried to remake the world in their own image, everything might not have gone so horribly.

You have to have internal mastery (control over yourself) before you can have external mastery. (control over everything else). If only Hammond had *both* aspects of power, maybe far fewer people would have died.

I Won't Be Sponsoring Your Park

John Hammond, the eccentric billionaire CEO of InGen, created the Jurassic Park theme park for many reasons, ranging from his desire to create a real, fantastic attraction to his desire to make children happy (and make lots of money!). One key motivation stands out—Hammond wants to bring dinosaurs back from extinction because *science enables him to*. He wants to bring them back simply because he can! Unfortunately, Hammond learns early on that his creations are less controllable than he hoped.

After a velociraptor kills a park employee, the park's investors want to know for sure that the park is safe. A team of experts is brought in—and Hammond's grandchildren. When the park's security is deactivated, what was a casual tour of the facility becomes a gruesome race to escape a death trap.

In *Jurassic Park* and its sequels, one thing is made perfectly clear—while humans had the scientific and technological mastery to recreate extinct species of dinosaurs, they failed to recognize their ultimate inability to control their own creations—and this lack of mastery produced terrifying and deadly consequences.

In his life, Friedrich Nietzsche (1844–1900) did not trust systems, and he often challenged them. Nietzsche developed the idea of the *will-to-power*. The *will-to-power* is the desire for power in the external world (and to create the world, godlike, in the way you want). Bringing back dinosaurs from natural extinction just because you can is an act of will-to-power—you resurrect long dead, majestic species simply because you want to and are able to. In fact, Nietzsche accepts the will-to-power as the only legitimate standard to live by, and rejects morality and religion as true or legitimate guides. Instead, he tells us that morality really is the way mediocre people try to repress the will-to-power of others—like investors trying to hold Hammond back from his miraculous creation.

Nietzsche argues that life *is* the will-to-power, which is a part of the motivation (to different degrees) of all living things. Life itself is "instinct for growth, for continuance, for accumulation of forces, for *power*." Like the dinosaurs of Jurassic Park, life struggles, fights, and kills to gain supremacy. To Nietzsche, "good" is really all that expands the feeling and exercise in power. He felt this so strongly that the "first principle'" of his "philanthropy" is that "the weak shall perish." So the strong make the world as they wish and the weak die in it. The best thing that anyone can do is to become the best possible version of herself, without resentment, and to recreate the world as she sees fit. But Nietzsche's philosophy isn't all about crushing others underfoot; it's also essential that we take responsibility for our own self creation—*self*-mastery.

Creation Is an Act of Sheer Will

John Hammond and the scientists responsible for resurrecting dinosaurs in *Jurassic Park* might be considered extremely eccentric by any standard, but his desire to clone giant, dangerous, long-dead beasts comes from more than Hammond's eccentricity (not to mention his wealth). Hammond is captivated by the majesty of the technology that brings back dinosaurs *and* the desire to allow humanity to see them after so many years.

Hammond's desire to create the park was sparked by his experience creating a flea circus. He wanted to build an attraction where he could show people "something that wasn't an illusion. Something that was real, something that they could see and touch. An aim not devoid of merit." His goal was beyond the creation of the mere *experience* of being around *fake* dinosaurs—he wanted to do the impossible and change the world through the re-creation of *real* dinosaurs.

Hammond highlights the excitement of children as the reason behind the idea for Jurassic Park. For him, the creation of Jurassic Park reflects an attitude to create something in reality that hadn't existed in the natural world in a very long time. To Hammond, "Creation is an act of sheer will"—science allows mankind the ability to transform nature into anything the human mind can create. His goal is similar to those of the Nietzschean "great man," using pure will to rebuild and change the world forever. For Nietzsche, through the active exercise of the "will to power," the *Übermensch* (the "great man"), raises himself up from the mundane mass of humanity to change the world. To Nietzsche, the human beings who rise to power in society are stronger than and superior to the rest of humanity, and gain mastery through creating the world in their own image, god-like.

A Taste for Hidden and Forbidden Powers

John Hammond's dream of building Jurassic Park is an absolute success and an absolute failure at the same time. On the one hand, his team of geneticists was successful in cloning several species of dinosaurs. On the other hand, they had planned to have a safe, secure, and profitable tourist attraction with that accomplishment. Their first goal was a complete victory, and the second was such a failure that its repercussions go far beyond the park. Dr. Malcolm highlights this failure when he criticizes Hammond and his team for being "so preoccupied with whether or not they could that they didn't stop to think if they should." Science can create technology, but not tell us how to use it appropriately.

Hammond counters that he doesn't "understand this Luddite attitude, especially from a scientist," and asks, "How could we stand in the light of discovery and not act?" By contrast with Dr. Malcolm, for Hammond the *ability* to achieve a scientific goal, like the resurrection of a species, creates a *duty* to achieve it. So, he clearly reflects the attitude of the Nietzschean "great man"—he wants to create the world in his own image towards his own purpose, and, at the same time, create himself as a free individual.

Nietzsche writes about this creative aspect of the will to power, where "The 'ego' subdues and kills: it operates like an organic cell: it is a robber and it is violent. . . It wants to regenerate itself. It wants to give birth to its god and see all mankind at his feet." Hammond's ego insists that even *natural* events that occurred without human influence can and should be manipulated if technology allows it. Decision-making belongs to the imagination, as long as the person doing the imagining can achieve those dreams. Hammond approaches nature, even at its most dangerous, as a passive object of human imagination and scientific and technological power. When he hears the potential dangers of this approach, he simply highlights the potential benefits of the project—it may make others happy, it may be a sound business venture, but the ultimate justification is the pure and simple unspoken declaration: "We can, so why shouldn't we?"

They Didn't Stop to Think if They Should

Hammond and his geneticists are amazed at their near-godlike ability to re-create functioning species from the discovered genetic material of long-dead beasts. Their enthusiasm far exceeds their caution. While they use game wardens, electric fences, tricky genetic security measures (like the attempt to prevent organic breeding by breeding only females . . . which, like the rest of their security measures, fails completely), none of these measures were enough to prevent dinosaurs from escaping to the human-snack bar. Scientists created something that far exceeded their ability to control it, so Jurassic Park is scientifically successful but wholly unsafe and, ultimately, *practically* unsuccessful. They *seemed* to be following the Nietzschean playbook—they reflected the external aspect of the will-to-power—but the experiment collapsed.

Remember Dr. Malcolm's criticism—that scientists were so preoccupied with their attempt to re-create dinosaurs that they failed to ask whether they *should*; here lies John Hammond's failure. Nietzsche said that creating the world in one's own image wasn't enough—the Übermensch must also have control over *himself*.

The human being who possesses his own independent and enduring will . . . this master of *free* will. . . with this mastery over himself, he has necessarily been given in addition mastery over his circumstances, over nature, and over all less reliable creatures with a shorter will.

Hammond and his scientists certainly mastered the *external* pursuit of the will-to-power, and they safeguarded it with every measure they could conceive of, to no avail. Nature was beyond their control. "Life finds a way" to reject their attempts to control it. The result? An island full of dangerous predators for whom the humans on the island are nice tapas. While they *thought* their security measures would be sufficient to prevent disaster, they were gambling with very dangerous stakes, assuming their own unproven mastery over nature. This is the failure to achieve *complete* mastery.

Hammond's control failed in many ways. For example, the park's security system is built around the expertise and control of one man, Nedry, who can then entirely shut down and bypass it by himself, at his leisure. Given that 1. their park's residents are among the largest and deadliest beasts Earth has ever known, and 2. they actually want to put people safely *in* that park *surrounded* by those residents, their security system ranks towards the top of the list of *World's Most Important Security Systems Ever.* Since Hammond could easily have hired a whole computer team to program and operate the park's security grid, and he could have established safety overrides to prevent an unsafe shutdown, this is one grave error (among many) within his control.

So can't we say that Hammond's "vice" is his lack of complete control? Nietzsche may argue that, if they'd had better control, this experiment would have been worthwhile, and the deaths have simply been small casualties on the way to greatness. Could John Hammond rely on this as his defense as a "great man" pursuing the "will to power"? If a few people get eaten along the way, that's just the result of the achievement of power. After all, you have to break a few bones to suck out their marrow. . . .

God Creates Man. Man Destroys God. Man Creates Dinosaurs. . . .

The sad, but "necessary" deaths argument might sway Nietzsche *if the Jurassic Park project could be controlled.* Hammond's enthusiasm ignored the very active variability in nature due to unforeseen problems—human (like Nedry's betrayal), natural (like the storm), or technological (like the inability to fully or reliably control behavior of the dinosaurs). But these uncontrollable, unforeseen variables have massive consequences (specifically turning a fun-filled theme park into a buffet for dinosaurs!)

Some of these unforeseen occurrences are the side effects of Hammond's own choices. First among these is the fact that the dinosaurs, originally bred female, changed sex. Hammond could have been more cautious and not spliced frog DNA into the dinosaur genetic code, or waited longer on a small popula-tion of dinosaurs to observe whether or not they were capable of sex-changes or reproduction. On the other hand, after cloning, he could not have controlled the dinosaur sex changes. But this only proves that he had no way to truly control dinosaur behavior.

Hammond's project relies entirely on his ability to protect Park visitors against tons of the largest, most deadly creatures ever to walk the Earth. Also, these creatures have never been observed or studied in the wild *before* Jurassic Park (because, you know, they were all dead). Hammond and his team assumed the big-dumb-beast hypothesis of dinosaur mental traits, formed by people who had also never studied real dinosaurs. To a huge degree, he and his team *underestimated* the strength of the dinosaurs *and* were constantly surprised by the adaptability and co-ordination abilities of dinosaurs like the velociraptors. Dinosaurs were creatures that, even in the best of circumstances, *Hammond should not have assumed he would have total control over.*

Under these circumstances, Hammond should have learned from Nietzsche's *self-control* that must come before attempts to gain power over the external world. Under the assumption that he had control, he willingly dove head-first into conditions he could never truly control, which is ridiculous because all he had to do was think about his lack of knowledge and lack of technology to know he shouldn't be so confident. His enthusiasm was based on his intentional ignorance of the forces he was dealing with and of the potential deadly consequences of failure. Had Hammond listened to Nietzsche's stress of self-mastery, these disasters would have likely been avoided before they began.

. . . if the Pirates of the Caribbean Breaks Down, the Pirates Don't Eat the Tourists

Jurassic Park highlights potential consequences of *undeserved* arrogance: specifically, humans playing with forces they cannot ultimately control. In Jurassic Park, John Hammond and his team of geneticists succeed in an undeniably fantastic project—they bring back from extinction several species of living, breathing dinosaurs. A project so dangerous is justified *if* Hammond's presumption that adequate safety precautions have been put in place. Unfortunately, these safety precautions fail miserably, showing that Hammond attempted to achieve control over the uncontrollable. He has no self-mastery; he is not honest with himself. He tried to do something that was impossible.

You see, to Nietzsche there really isn't anything wrong with arrogance. There is nothing wrong with knowing you are awesome, *if you are awesome*. But to think you have power that you don't, *that's just weakness*. Nietzsche and *Tyrannosaurus rex* both have no patience for weakness. If we lie to ourselves about our strength and the rest of the world crushes us underfoot (literally) because we were too busy trying to use power we didn't have, too bad. That's one thing we gotta give Nietzsche; while he isn't very compassionate for the weak and needy, he also has no tolerance for people who try to remake the world and fail. If you aren't strong enough to be honest with yourself, then you have no place creating the world (or dinosaurs).

Hammond neglected to see the limits of his power over nature because he did not want to see them—instead, he trusted his many assumptions. By assuming that his safety measures were enough to keep them all safe from his creations, he placed himself, his crew of geneticists, and his visiting guests in the middle of an isolated island, surrounded by the deadliest species the world has ever known (with the hope of inviting tourists to the island, and putting *them* in the middle of deadly creatures). Every major problem invites gruesome death—and they happened to have almost every possible security failure actually occur, and all at the same time. Hammond attempted to achieve the *external* component of the Nietzschean will-to-power, the capacity to create the external world in his own image, without accomplishing first the *internal* component, the development of self-mastery. A John Hammond with self-mastery may have controlled his enthusiasm for scientific power long enough to see the weaknesses in his actual ability to command nature. You see, to Nietzsche, Hammond's failure wasn't a *moral* one, it was a *weakness*. Hammond was too *weak* to control the external world because he didn't have control over his internal world.

Contemporary history is filled with examples of the wondrous capacities of modern science. Scientists are actively pursuing successes in cloning, lengthening human lifespans, and genetic modification of plant life and animals for food—significantly manipulating living organisms in ways that will probably impact the public long before they even know their full range of consequences. At the same time, scientists are developing numerous technologies that have military application or are primarily designed for military use, like "invisibility cloak" technology, deadlier weapons, and drones. All of them—scientists, politicians, and contractors—pursue this increasing destructive capacity without honest recognition of the terrible consequences that may result from those technologies.

John Hammond is an example (either dead or humbled, depending on whether you read the books or watched the movies) of what happens when humans try to control the world without knowing their own limitations first. This is always a danger of science, as it is with any other power. You don't fire a gun (even to save yourself from a *T. rex*) if you don't know which end shoots the bullet. And you don't make dinosaurs if you aren't honest with yourself about how much can go wrong.

If we are to become great, as Nietzsche demands, and build wonders, as Hammond dreams, we have to first look at ourselves, honestly, and master ourselves. We can't blame Hammond, or science, for not planning for every possibility, but we can blame them when they lie to themselves and to us when they say, "We have it under control."

24
How Much Are Your Grandchildren Worth?

JANELLE PÖTZSCH

Remorse, they say, comes late in life. So does insight. Perhaps that happened to John Hammond when he was encircled by those creepy compys in the book *Jurassic Park*. I can't help but wonder if insight finally came to Hammond as their poison paralyzed him—or perhaps while they were eating him. Probably not. But I bet he regretted his little walk in the woods.

Really, the fault seems to lie in Hammond's way of thinking. Self-doubt was never one of his problems. Even after everyone else realizes that Jurassic Park just won't work, Hammond still clings to the idea that his great plan has simply been poorly carried out. It doesn't cross his mind that something might be wrong with his idea itself.

In refusing to accept that nature's simply too complex to be planned, Hammond becomes a danger to everyone around him. And I suppose we should give Hammond this: he didn't risk his grandchildren's lives just for a little money—he risked their lives for a *whole lot* of money.

Philosophy Meets Chaos Theory

The mathematician Ian Malcolm is scandalized by the arrogance of Hammond and his researchers. Their mindset causes him to state: "Scientists . . . never stop to ask if they *should* do something. They conveniently define such considerations as useless. If they don't do it, someone else will. Discovery, they believe, is inevitable" (*Jurassic Park*, p. 284). In questioning the aim of Hammond's research project, Malcolm's views repeat the ideas of the German philosopher Hans Jonas (1903–1993).

Jonas argues that we need new ethics because former moral theories (either religious or philosophical) focused on a person's immediate surroundings, like neighbors or fellow citizens. We've all heard, "Love thy *neighbor*." But because of the huge advances in modern technology, our actions no longer affect only those who are in direct contact with us. Nuclear weapons affect the whole world, not just nearby countries. And some of the smaller dinosaurs Hammond created managed to escape and run amok on the rest of the island, harming those who had nothing to do with his freaky zoo.

Because of the enlarged range our actions can have, our earlier moral theories are not good enough today. Jonas emphasizes that we need new moral guidelines that fit the fact that we can do a whole lot more damage, to people *much* farther away—a problem that came with modern technology. For that purpose, he formulates a new moral rule to include the possible negatives of technological progress: "Act so that the effects of your action are compatible with the permanence of genuine human life."[1] In other words, my actions *today* should not conflict with human beings' continued existence *in the future*. And I'm pretty sure that creating genetically engineered monsters and then releasing them into the world *does not* help human "permanence"!

Control

At first glance, Jonas's pessimism seems a bit over the top. After all, human beings always developed and used some sort of "technology." If we didn't, we wouldn't have survived for long. But our modern technology marks a clear turning point in human history.

Early technology simply enabled us to survive. It allowed us to make use of nature, but we still had to conform to it. Early humans could use their ploughs to plant seeds, but whether and what they sowed depended on the seasons. They were constantly reminded of their dependence on nature. This relation-

---

[1] Hans Jonas, *The Imperative of Responsibility* (University of Chicago Press, 1984), p. 11.

ship has changed with the further development of science and technology. Nowadays, nature has become increasingly vulnerable to human intervention (through, for example, climate change, nuclear power or genetic engineering). Due to our increased power over nature, Jonas claims that we now bear responsibility for the whole biosphere of the Earth.

Malcolm also sees the connection between power and responsibility: "Most kinds of power require a substantial sacrifice by whoever wants the power. . . . But scientific power is like inherited wealth: attained without discipline" (*Jurassic Park*, p. 306). This is because a person's research usually builds on the research of another person. So a scientist always has some kind of reliable starting point (the work of others), which makes it easy to proceed. All that's required of scientists is to take the next logical step; they don't start from scratch.

Malcolm thinks that because this progress is so easy, scientists aren't mature enough to think about the implications of their power. This is why Malcolm points out: "Scientists . . . are focused on whether they can do something. They never stop to ask whether they *should* do something." To be able to ask (or even think of) such a question requires wisdom. Sadly, John Hammond and his team of scientists are far from possessing wisdom. Instead, they represent what Malcolm calls "thintelligence": "They think narrowly and they call it 'being focused.' They don't see the surround" (p. 284).

Thintelligent Thinking

Narrow focus is the main problem of our modern technological age. But Jonas points out that our outlook on our actions is *always* limited. Whether we are optimists like Hammond or not doesn't make a difference—modern technology simply overtaxes our imaginations. If it didn't, a talented geneticist like Wu would have thought of the weirdness of amphibian DNA. Because of our lack of foresight, Jonas asks us to display something that is far more difficult to achieve than wisdom: humility.

The demand for humility seems to be at odds with Jonas's earlier claim that humanity possesses *too much* power. Why should we be modest, given that we developed abilities that were formerly unimaginable? Jonas says that that's exactly the problem! Our new technological power has turned idle speculation "into competing blueprints for projects" (p. 21). Hardly anything is impossible nowadays! The humility Jonas asks for would be based precisely on our immense abilities: we should be humble enough to realize that we can't know the ultimate consequences of our actions, and so we should restrain ourselves. No matter how often or firmly Hammond asserts that "it was all very simple," they were all still trapped on an island full of bloody (and bloodthirsty!) velociraptors. He should have been humble enough to know that some consequences can't be foreseen. . . .

To avoid being overwhelmed (or eaten) by our technological innovations is no piece of cake since there is a considerable "gap between the ability to foretell and the power to act" (p. 8). This gap is mostly due to the enormous speed of technological progress, which makes their course very uncertain and so impossible to predict. Because of their alarming pace, technological innovations tend to develop dynamics of their own and end up overtaking the plans and wishes of their creators. (Who would have thought that the dinosaurs could find other sources to satisfy their need for lysine?)

What's more, this speed also makes it increasingly difficult to intervene if things don't turn out as expected. That's why Jonas claims that we should always act according to the worst-case scenario rather than the optimistic one. But such a cautious, even pessimistic, attitude isn't too popular among people with a strong belief in technology, like Hammond and Wu.

Malcolm claims that scientists' belief in their ability to control everything stems from "Western attitudes that are five hundred years old" (*Jurassic Park*, p. 312). The scientific movement of the early seventeenth century was characterized by a strong optimism about the future and about improving human life through science. The ultimate aim was to gain enough knowledge to conquer and use nature. That's the meaning of Sir Francis Bacon's famous adage "Knowledge is power." You may dream about how cute it would be to have a tiny raptor as a pet, but you can only breed one if you're really good at biology, especially genetics. If you've got that know-how, you can do pretty much whatever you want.

Now, we could wonder why Jonas regards this way of thinking as problematic. After all, the scientific development that got going in the sixteenth century turned out to be quite useful for us. If all scientists were as cautious as Jonas, we probably would still have to do without antibiotics or even vaccines. That's why Jonas claims that Bacon's program was *too* successful. We now witness in *Jurassic Park* the ultimate triumph of Bacon's ideals because we are able to control nature so much that we can outwit it and re-create dinosaurs.

Who Needs Speed Limits?

Jurassic Park illustrates that we've undertaken too much: We may control nature, but we don't control our power over it. According to Jonas, we don't just *develop* new abilities—we also feel compelled to make use of them. Once you've bought a Porsche, speed limits seem quite annoying. Similarly, it's not enough just to *decipher* DNA (which is impressive enough), we also want to do something with it. Something great and astonishing, like "real" dinosaurs—whatever that means.

All Hammond can think about is how to carry out his plans and make use of the scientific possibilities he has at his disposal: Use it or lose it. But his attitude puts an awful lot of people at great risk, not only Hammond's guests but also the natives of Costa Rica. (Remember that chapter with the newborn nursery and the rise in infant mortality? Exactly.) That's why Jonas says we need a force to keep people like Hammond, who do things simply because they can, in check: fight fire with fire and power with power.

A System Screwup

This power must come from society, "as no private insight, responsibility, or fear can measure up to this task" (p. 142). The risks of modern technology need to be dealt with collectively, especially because the private interests of individuals can be different from everyone's good (Hammond isn't totally honest with his investors for a reason!). Jonas concedes, though, that it takes a certain form of society to handle this issue. Unlike Malcolm, Jonas is less concerned about the after-effects of the Renaissance and more concerned about our modern economic order: Capitalism.

That may be hard to believe since most of us were raised on the idea that capitalism is awesome, and it is in *some* ways.

After all, people are free to purchase, invent, and sell whatever they like. Unlike in communist states, there is no imposition on what people ought to produce or buy. The only driving force is supply and demand. But according to Jonas, that's precisely the problem. The law of supply and demand suffers from a loophole: everything depends on the goals a person has.

And since our goal in our system is to make as much money as possible, we tend to cater especially to those demands that promise the most money. That's part of why Hammond was willing to take such a *huge* risk to make *a lot* of money! But what if we relied, instead, on a need-economy rather than a profit economy? Without a profit motive, we would deal more carefully with our natural resources. Imagine what could have been done with the huge sums of money Hammond spent on his Jurassic Park! Do we really need dinosaurs more than we need to fix the US energy grid, cure cancer, or solve world hunger?

Jonas thinks that if we'd banish the profit motive from our economy, we would also act more reasonably because we would be less eager about making a fortune. Maybe Hammond wouldn't have even thought about an amusement park with dinosaurs if he hadn't been so keen about the financial gains. He created a need we don't really have, so that we would pay to fill it. That's a pretty significant system-wide problem.

In some ways the consequence (live dinosaurs!) was pretty cool, but shouldn't the *risks* have been taken into better account? Did we really *need* dinosaurs so much that we are willing to risk lives, not to mention the ecosystem as a whole? Hammond's drive (one that most of us share) for money was so strong he was willing to risk his own grandchildren to make it work. He didn't need the park, nor did anyone else, but he wanted the money, and he paid for it with his life and the lives of a lot of other people.

Hammond's attitude is a problem for two reasons: First, we spend time and money on unnecessary things like parks full of dinosaurs instead of catering to the 'real' needs of people. Second, even though capitalism provides us with a ton of goods and services for our tastes and wants, it makes us (as consumers) prisoners. This isn't as paradoxical as it may sound: like technology, our economy also tends to make itself independent. Its starting point may have been to fulfill actual needs, but because it is driven by the profit motive, everything is now about selling the latest fashion, cell phones, or tickets to a new kind of zoo. As soon as you've bought one, you already need the *newer* one!

So we're pretty much prisoners to the constant demand that is placed on us to purchase new things. We work harder and harder for new phones, more channels, and extra accessories, when what we had before was fine. It might be pretty liberating to *reduce* our wants rather than giving into them. Perhaps that's why Malcom answers Ellie's amazed question about whether he isn't bored with wearing only two colors: "Not at all. I find it liberating. I believe my life has value, and I don't want to waste it thinking about *clothing*" (*Jurassic Park*, p. 72).

Damned Bureaucracy Is All It Is

If Jonas is right, our consumer culture is anything but sparing—especially with regard to natural resources. To avoid putting our (or a later generation's) livelihood at risk, we actually should try to do with less. But since such frugality is very much against our habits, governments might even have to impose certain measures to make us more frugal. In contrast to this, our capitalist society is about what's good for the economy and what consumers might like to buy. We're keen on economic growth and new product lines because we've been told that that's the only way to have a life worth living.

Our current social system is highly individualistic, so it has a strong focus on the present rather than the future: We admit that people do what they consider good for themselves without pondering whether their actions cause harm for society. That's because we value individual freedom. Hammond could have conducted his little experiment in the US, and despite the EPA closely watching him, he wouldn't have been charged with doing anything illegal. This cat-and-mouse game between Hammond and the authorities illustrates that we need more than well-intentioned watchdogs.

This thought might have you yelling "Communism!" with a fist upraised in anger, but seriously, isn't capitalism exactly what *allowed*—even pushed—Hammond to pursue his insane dream? And was it our selfish individualism that made him think it was morally acceptable? What kind of government, and

what kind of upbringing do we need so that people like
Hammond develop a sense of morality that protects the basic
rights of his fellow citizens (and also of future generations)?
Because so far, it seems that our system doesn't discourage people from being like Hammond; it encourages and rewards them
for behavior that risks the welfare of humanity's future, not to
mention the rest of us *today*. Massive, and massively expensive, cloned carnivorous monsters the size of houses seem
worthwhile when untold billions are on the line—in fact almost
any action seems worth the risk if there is enough money
involved!

Killing Time

Many of us feel like Ellie Sattler, who replies to Malcolm's
scathing criticism of Hammond's mindset with a bantering,
"You want to turn back the clock?" But Malcolm and Jonas
don't want that. They simply "want people to wake up" (p. 285).
In the final chapter of his book, Jonas underlines that people
who charge him with being against science and technology
miss the point. He doesn't condemn science. No one could sen-
sibly do that. Instead, Jonas want to balance out our thoughtless optimism we have regarding technology and science. He
wants to call our attention to the fact that there is a dark side
to everything, even to things that so far have been very beneficial for us.

And it's worth asking ourselves whether the benefits of
modern science are exactly benefits. As Malcolm is eager to
point out: Despite a whole army of household appliances,
women still spend roughly the same amount of time on house-
work as they did decades ago. According to Malcolm, people of
the stone-age had a more pleasant life: "Thirty thousand years
ago, when men were doing cave painting at Lascaux, they
worked twenty hours a week to provide themselves with food
and shelter and clothing. The rest of the time, they could . . . do
whatever they wanted" (p. 285). In other words, my computer
hasn't really reduced my work load, it has *increased* it—no
caveperson ever had to worry about making a writing deadline!

Our enthusiasm for certain developments shouldn't make
us blind to their possible drawbacks, like creating a devastating illness, destroying the environment, or just being eaten by

something with very pointy teeth. But the solution to the threats of modern technology can't be to *halt* technological development. Rather, we should try to *thoughtfully restrain* it. Hopefully, this leaves us enough time to ponder the possible consequences of our next step forward, and whether that's what we really want.

Because some things, once they're out there, can't be put back into their cages.

25

Chaos and the Inevitable Collapse

David L. Morgan

Y*ou crouch in the dark, your back pressed against an overturned amusement park SUV. Directly in front of you lumbers a full grown adult* Tyrannosaurus rex. *Its head swings slowly side to side—searching for you. Its eyesight is poor, triggered more by motion than outlines, so it's hunting you by scent. If the slightest breeze wafts your odor in its direction, you are a goner. Luckily, earlier in the day, a butterfly had landed on a flower just on the other side of the clearing. Its tiny wings jostled the air, creating a tiny whirl that added to a growing breeze. The air shifts. The wind swirls. The* T. rex *catches a scent off to its left and thunders away into the jungle. Whether you know it or not, you have just been saved by chaos.*

Unless you're a mathematician or a scientist yourself, there's a good chance that you first encountered the idea of "chaos theory" in one of two places. One is James Gleick's 1987 book *Chaos,* one of the first popular books written for regular folks curious about this emerging area of scientific and mathematical study. But it's even more likely that you first heard the words from the mouth of Ian Malcolm, the black-clad, rock star mathematician from the pages of Michael Crichton's novel *Jurassic Park*, played by Jeff Goldblum in the movie.

From his first appearance, Malcolm proclaims chaos theory as the ultimate reason that the park is doomed to fail, and his predictions seem to be vindicated when the prototype theme park collapses in an orgy of prehistoric terror and bloodshed. But what is chaos theory really about? And could a purely mathematical theory give someone such a deep insight into the inevitable downfall of a real-world system like Hammond's dinosaur theme park?

Science and Certainty

Modern science uses mathematical equations and formulas in order to make precise predictions about what goes on in the natural world. This way of thinking about the natural world really started with Isaac Newton's development of physics. Using a few simple laws of motion that describe how forces affect the motions of objects, and a simple law to calculate the gravitational force between massive objects, Newton almost-singlehandedly transformed what had been largely unexplained motions of the Solar System into an orderly and predictable system.

Armed with Newton's physics, it seemed possible to feed in the current state of some physical system, turn a mathematical crank, and with a bit of effort, predict what the system would be doing at any point in the future. The mathematical effort might be huge, but it was finite. And while the future of a physical system might be difficult to predict, that was only a result of our limited knowledge and our limited calculating ability. Since nature was based on physical laws, and these laws were straightforward cause and effect relationships like, "If *this* happens, then *that* happens," we could, in theory, know the future just as certainly as we can know the present.

According to this way of looking at things, the destruction of the dinosaurs by an asteroid 65 million years ago was already preordained billions of years earlier, when the Solar System first formed. (Sadly, had the dinosaurs had a telescope and a copy of Newton's book, they might have been better able to prepare.)

This view of the future is called "causal determinism." According to causal determinism, the future state of the universe is completely determined by its present state. And if nature is completely governed by simple cause-and-effect laws, then everything about the future is potentially predictable if we know those laws, and if we have enough information about the present. This view may have reached the pinnacle of expression when Pierre-Simon, Marquis de Laplace (1749–1827) wrote in his *Philosophical Essay on Probabilities*,

"We may regard the present state of the universe as the effect of its past and the cause of its future."

He imagined a powerful being who "at a certain moment would know all forces that set nature in motion, and the respective positions of all items of which nature is composed," and he concluded that such a being, if it was smart enough and had enough time, could calculate everything that would happen next. In other words, if we know exactly where everything is now, and we know the physical laws that govern the universe, it's a simple matter of calculation to determine what will be happening in the future. It might be a difficult calculation—requiring either a God-like intellect or a computer the size of a galaxy—but it's ultimately a solvable problem.

A strictly deterministic view of the universe—where the future is no less certain than the past—has far-reaching implications. For example, it causes quite a problem for the idea that humans can have free will. Religious thinkers pondered whether even God has the freedom to act in a universe that follows exactly from the rules and conditions that were laid down at its creation. But does science make us overconfident in our ability to predict the future? Might there be, as Ian Malcolm suggests, "great categories of phenomena that are inherently unpredictable"?

Complexity and Non-linearity

One reason that Newton's classical physics is so successful at describing and predicting the behavior of the natural world is that many processes in nature seem to obey equations that are linear. Many of the equations of physics are simple, like Newton's $F=ma$ or Einstein's $E=mc^2$.[1] If you double a term on one side of the equation—say the force in Newton's law—then the quantity on the other side, the acceleration, will double in response. This means that a small change in one quantity usually leads to a small change in the other quantities. To put it in more physical terms: Throw a ball a little harder, it goes a little farther.

---

[1] Remembering your high school math, you may think that the square in this equation would make it not "linear," but the c in $E = mc^2$ is not a variable, it's a constant—the speed of light. So c^2 is just a number. The equation describes a linear relationship between energy and mass.

But not all natural phenomena obey simple linear equations. Chaos theory deals with the behavior of non-linear equations—where throwing the ball just a little harder makes it go *a lot* farther. The technical definition of non-linear behavior is pretty complicated, but to make my point it is enough to say, systems with very many interacting elements and intricate feedback loops tend to behave in a non-linear way. And non-linear behavior is the raw material for chaos.

One characteristic of chaotic systems is that they tend to exhibit a feature called "sensitive dependence." With linear systems, small changes in their initial conditions lead to small, easily predictable effects. But with non-linear equations, a tiny change in the initial setup of a system can lead to wildly different behavior. This makes the behavior of non-linear systems difficult to predict. Ian Malcolm explains sensitive dependence to Gennaro using the example of the weather. "if I have a weather system that I start up with a certain temperature and a certain wind speed and a certain humidity—and if I then repeat it with almost the same temperature, wind, and humidity—the second system will not behave almost the same. It'll wander off and rapidly will become very different from the first. Thunderstorms instead of sunshine. That's nonlinear dynamics. They are sensitive to initial conditions: tiny differences become amplified." This sensitivity of non-linear systems to small changes in their initial conditions is sometimes called "The Butterfly Effect," a term coined by the American meteorologist Edward N. Lorenz (1917–2008). Lorenz was one of the pioneers in the study and simulation of complex systems and in the application of computer modeling to the prediction of the weather. Malcolm summarizes Lorenz's basic idea simply as— "A butterfly flaps its wings in Peking, and weather in New York is different." Small changes can have big effects.

Models versus Reality

Systems that exhibit very sensitive dependence on their initial set-up thwart the usual way of doing science. We can't start with the initial conditions, turn a mathematical crank, and predict what the system will be doing in the future, because we can never hope to have knowledge of the initial conditions that is 100 percent accurate. If we are off in even the tenth decimal place initially, when trying to predict the behavior of a chaotic system, then our prediction will turn out wrong. And not just a little bit off, but way, way off!

So, even if the universe is strictly deterministic, it may not be predictable. And think about what that means: even if everything in the universe does happen for a reason (the past causes the future), we still can't predict with any confidence even the most mundane events!

This lack of predictability is the source of the tension between Malcolm and Hammond. A theme park containing many species of dinosaurs and many individuals of each type—each with its own requirements for food and safety and its own unique set of instinctual behaviors—can't be described in terms of a simple equation like $F = ma$. And it sure seems like Hammond thinks it can be predicted and therefore *controlled*. Just let money be m and let cloned dinosaurs be d, and "control" be c, and you get c *times d equals a whole lot of m!* But Jurassic Park is what's sometimes called a "complex dynamical system," and one thing about complex dynamical systems is that they tend to display the telltale features of chaos—a sensitive dependence on their initial conditions, and often rapid and unpredictable changes in behavior.

How do you go about studying the behavior of chaotic systems, if not by trying to predict their behavior exactly? You do it by modeling them, usually with computer simulations, and studying the broad types of behaviors that the system is capable of. This is what we are to suppose that Ian Malcolm had done before he arrived at Jurassic Park. But what exactly are we to imagine he had simulated? He certainly didn't input the location of every velociraptor and compsognathus, . . . every jeep and electric fence, . . . every power station and port-a-potty, . . . and then run a deterministic simulation of the park. That's not how modeling works.

When Malcolm talks about his results in terms of the "movement of the system within phase space," he is describing the mathematical behavior of some highly abstract and simplified simulation of the park taking place on a computer. So why should Hammond believe him when he makes claims about the relationship between his model and the viability of the real Jurassic Park? This is one of the main philosophical questions raised by the whole idea of chaos theory. How seriously should we take generalizations about the real world that originate from numerical calculations taking place inside of a computer? To put it another way— is the mathematical behavior we call "chaos" an inherent property of nature? Or is chaos only a property of the mathematical models we use to approximate nature?

Evolution and Certainty

The process of evolution seems far from deterministic, and the unpredictability of evolution is another theme addressed in *Jurassic Park*. Scientists and mathematicians don't agree on the proper way to think about the relationship between the chaos exhibited by mathematical models and the complexity of the real world. But we do know that nature can be complex and difficult to predict, and that theories like Natural Selection must approach nature in a way very different from the way physics does. In *Jurassic Park*, Crichton connects the unpredictability of evolution itself to the unpredictability of chaotic systems.

The process of evolution, is governed by Charles Darwin's theory of Natural Selection—a process that's too complex to model using some simple set of equations. From the unfolding of a set of genetic instructions, to the specific behavior of an individual creature, to the daily dice roll of survival-of-the-fittest, Natural Selection relies on a complex chain of possibilities. And while these possibilities may not be not truly "random," they are so complex and interconnected that there's no hope of predicting whether or not any particular individual or population will survive any particular generation.

The one certainty allowed by Darwin's model is that those who *do* survive will, over time, find themselves well-adapted to their environment (since it's differences in survival over time that are responsible for the characteristics of the current population). Evolution has no "goal" or "purpose," but if it did have a purpose, it would be nothing other than adaptation for survival. In the novel, Malcolm presents this view of life by pointing out that "the history of evolution is that life escapes all barriers. Life breaks free. Life expands to new territories. Painfully, perhaps even dangerously. But life finds a way."

Malcolm says this to suggest that any attempt to try to "control" life and squelch the power of evolution the way that Hammond was attempting to do with his park was ultimately doomed to fail. Life adapts to changing environments, and the complexity of the relationship between organism and environment is the force that drives evolution. This complex relationship leads to chaotic behavior and inherently unpredictable results. While it's true that life is bound to evolve whenever it's free to reproduce and subject to selective pressures, it's a far cry from this claim to say that dinosaurs are bound to run amok and destroy your island theme park.

In fact, Malcolm's certainty in his doomsday prediction for the Jurassic Park venture seems to involve a paradox. If his whole point is that complex systems are chaotic and unpredictable, how can he be so sure of one particular out- come? Yes, as a chaotic system, the park is subject to the snowballing of tiny unknowns as in the butterfly effect, but the snowballing effects of the butterfly's flapping can just as often lead to a calm, sunny day as a devastating hurricane. Who's to say that the dinosaurs won't respond to captivity by evolving traits of submission and a desire for human companionship, the way that wolves and wild felines became our domestic dogs and housecats?

What Malcolm does get right is the overall idea that evolution is deeply contingent. In other words, the complexity of the relationships between organisms and their environment virtually guarantees that the outcome of the evolutionary process is unpredictable. (The late evolutionary biologist Stephen Jay Gould explored this scenario extensively in his book *Wonderful Life*.) If you were to rewind the evolutionary history of the Earth to some point in the past—to the Precambrian, say, or the Jurassic era— and then allow evolution to proceed again from the same starting point, the process would be very unlikely to result in the familiar world we see around us. As with the butterfly effect of chaos theory, tiny changes in the expression of particular genes, or the chance survival of specific individuals would provide Natural Selection with slightly different raw material, leading over time to completely different species and completely different adaptations and strategies.

In this sense, chaos theory predicts unpredictability. Malcolm was right when he declared, "Life finds a way." But the correct interpretation of his warning is not necessarily, "Chaos theory proves that life will find a way to destroy your dinosaur theme park." Rather, the lesson we should take away from chaos theory is that, when we choose to ignore tiny factors in a complex system, we shouldn't be surprised when those small changes blow up into big effects that can come back—quite literally, perhaps—to bite us.

26

A *T. rex* Swallowed My Pride

MICHAEL D. STARK AND A.G. HOLDIER

If I were Ian Malcolm—and had just watched a sixty-five-million-year-old monster rip apart both a lawyer and a Land Cruiser before having my own leg shattered by the beast—I would be more than just "fairly alarmed" to realize the implications of the rippling pool of rainwater next to my broken body. But I wouldn't be surprised. Just as Dr. Malcolm had predicted, chaos reigned supreme and, despite the best laid plans of John Hammond and his staff, the man-made *Tyrannosaurus rex* broke free from its man-made prison to enjoy, for the first time in the history of the planet, the taste of man.

As he was always quick to point out, Hammond's InGen Corporation spared no expense in building the prehistoric zoo, but years of planning with the latest science still could not guard against the most destructive force the planet has ever seen: human pride. That's right; the *T. rex* might have jaws that can turn a car into tissue paper, but when compared to the damage that arrogant humans have done in our relatively short time walking upright, such strength is as unimpressive as the idea of using a bamboo bathroom for a defense bunker. The problem of Jurassic Park lay at its core: the vanity of the whole project all but guaranteed its failure.

What Have They Got in There—King Kong?

On Isla Nublar, we see a venture capitalist leading a company into very questionable ethical waters without considering much beyond the price tags of the lunchboxes in the gift shop.

With the carelessness and greed of men like Hammond or the "blood-sucking lawyer" (and eventual *T. rex* treat) Donald Gennaro on full display, questions of appropriateness were never even considered.

With one important exception.

Since even before the audience met him in the helicopter, Ian Malcolm constantly (and loudly) voiced his concerns over InGen's arrogance before nature and repeatedly predicted the tragedy it led to. Unmoved by the ambitious scope of Hammond's vision or the dollar signs in Gennaro's eyes, Malcolm maintained a healthy skepticism of our ability to play God. In his own sarcastic way, Malcolm—philandering, cynical, and arrogant—is the model of virtue in the park, which doesn't say a whole lot about the virtue of everyone else.

A Deplorable Excess of Personality

Admittedly, Ian Always-on-the-Lookout-for-a-Future-ex-Mrs. Malcolm doesn't seem to be the honorable and virtuous guy we should all try to be like. He is confrontational, flirtatious, and extremely blunt . . . yet behind that swagger we find the only consistently moral perspective against the pride of Jurassic Park.

When he discovers Hammond's (re)creation of dinosaurs, Malcolm is unsettled by how quickly scientists brought life from death. Even before his own "house of horrors" tour through Jurassic Park begins, Malcolm is strongly critical of Hammond's failure to even consider the consequences of his actions. Over lunch, while listening to Gennaro and Hammond discuss the bathtubs full of money that they'll be able to make off of the park, Malcolm explodes with frustration at the entire idea, trading barbs with the two businessmen in an exchange that builds to:

MALCOLM: You stood on the shoulders of geniuses to accomplish something as fast as you could, and before you even knew what you had, you patented it, and packaged it, slapped it on a plastic lunch box, and now you want to sell it! *Sell* it!

HAMMOND: I don't think you're giving us our due credit. Our scientists have done things which nobody's ever done before.

MALCOLM: Yeah, but your scientists were so preoccupied with whether or not they could *that they didn't stop to think if they should!*

Dressed in black leather (against Hammond's clean, white suit), the confident Malcolm is the only one to initially recognize the dangers of a human playing the role of a god.

Man Destroys God, Man Creates Dinosaurs

From beginning to end, what the Jurassic Park project lacked is virtue, or "the ability to know when dead gigantic meat-eating monsters should stay dead." To be more specific, a virtue is a positive character trait that encourages habits that make a person become a better person. A virtue is not something that helps you get eaten by a prehistoric beast you defiantly brought back to life.

We don't have to travel sixty-five million years into the past to find the answer to the question, "What went wrong with Jurassic Park?"—only a few hundred, to Paris in the thirteenth century. Just like Dr. Malcolm, medieval philosopher Saint Thomas Aquinas (1225–1274) would diagnose the problems of Jurassic Park without hesitation: they all arise from human arrogance and pride.

In general, Aquinas is not as concerned about the particular actions that someone performs as he is about the overall character of the person doing the action. This lands him squarely in the field of "virtue ethics"—mostly concerned with the type of people we are and who we try to be, not just our obligations and the consequences of our actions. Look at Dennis Nedry and imagine if his plan to shut down the computer system had failed: no dinosaurs would have broken free and no one would have died, but he would still be the same sneaky, selfish weasel that he ever was. Even if his actions did not end up killing a bunch of people, he would still lack virtue and still not be a "good" person.

Or think of Dr. Grant's promise to Lex and Tim that he would stay awake all night in the tree to guard them. Given the context, this was almost certainly a lie—and lying is bad, right? But Aquinas would say that Grant's compassion for the children's nerves and concern for their well-being would make that lie acceptable; it's not that the *act* is considered right or wrong in that situation; it's the *character* of that act—the choice of valuing the children's sense of security—that is most important.

Aquinas based all virtues on Natural Law—a set of laws (like the laws of physics) that are accessible to every person and allow humans to live well. Aquinas believed that human beings, as rational animals, only live well if they are living up to what it means to be rational animals. Virtues are the things that allow us to reason well.[1]

However, not all virtues are created equal! Aquinas considered certain virtues to be more fundamental than others, with "prudence" being at the very top and "temperance" trailing not far behind. Because he shows both of these virtues, Dr. Malcolm, despite his oh-so-charismatic style, might actually be the most ethically-minded of the whole lot of characters!

Prudence is the feature of humanity that guides judgments about what actions are right and wrong. This is more than simple "street smarts." It guides how we make difficult decisions, such as whether or not it is sensible to bring a species that has been extinct for millions of years back to life! If you're prudent, then you'll know the proper thing to do, no matter what situation you find yourself in.

Temperance is the restraint of excess, enjoying just the right amount of something. For example, John Hammond might have been tempted to overindulge his celebratory drink when he first meets Dr. Grant in person, but such drunkenness and loss of control would hardly be virtuous. The drunkenness is the excess; the restraint from drunkenness is the virtue of temperance. Aquinas writes, "Temperance withdraws man from things which seduce the appetite from obeying reason." In fact, Aquinas connects our two virtues together here very nicely. Prudence guides a person practically while temperance fights off the things that skew our ability to think clearly and make good decisions.

So, is Dr. Malcolm the virtuous character? The opposite of living by the virtues is living by vices—the character traits that lead one to become an evil person, rather than good. To Aquinas, the absolute worst evil is the greedy, thoughtless, self-centered vice of pride. This is what we see in *Jurassic Park*. Ian Malcolm operates virtuously with prudence and temperance (in far more than just alcohol consumption). John Hammond

---

[1] The substance of Aquinas's great work, *Summa Theologica*, has been edited and compiled in a readable short text—Peter Kreeft's *A Shorter Summa: The Essential Philosophical Passages of Saint Thomas Aquinas's* Summa Theologica (Ignatius Press, 1993).

and Donald Gennaro act almost exclusively out of pride. So, while Dennis Nedry's prideful selfishness might be the immediate reason for the Isla Nublar incident, blaming the obvious fool of the story is easy; we want to focus on examples of vice which are more difficult to identify. In our view, these vices are often the most damning, especially in the case of Jurassic Park.

God Help Us, We're in the Hands of Engineers

In the movie, Hammond is depicted as a friendly grandfather whose prideful ambition, though clearly present, is not as central to his personality as it is in the book. In the novel, the character's vice is far more clear, because he is far less kind. Explaining why he spent his fortune on creating an amusement park and not some humanitarian effort, Hammond exclaims: "Would you make products to help mankind, to fight illness and disease? Dear me, no. That's a terrible idea. A very poor use of new technology. . . . Personally, I would never help mankind."

Throughout the story, Hammond acts with the terrible vice of imprudence, never stopping to consider the propriety of his actions—and Malcolm doesn't hesitate to call him out on it. Let's return to that fateful lunch scene:

> MALCOLM: Don't you see the danger, John, inherent in what you're doing here? Genetic power is the most awesome force the planet's ever seen, but you wield it like a kid that found his dad's gun. . . . I'll tell you the problem with the scientific power that you're using here: it didn't require any discipline to attain it.

Malcolm makes a good point about Hammond's thoughtlessness, but what does Hammond do? He laughs and shrugs it off. Even after chaos breaks out in the park and his grandchildren are lost inside, Hammond still tells Dr. Sattler (in between endearing licks of ice cream) that he would try again, because "that's all correctable for the next time around."

Aquinas would shudder at the magnitude of Hammond's prideful God complex. With his vast fortune and gang of engineers and scientists, he is so arrogant—because he has the ability to (re)create a species that has been extinct for millions of years! In gaining the upper hand on nature and evolution, the mastermind of Jurassic Park never stopped, even for a minute, to ask whether bringing back dinosaurs was the *right* thing to do. Hammond completely ignored the importance of analyzing his motivations; from this, we know the virtue of prudence is something Hammond just doesn't have.

Not to mention, Hammond's interest in fame and fortune drove him to hurry the creation of the park and its captivating creatures. These characteristics reveal his imprudence rather than his discretion. A virtuous person of prudence would have allowed reason to guide her in a more thoughtful process. She would ask if it is ethically right to bring creatures back from the dead, and, if it is even permissible, what the best way is to do it *safely*. Hammond's haste and his inability to carefully reflect on Malcolm's criticism lead not only to his downfall as the CEO of InGen, but also directly contribute to the story's disaster (and, in the novel, his own death).

The movie version of Hammond does seem to take responsibility for the accidents at Jurassic Park. Despite at one point muttering to himself about his hatred of Ian Malcolm, Hammond seems to recognize the soundness of the mathematician's objections and course-corrected his vicious attitude towards prudence. Consider the final spoken lines of the film:

GRANT: Mr. Hammond, I've decided not to endorse your park.

HAMMOND: So have I.

Yet by the time *Jurassic Park: The Lost World* came around, Hammond was up to his old tricks again.

The Blood-Sucking Lawyer

However, the downfall of Jurassic Park lands not only on the easily blamable John Hammond. Donald Gennaro, the attorney sent to evaluate the park's safety on behalf of its investors, also provides a great example of vice. Recall Aquinas's key virtues: while Hammond easily represents imprudence, Gennaro is the model of intemperance. Even more than the venture capitalist, the lawyer has dollar signs on his mind. Consider Gennaro's very first words upon seeing a real-life dinosaur: "We're going to make a fortune with this place!" This stands in stark contrast to Malcolm's initial, and far less selfish, reaction: "You did it. You crazy son of a bitch, you did it!"

Remember the lunch meeting where Gennaro talks about charging two to ten *thousand* dollars a day for admission and, when Hammond chastises him, Gennaro suggests "coupon day"? Malcolm is right to be horrified. At this point, unable to contain his disgust, Malcolm spits out, "Gee, the lack of humility before nature that's being displayed here, um . . . staggers me." They are surrounded by gigantic *predatory* animals that are powerful beyond our imaginations and have been *dead* for more than sixty-five million years, yet Gennaro and Hammond are talking about money!

Remember—temperance is the virtue that helps someone refrain from excess. The excess here is money, and lots of it! If Gennaro (and the companies he represents) had a more temperate attitude about reincarnating dinosaurs, then perhaps the approval process for the park would have involved more scrutiny and created a safer environment. Money, in itself, is not bad; the vice is the tunnel-vision approach to gathering large sums of it very quickly. Gennaro, while sent to focus on the park's safety, is wholly distracted by the money. His intemperance leads to imprudence and, since thin bamboo walls rarely keep people safe against a predator the size of a building, his death.

With Hammond and Gennaro as models of the vices of imprudence and intemperance, Malcolm remains a virtuous skeptic throughout the story. With his rock'n'roll personality, one might think he would be excited for a speedy debut of Jurassic Park. But he isn't. He keeps his pride in check and allows Aquinas's virtues to guide his ethics and actions. He asks questions that must be asked.

Life Will Not Be Contained. Life Breaks Free . . . Life Finds a Way

Dr. Malcolm continually demonstrates wisdom—Aquinas's definition of the virtue of prudence. We've said quite a lot here about Malcolm's doubtful attitude towards the park and Hammond's ability to prevent the inevitable outbreak of chaos that comes to pass. Unlike the scientists and their financial backers, Malcolm recognizes the importance of questioning human activities—even those done in the name of some good (since "discovery" equals "the rape of the natural world" to the mathematician). He only supports those activities that are appropriate to the particular situation, which is an attitude that fits perfectly within Aquinas's understanding of prudence, where "the right thing to do" is always dependent on the situation.

For example, who would really want to draw attention to themselves in the middle of a rampaging *Tyrannosaurus rex* attack? But the virtuous Malcolm did precisely that, because he realized that potential self-sacrifice for the sake of protecting children was better than prideful self-preservation: by the application of reason to the situation, he naturally understood what to do and acted accordingly. Incidentally, Aquinas's other two Cardinal Virtues are Justice and Fortitude (or Courage). Malcolm's bravery in the face of the prehistoric predator is, indeed, evidence of his valor and further proof of his virtuousness.

Malcolm's entire point in the lunchroom scene is not simply that InGen has proceeded down this shady path, but that the company has fully given up any possibility of prudential virtue, because no one has ever even tried to ethically analyze the situation at all. For Malcolm, who appreciates the power of nature at work and recognizes that the dinosaurs were selected for extinction, it is clear that the ambitious undertaking of Jurassic Park is no different than the idea of re-arranging Earth's tectonic plates or changing the value of *pi* throughout the universe; even if such things are possible, they sure do seem like "destructive, penetrative" acts!

And neither does the promise of great wealth distract the temperate Malcolm from his focus. Unlike Gennaro, Malcolm fails to get caught up with the material things of the world. In the novel, he comments on his drab wardrobe (that consists wholly of black and grey hues) as efficient, allowing him to ignore fashion and have more time to work and care about genuinely important things. Even with his flirtatious advances towards Dr. Sattler (which Aquinas would certainly not approve of) Malcolm eventually recognized their inappropriateness in light of the circumstances and, once again, made the prudent choice to be temperate and hold back from working his rock star vibe with her. Of course, having his leg broken by a dump-truck-sized animal was very likely helpful in this effort, as well.

Altogether, Ian Malcolm serves as the conscience of Jurassic Park, whispering seeds of virtuous doubt that, up to that point, Hammond, Gennaro, and the rest of InGen had been ignoring. He stresses Aquinas's concern for prudential sensibility and chastises the company men for their single-minded, intemperate concern for the almighty dollar. Dr. Malcolm, for all his excess of personality, has his heart in the right place. But, boy, does he "really hate being right all the time!"

That Is One Big Pile of Shit!

Coming across a massive pile of Triceratops dung, Dr. Sattler dives in elbow-deep to solve dinosaur health problems. We've also been dealing with a rather messy situation: both Hammond and Gennaro are clearly full of, well, shit. Their unvirtuous character not only limits their ability to do the right thing, but the horrible stench of their vice seeps out and makes the entire project reek! Even if the opening of Jurassic Park had gone flawlessly, it's still pretty obvious that these are thoughtless, selfish people who are unwilling to use basic reasoning to restrain their own greed!

Dr. Malcolm has developed character traits like prudence and temperance, but he still has his faults, too! Virtues will never make a perfect person. It's not as if one ever reaches a point in life and rightly says, "I'm virtuous enough." The virtues are a guide, a kind of course correction that keeps vicious characteristics in check as you go about your life. The task never changes: we must continually develop into virtuous characters.

It's a lifelong task—or, as the nineteenth-century Danish philosopher Søren Kierkegaard once said, "To be finished with life before life has finished . . . is precisely not to have finished the task."[2] Though a person will never be perfect, we can, like Dr. Malcolm, make good judgments in difficult circumstances (and those were pretty *difficult* circumstances) if we are just willing to *think*.

---

[2] Søren Kierkegaard, *Concluding Unscientific Postscript* (Princeton University Press, 1971), p. 147.

27
How to Avoid Extinction

TRIP MCCROSSIN

Terrified and exhausted, Lex, Tim, and Dr. Grant huddle together, up in a tree, in the dark of night. Their hope: to escape a seriously gruesome death in the clenching jaws of a dinosaur.

Lex, though, in spite of her fear, just can't help worrying about Drs. Grant and Sattler. Now that they "don't have to pick up dinosaur bones anymore," what *will* they do? Grant reassures her and her brother that the good doctors will "just have to evolve, too." They are reassured—and we in the audience are as well. What's more, though, we're also reassured about something *much bigger*.

Grant is talking to Lex and Tim, but also *to us*. He's talking about himself and Sattler, but also *about us*. We—as in *humanity—will also just have to evolve!* Better yet, he's telling us that we'll just have to evolve *too*, and is confident that we *can*. It's only the next morning that Grant discovers, with childlike wonder, a nest of hatched dinosaur eggs, but even the night before, he must believe *already* that "Malcolm was right," that "life finds a way." In talking *to us*, *about us*, he's surely telling us that this isn't true *just* for the dinosaurs, but also for *us*.

But *how* will life find a way for us? The answer, Malcolm believes, lies in a deeper understanding of *extinction*. How and why do certain species *fail* to evolve successfully? Malcolm thinks he knows, and so is curious to see if the "lost world" of Isla Sorna proves him right. It's true that the cause of extinction is sometimes some catastrophe, like with the meteor that helped kill off the dinosaurs in the first place. But it may also

267

sometimes be because of the species's behaviors, which also might be happening to us right now!

Malcolm's curiosity (and ours) is only partly about dinosaurs. Let's say Isla Sorna's dinosaurs were to die off. And let's say that we notice a behavior that caused it. In fact, Malcolm tells us about some real behavioral scenarios where behavior does cause a downfall: the "Red Queen" and "Gambler's Ruin" scenarios. Then yes, if we understood behavior-caused extinction, we'd certainly know more about dinosaur extinction. But more importantly, we might *also* know more about how *our* behavior may threaten *our* extinction, and what we might *do* about this. That's the hope, anyway!

Alice in Isla Sorna

Malcolm is struck, as we all should be, by life's fantastic complexity. The interaction of only a small number of objects is already bewilderingly complex, he notes, but "inside the cell, there's *one hundred thousand things* interacting. You have to throw up your hands. It's so complex—how is it even possible that life ever happens at all?" His answer: that "living forms organize themselves. Life creates its own order, the way crystallization creates order."

Most of us recall fondly the experience of staring at crystals forming in a petri dish in chemistry class or around the kitchen table on a rainy weekend, at snowflakes gathering on a mitten in wintertime, and so on. We're amazed by how beautiful and seemingly perfect their various shapes and patterns are, so maybe we look for some sort of controlling process. But Malcolm thinks this is all wrong, that it's much more likely they're simply *self-organizing*. "So maybe living forms are a kind of crystallization," he imagines, "maybe, like crystals, there's a characteristic order to living things that is generated by their interacting elements," which, for better or worse, can happen *very fast*.

"If you map complex systems on a fitness landscape," he continues, "you find the behavior can move so fast that fitness can drop precipitously." Not because of meteors falling from the sky, or diseases getting out of hand, or anything especially cataclysmic, but "just behavior that suddenly emerges, and turns out to be fatal to the creatures that do it." Malcolm's real worry is what this can teach us *about ourselves*. "Human beings are transforming the planet," he worries, "and nobody knows whether it's a dangerous development or not"—whether it might actually be leading to our own extinction. But wouldn't it be nice to *know*, so as to change course and survive instead?

Malcolm doesn't give us great odds. "We are stubborn, self-destructive conformists," he complains, and frankly it's hard to disagree. But then again, he's also the one telling us "life finds a way." So what might this look like? A natural place to start would be Malcolm's attempt to explain his general scientific outlook using the Butterfly Effect—a "butterfly can flap its wings in Peking" and, without obvious connection, change the weather in New York City. Unfortunately, this doesn't help his companions, and without additional detail, it doesn't really help us, either.

Let's take child-rearing, for example. Faced with the dizzying complexity and nerve-wracking unpredictability of raising a child, parents sometimes take comfort in the Butterfly Effect. They're prepared to do their best, they say. But they're also prepared for some small and seemingly unimportant thing in their kid's life to have some gigantic effect later on—good or bad—which overcomes a lot of (if not *all* of) their parental efforts. Or things that seem huge and life-changing early on may have only small and seemingly unimportant effect later on. Still, they do their best. But what about when we're talking about behavior on a grander scale, as Malcolm is when talking to us about extinction? Here, when it's about "doing our best" *together as a species*, to intervene positively in our own evolution (instead of causing our own extinction), the Butterfly Effect just doesn't seem all that helpful. And so we look to Malcolm's Red Queen and Gambler's Ruin.

Evolution is a sort of "arms race." Plant and animal species survive by continually evolving new defenses against new forms of aggression from competing species. The Red Queen phenomenon gets its name from a passage in Lewis Carroll's *Through the Looking-Glass*, in which the Red Queen famously explains to Alice that, in Wonderland, "it takes all the running you can do, to keep in the same place." And so it is in nature.

Let's say something goes wrong—even in a small way—and as a result, Alice (the species) has to slow down, and can no longer "keep in the same place." Why can't she just slow down for a bit and catch her breath, and then catch herself back up again? Sometimes she can. But other times, according to the Gambler's Ruin, things continue to go wrong, slowing her further, making it all the more difficult to catch herself up. A gambler playing a fair coin-toss game, Malcolm explains, winning on heads and losing on tails, may think they'll come out even in the end, but instead the gambler is always eventually ruined. "Everything in the world goes in streaks," he concludes, and once "things go bad, they tend to stay bad. . . . Bad things cluster. Things go to hell together. That's the real world." Once Alice stumbles, in other words, not only is she unlikely to catch back up to where she was, but she's likely to stumble again and again as she struggles to do so.

Bad things cluster and go to hell together, and this can happen *very fast*. This is a big deal! So, how might we help ourselves? How do these phenomena happen in *human* evolution, too? We're "so destructive," Malcolm complains. Again, it's hard to disagree. That means we're not so different from other species that survive by destroying the competition. What makes us different, though, is that we're also *self*-destructive. We tend to destroy other species and our shared environment, *aware* that in the process we're destroying ourselves. Like other species, we have to develop continually new defenses against their aggression. Unlike them, though, we must do so also against *our own*.

For us, unlike other species, an essential part of running as fast as we can in order to stay where we are, is running as fast as we can *away from ourselves*. So, human survival is more exhausting—and less likely because of that fact. What about the Gambler's Ruin? Well, for one thing, because of our *self*-destructive nature, we actually gamble in an attempt to win while *also* making it so that we can't.

Imagine that Malcolm's a poker player. He's just sat down to a weekly poker game with the game's four other regular players. They know each other so well that they all figure they'll be able basically to break even by the end of the night. This is actually the way they *want* it to be, because the best way for the game to continue into the future is for everyone to enjoy playing, which will occur most naturally if at the end of the night everyone's won or lost only a little bit. Ideally, each player will win roughly an equal number of hands, for roughly equivalent winnings overall.

But a problem arises. A sixth player joins the game who doesn't care about playing weekly; he just wants to win as much as possible in tonight's game. He doesn't care what the cost may be to the five original players—even if, in the extreme, the weekly game ceases to exist after tonight as a result. Even worse, the new player sets a new rule for the night's play: in order for Malcolm to win a hand, he has to beat all five other players. But there's more. The more often he beats the four other original players, the easier it is for the new player to beat them, *and* to beat Malcolm.

So how does Malcolm avoid letting the new player win and destroy his weekly game? First, he would want to protect the original players, by encouraging and even helping them to win, in order to reduce the influence of the new player. Second, he would want to play as aggressively as possible against the new player to make them even less of a threat. Success would be all six players breaking even, disappointing the new player and letting the five original players go back to enjoying the business of competing, just the five of them, weekly to a draw.

How might *we* similarly avoid ruin, not as individual card players, but as a species? The game is a metaphor for life on Earth. Simply put, we need to keep ourselves from "winning" at the cost of actually losing by ending the game. We need to keep our actions in check so that we don't cause a system collapse that leads to our own extinction.

Fences Are Failing All Over

At first, we learn that Hammond has "successfully" cloned dinosaurs, and we're truly amazed. So why worry? They're cloning raptors; that's why! We might have been able to handle *all* of the other potentially dangerous beasts, even though all the same precautions are in place to make sure that nothing goes wrong, but *this one*'s one too many, and things do go very wrong.

This flaw in human behavior, called the Tragedy of the Commons, first observed by William Forster Lloyd (1795–1852), is increasingly dangerous to human survival.[1] Every part of

---

[1] *Lectures on the Checks on Population* (1733), available at archive.org and books.google.com. The Tragedy of the Commons is now known primarily

the natural world (and by extension the whole world) has a limit to the number of lives it can maintain without damage. Once this limit is reached, Lloyd observed, a tension arises. Let's say Sattler and Grant make good on his promise to Lex, retire from digging up bones, and take up sheep herding. Each lets their flock graze on a common pasture ("the commons"). If they both add an additional sheep—to up their yield of wool or mutton, enjoy the added company, or for some other reason— they can reasonably believe that this upside outweighs whatever downside the other may experience.

But what if other herders join Sattler and Grant on the commons, and now all of them decide to add an additional sheep to their flock? They might still all believe that the upside for them outweighs the downside for others, but their belief is no longer reasonable. The pasture will become "bare-worn," as Lloyd observed, the sheep "puny and stunted," and Sattler, Grant, and their fellow herders hungry and poor.

The solution we have historically used is to manage the commons by means of *enclosures*—from actual fences surrounding plots of land, to more symbolic fences, in the form of laws. The idea has been historically controversial (and rightly so when motivated by greed, power, class, and the like), but when it comes to the Tragedy of the Commons in particular, good fences do seem to make for good neighbors. As sheep numbers swell in Grant and Sattler's pasture, they will be reminded of what the Red Queen says to Alice about running as fast as she can in order to stay in place. That means enclosing some portion of the commons, building a fence around it, to protect themselves from others' aggression. But at the point when they're most in need, they find that "fences are failing all over."

We remember the ominous drama of a commons shared by humans and dinosaurs in the first movie, early in our stay on Isla Nublar. There's the missing goat, the sudden appearance of the tyrannosaur feasting on it, the twanging of breaking cables as the paddock fence fails, the massive eye staring at Lex, all

---

through Garrett Hardin's essay by the same name, available at garret-thardinsociety.org, including a useful pair of cartoons illustrating the phenomenon. Thanks to Deborah Greenwood for introducing me to this concept, and to a deeper appreciation of environmentalism in the process. The conclusions I derive from it here, though, are my responsibility alone.

hell breaking loose. But when *that* fence fails, another remains in place, which is the island's coastline. In the movie's closing scene, for example, our heroes are being ferried to safety by helicopter. They see through the window that they're not alone in the sky. They're being shadowed by what look initially like pterodactyls, but are really only pelicans. They fly alongside for a while, and then over the ocean and into the setting sun, reassuring us that nothing properly dinosauric has jumped the fence. When our artificial fences fail, we don't worry because natural fences will always ultimately save us.

The second movie makes us question this, though, when the commons is extended to include Isla Sorna and San Diego, and a different fence is required. In the final scene, we hear from a news anchor that an "ever-growing" Navy escort is accompanying the ship returning the kidnapped tyrannosaurs back behind the natural fence that is the coastline. Then, as the film closes, we learn from Hammond that still more is needed. "It is absolutely imperative that we work with the Costa Rican Department of Biological Preserves," he insists—the "we" presumably the corporate side of a corporate-government alliance—"to establish a set of rules for the preservation and isolation" of Isla Sorna.

And *again*, we have to question how well enclosures work in the third movie. The island's isolation is undone by petty greed and family dysfunction. A still stronger fence is needed. By the time Grant and company escape Isla Sorna, the Navy's no longer enough. To Erik's delight, Sattler has sent "the Navy *and* the Marines." Survivors are evacuated again by helicopter, as in the first movie, but this time by *military* helicopter.

And yet, the film ends with our faith still not entirely reassured: again our heroes find that they're not alone in the sky, but instead of pelicans, pterodactyls have breached the fence, first by escaping their aviary, and then by leaving the island altogether. "Where are they going?" Erik asks. "Maybe looking for new nesting grounds," Grant replies, adding that it's "a whole new world for them." Fences are failing *all* over. The dinosaurs are out, and so the commons has been extended yet again. This time, though, unlike the "incident in San Diego," the situation is *not* under control. "I dare them to nest in Enid, Oklahoma," Erik's mom mumbles half-jokingly. But there's a serious note here.

One way to interpret her is as simply boastful, but there's another, more charitable way. She's asserting *herself* as the solution. If Jurassic Park reflects the Tragedy of the Commons, and if corporations and governments are going to fail us—as it seems they have, in film and in real life—then she, and presumably regular folks like her *are* the fence that will ultimately save us.

As Malcolm points out, extinction is in many ways about behavior. We tend to think of it as something that happens when a species *physically* can't keep up with changes around it. But he reminds us that environmental changes may require behavior changes more than they require physical changes. So the real question is, can we learn new behaviors quickly enough as the world changes around us? Or do we too just become fossils?

In order to stay where we are, to survive, we're running as fast as we can from species trying to harm us, which in this case we ourselves have made. So we evolve stronger and stronger defenses, apparently against their evolving destructiveness, but since we made them, really against our own evolving *self*-destructiveness. We run and we run, as fast as we can, from dinosaurs, but really from *ourselves*.

What we need is to realize that we don't *need* to be self-destructive, but rather we *allow* ourselves to be. We do this when we ignore that the commons, fundamental to our survival, is tragically endangered whenever we do what's best for ourselves (or allow others to do what's best for themselves) without concern for what's good *for all*.

Daring *ourselves* to work together, to learn not to do this, is the fence that makes all other fences work.

Velociwriters

ADAM BARKMAN is an associate professor of philosophy and chair of the philosophy department at Redeemer University College (Canada). He is the author and co-editor of many books, most recently *Imitating the Saints, The Culture and Philosophy of Ridley Scott,* and *The Philosophy of Ang Lee.* When not doing philosophy, Barkman enjoys helping his son Tristan dig for fake dinosaur bones while humming the theme to the "Daddy-Chechi Song" (the *Jurassic Park* theme).

VINCENT BILLARD was born in Vietnam during the American war. He grew up in France and he's a graduate from Sorbonne University. He's now a professor of philosophy in Paris. He has already published one book in Canada: *iPhilosophy* (philosophy of Apple, the world-famous computer brand). He is a great fan of *Jurassic Park* but unfortunately the only living dinosaurs he ever met in Paris were some old French philosophers at the university.

EVAN EDWARDS is a PhD student at DePaul University in Chicago. While he spends a lot of time thinking about German Idealism and the mind-numbing lists of conceptual distinctions in Husserlian and post-Husserlian phenomenology, he's more happy thinking about real-world problems, like, "Can I conceivably ride a velociraptor like a horse?" or "What would an apatosaurus burger taste like?"

JEFF EWING is a graduate student in sociology at the University of Oregon. Jeff wonders if, in a world where dinosaurs never went extinct, they would have evolved dinosaur-versions of the great philosophers, like Plato and Nietzsche and Marx. He hopes the next *Jurassic Park* movie will address that important question.

Born and raised in Canada, KENN FISHER lives in Toronto where he works in film and television production. He graduated from the University of Toronto with a degree in Philosophy, and contributed to *The Wire and Philosophy: This America, Man* (2013). When he saw *Jurassic Park* for the first time as a child while it was in its original theatrical release, it scared the hell out of him.

JOHN R. FITZPATRICK is a lecturer in philosophy at the University of Tennessee, Chattanooga. He received a PhD in Philosophy from the main branch of the University of Tennessee in Knoxville in 2001. He is the author of *John Stuart Mill's Political Philosophy: Balancing Freedom and the Collective Good* (2006), and *Starting with Mill* (2010). He is a contributor to several Popular Philosophy books which does not necessarily make him a friend to extinct and endangered species, but does indicate that he is involved in a criminal conspiracy to murder innocent trees.

DAVID FREEMAN is a graduate student in history at the University of New England. In one version of his past, he received a BA in history and English lit from the University of Queensland, where he later undertook graduate work in philosophy. He previously published an article in the journal *History in the Making* on phrenology and madness (which may explain many of his ideas). A tiny percentage of the atoms comprising him probably belonged to some kind of dinosaur millions of years ago, which technically makes him a reconstructed dinosaur studying itself.

A.G. HOLDIER took an MA in the philosophy of religion from Denver Seminary and currently teaches high school theology courses in the lost world of southern Idaho. His research in metaphysics, mythopoesis, and the ontology of fiction is very probably more than just a clever excuse to read comic books. Like Dr. Malcolm, he also hates being right all the time, although his wife assures him that he doesn't really need to worry about that.

ROGER HUNT studied philosophy in Montana, New Zealand, and Boston, and is currently in psychoanalytic training in Boston. He also works with several private foundations and universities to organize high-school philosophy programs including the Boston Regional High School Ethics Bowl. In Kindergarten he made a massive papier mâché pterodactyl, which made the end of J2 extra special.

TIM JONES is Associate Tutor in Literature at the University of East Anglia in Norwich, England. He hopes that future people will enjoy his chapter or, if they think it's rubbish, that that's the worst they have to worry about. Or, at least it will give them something else to worry about between global warming and dinosaur attacks.

LISA KADONAGA is a geographer who researches and teaches at the University of Victoria on Vancouver Island. Some observers suspect that Lisa's preoccupations exhibit a morbid streak: global environmental change, endangered crop biodiversity, food security in Afghanistan, the Time of Thirty Tyrants in third-century Rome, the interpersonal repercussions of selling crystal meth (she contributed to *Breaking Bad and Philosophy: Badder Living through Chemistry*). And now, giving the thumbs down to the resurrection of *T. Rex*. But she persists in cheerily affirming that human life will find a way. In all probability.

JOHN V. KARAVITIS, CPA, MBA, is a financial analyst in the Chicagoland area. Besides contributing essays to Popular Culture and Philosophy books, John's other passion is competing in 5K races. His training runs on forest preserve trails are always very early in the morning, pre-dawn, since he knows that velociraptors only hunt during the day. He hopes.

BRANDON KEMPNER is Associate Professor of English at New Mexico Highlands University. Despite the science, he refuses to believe velociraptors had feathers, and no one is going to convince him otherwise. Chapters by him have previously appeared in *The Walking Dead and Philosophy: Zombie Apocalype Now* (2012) and *Neil Gaiman and Philosophy: Gods Gone Wild!* (2012).

CHRISTOPHER KETCHAM is a reformed academic of the university species. However, exposure to the rigors of science does not prevent him from selfishly coveting his own genes. In his bid for immortality he has elected himself to give the commencement address for the first graduating class of the College of Raptors.

SKYLER KING is studying English and philosophy at the University of Missouri, Kansas City, and plans to continue studying these two topics in graduate school. He has contributed chapters to several Popular Culture and Philosophy books. He also likes to think that he's charming and witty like Dr. Malcolm, but he managed to realize his mistake before a hungry *T. rex* attacked him—barely. But, hey, that's chaos theory. Oh, and if you would like to see more of Skyler's friendly philosophical musings, visit his blog at www.unmitigatedreasoning.wordpress.com.

DANIEL KOKOTZ is a doctoral candidate at the Ruhr-University Bochum in Germany. He's working on the philosophical problems of the extension of the human lifespan, having realized way too late that Hammond's dinosaurs already work for the drastic shortening of said lifespan.

If **GREG LITTMANN** could be a dinosaur, he would be an armor-plated Ankylosaurus, smashing the hell out of everything with his club-like tail. He wouldn't give up his job as an associate professor of philosophy at SIUE and would continue to teach metaphysics, philosophy of mind and epistemology, but everyone would fear him and nobody would give him any crap. By pecking at the keyboard with his small, leaf-shaped teeth, he would continue to publish in philosophy of logic and evolutionary epistemology, as well as adding to his list of over twenty chapters written for books relating philosophy to popular culture, including *Breaking Bad and Philosophy: Badder Living through Chemistry* (2012), *Frankenstein and Philosophy: The Shocking Truth* (2013), *and Planet of the Apes and Philosophy: Great Apes Think Alike* (2013). Then, when he wanted a break, he would wander campus, roaring and smashing things with his tail.

TRIP McCROSSIN teaches in the Philosophy Department at Rutgers University, where he works on, among other things, the nature, history, and legacy of the Enlightenment. He's been heard to say, as students are entertaining themselves before class, "Oh, yeah. Oooh, ahhh, that's how it always starts. Then later there's running and screaming."

NICOLAS MICHAUD recently edited *Frankenstein and Philosophy* and is excited about his current project, *Adventure Time and Philosophy*. Ironically, Nick hates adventure. In fact, visiting Isla Sorna is his worst nightmare. Between the turbulent helicopter flight, the giant, prehistoric mosquitoes, and a massive hurricane, he'd rather just stay home. The fact that there are dinosaurs rampaging across the island comes as no surprise to him as all of his so called 'vacations' have ended in similar chaos. When excavators unearth his remains a thousand years from now, they will find him seated in his recliner, clutching his remote control in his cold, dead fist, refusing to go anywhere, dammit!

DAVID L. MORGAN received his PhD in theoretical particle physics from William and Mary, and his research has appeared in *Physical Review* and the *Astrophysical Journal*. He is the recipient of a Sloane/EST commission for his play, *The Osiander Preface*. His chapter on the physics of time travel appeared in Open Court's *Planet of the Apes and Philosophy: Great Apes Think Alike* (2013).

MICHAEL J. MUNIZ is an adjunct professor of philosophy at several colleges in South Florida. He can be seen writing in his journal while sunbathing on the beautiful beaches of Miami. He fears that one day the carcass of a megalodon will shore up as a result of suntan oil pollution brought about by Hawaiian shirt-wearing tourists.

JANELLE PÖTZSCH earned a degree in philosophy and English at Ruhr-Universität Bochum, Germany. She has contributed essays to *The Big Bang Theory and Philosophy* and *Frankenstein and Philosophy*. As a moral philosopher, she, of course, would never fall for the temptations of big money, as Hammond did. Never.

TIMOTHY SEXTON has published two novels, *Antichrist Superstar: The Musical* (2000) and *Bizarre Love Triangle* (2001), as well as contributing chapters to *Sherlock Holmes and Philosophy: The Footprints of a Gigantic Mind* (2011) and *Jeopardy! and Philosophy: What Is Knowledge in the Form of a Question?* (2012). He stands firmly by his contention that he did indeed predict that Dr. Grant would suddenly jump out of a moving vehicle.

TRENDAN SHEA teaches philosophy at Rochester Community and Technical College in Rochester, Minnesota. His main areas of teaching and research interest include the philosophy of science, logic and inductive reasoning, and bioethics. He encourages any aspiring billionaire dinosaur-theme park founders to get in touch with him regarding an on-location ethics consult. This is because, you know, he secretly thinks that it would be awesome to see some dinosaurs.

MICHAEL D. STARK is an Affiliate Professor of Philosophy at Colorado Christian University. He has an MA in philosophy from Denver Seminary and in 2013 was a summer research fellow at the Hong Kierkegaard Library at St. Olaf College. His research includes Kierkegaard, epistemology, and virtue theory. When he's not musing over Kierkegaard, he ponders why anyone with a *juris doctorate* thought that a portable toilet would protect him from a *Tyrannosaurus rex*.

RICK STOODY teaches philosophy at the University of California, Santa Barbara. He can often be found at home stomping around his two kids, with his elbows tucked to his sides, roaring loudly, thinking to himself, "So *this* is what it's like to be a *T. rex!*"

NATHAN VERBAAN is an independent scholar whose philosophical interests include ethics, metaphysics, and discussing the finer points of when it is obviously a *really* inappropriate time to eat ice cream—yes, even if it's melting!

SETH M. WALKER teaches courses in religious studies, philosophy, and humanities at the University of Central Florida and the University of South Florida. He's also one of the founding editors of *Nomos Journal*—an online journal engaging the intersection between religion and popular culture. He hopes that if dinosaurs do return one day, they'll be treated with equal moral consideration . . . and that "the monkeywrench" soon becomes a popular dance move.

JESSICA WATKINS (in private life, now Watkins-May!) is an adventurer who tends to foolishly believe that everything will be just fine, and that she (probably) won't be eaten by anything with large, pointy teeth. In fact, Jess ventures into a misty land of monsters daily to teach middle school. Like velociraptors, seventh-graders are a dangerous species to study, and the answers we've reached about them are theoretical, at best. Every day with them, her husband, and her family is an adventure, and she'd have it no other way.

Genetic Markers

altruism, 34, 181

amber, 11, 23, 63, 88, 145, 160

Animal Liberation Front (ALF),
168

Aquinas, Saint Thomas,
259–265

Aristotle, 41, 123, 124, 126, 128,
189, 190, 192, 193, 194

arrogance, 4–8, 10, 78, 79, 117,
121, 151, 235, 257, 258, 259,
261

asteroids, 45, 250

Baudrillard, Jean, 113–120

Bentham, Jeremy, 76, 147, 204

Brachiosaurus, xi, 21, 23, 137,
181, 188, 221

Brontosaurus, 112, 116, 118

Brown, Justice Henry Billings,
164

capitalism, 35, 81, 82, 86, 87, 88,
243, 244, 245

Carr, Eddie, 171, 172

Carson, Rachel, 74; *Silent
Spring*, 74

chaos, 6, 19, 32, 35, 4, 84, 117,
148, 182, 211, 239, 249,
251–57, 261, 263, 277, 278

Cleanthes (David Hume), 31, 32

clones, 3, 11, 22, 28, 29, 33, 39,
40, 41, 42, 44, 45, 46, 47, 56,
85, 88, 111, 120, 190, 220, 221,
222, 223, 224, 225, 227, 230,
246, 253, 271

consciousness, 17, 40, 101, 104,
105, 108, 109, 128, 132, 136,
138, 141, 156, 160, 162

conservation, 12, 13, 14, 146

conspicuous consumption, 145

control, 6, 8, 27, 29, 30, 34, 37,
39, 44, 48–50, 55, 60, 69, 71,
74, 75, 82–84, 86–89, 118,
121–23, 149, 157, 167, 183,
184, 187, 189, 190, 199–203,
229, 230, 232–237, 240, 243,
253, 260, 273

Cook-Greuter, Susanne,
161–62

Cretaceous, 13, 27, 66, 148

Crichton, Michael, xi, xii, 3, 4, 5,
6, 9, 25, 27, 65, 73, 74, 75, 79,
80, 92, 95, 108, 115–120, 249,
254; *Eaters of the Dead*, 120;
The Lost World, 18, 26, 27, 27,
68, 94, 95, 97, 98, 115, 117,
122, 124, 125, 126, 147, 167,
178, 179, 181, 182, 183, 202,
204, 206, 262; *State of Fear*,
79

Curtis, Kelly, 95

Darwin, Charles, 32, 33, 34, 67, 68, 69, 70, 71, 198, 200, 254

Dawkins, Richard, 155, 156; *The Selfish Gene,* 155

de Waal, Frans, 133

de-extinction, 11, 14, 16, 18, 19, 54–60, 64, 65, 68, 151

Deinonychus, 116

Descartes, René, 134–36, 138, 139, 199

determinism, 253, 254

Dilophosaurus, 144

DNA, 11, 12, 13, 23, 24, 25, 26, 30, 34, 37, 40, 55, 58, 65, 66, 68, 70, 87, 98, 101, 102, 110, 137, 145, 149, 160, 188, 190, 194, 202, 203, 224, 225, 234, 241, 243

Dodgson, Dr. Lewis (head of BioSyn), 123, 204

dualism, 102, 103, 110

Earth First! (EF!), 167, 168, 175

Earth Liberation Front (ELF), 168

ecology, 14, 15, 16, 170, 171, 172

Einstein, Albert, 8, 135, 251

Elliot, Robert, 77–78

emotion, 92, 96, 97, 98, 127, 212

Engels, Friedrich, 82

Enlightenment, 6, 179, 180, 182, 278

ethics, 12, 17, 39, 41, 42, 47, 48, 49, 50, 57, 60, 75, 77, 78, 79, 80, 84, 124, 132, 139, 140, 148, 149, 172, 174, 175, 178, 198, 200, 201, 205, 207, 209, 210, 211, 213, 215, 219, 240, 257, 259, 260, 262, 263, 264, 276, 279

evolution, 13, 29, 32, 33, 34, 35, 36, 37, 45, 67, 69, 70, 87, 133, 162, 187, 200, 254, 255, 261, 269, 270

exploitation, 15, 84, 86, 88, 89, 95, 160, 182

extinction, xii, 4, 5, 11, 13, 14, 16, 18, 19, 44, 45, 50, 54–60, 63–65, 68, 74, 143, 144, 146, 147, 151, 164, 187, 215, 219, 220, 227, 229, 230, 235, 264, 267–69, 271, 274

flourishing, 16, 31, 50, 55, 60, 215, 216

Foreman, Dave, 168

fossils, 21, 22, 24, 28, 31, 58, 98, 103, 112, 113, 115, 116, 119, 120, 167, 175, 274

Gambler's Ruin, 268–270

genetic engineering, 12, 14, 21, 34, 35, 36, 103, 131, 241

Gennaro, Donald, 84, 85, 98, 101, 123, 252, 258, 261, 262, 263, 264, 265

Gila crassicauda, 143, 144, 146–47, 149

Gilbert, Bil, 145, 147, 223, 226

Gleick, James, 249; *Chaos,* 249

God, 3, 5–8, 29, 31, 32, 43, 44, 46, 67, 70, 73, 86, 97, 115, 134, 158, 160, 192, 198–203, 207, 210, 251, 258, 259; Playing God, 53–61, 229–237

Godzilla, 97, 115

Gould, Stephen Jay, 255

Gorman, James: *How to Build a Dinosaur,* 23

Grant, Dr. Allen, 13, 14, 21, 22, 35, 54, 56, 57, 58, 60, 64, 83, 84, 95, 121, 122, 126, 127, 129, 130, 133, 135, 137, 140, 151, 155, 160, 181, 182, 183, 191, 197, 199, 202, 212, 214, 220, 259, 260, 262, 267, 272, 273

greed, 9, 10, 81, 88, 189, 219, 258, 260, 265, 272, 273
Guardians of the Future, 178–180, 182, 185

Hammond, John (head of InGen), 133, 140, 145, 146, 148, 150, 167, 169, 171–75, 177, 178, 179, 180–85, 187, 188, 190, 193, 195, 198, 201–03, 210, 214, 222, 225–27, 229–237, 239–246, 250, 253, 255, 257–263, 265, 271, 273, 277, 278
Harding, Sarah, 171, 183, 213
Haywood, Bill, 168
Homer, 76
Horner, Jack, 23, 118
humility, 5, 6, 8, 9, 131, 147, 183, 236, 241, 242
Hume, David, 31, 32
hyperreality, 113–120

Iguanodon, 22
InGen (corporation), 24, 30, 31, 35, 36, 37, 58, 64, 91, 122, 123, 124, 125, 126, 144, 167, 169, 170, 171, 173, 174, 175, 180, 181, 182, 210, 229, 257, 258, 262, 264, 265
Isla Nublar, 21, 64, 104, 105, 124, 158, 181, 257, 261, 272

Jean-Jacques Rousseau, 6
Jonas, Hans, 67–70, 240–46

Kant, Immanuel, 124, 126, 129, 134–36, 139, 179–182, 184
Katz, Eric, 78, 79
Kierkegaard, Søren, 265, 279
Kirby, Eric, 95, 98, 184

Language, 12, 36, 105, 134, 137–39, 159, 161, 211, 214, 223
Larsson, Hans, 23
Leopold, Aldo, 75–77; *A Sand County Almanac*, 76
life finds a way, 4, 32, 44, 55, 67, 189, 233, 254, 255, 263, 267, 269
Light, Andrew, 79
Lloyd, William Forster, 271, 272
Lorenz, Edward N., 252
lysine, 48, 123, 149

Malcolm, Dr. Ian, 4, 5, 12, 15, 16, 21, 27, 30, 31, 32, 33, 34, 35, 36, 37, 43, 44, 45, 46, 48, 50, 54, 55, 56, 57, 59, 64, 69, 70, 71, 75, 95, 102, 123–25, 131, 140, 146, 155, 157, 171, 181–83, 198, 200, 203, 211, 223, 231–33, 239, 241–43, 246, 249, 251–55, 257–265, 267, 268, 269, 270, 271, 274
Marx, Karl H., 82, 86, 275
Megalosaurus, 22
memes, 29, 34–37
Mendel, Gregor, 34
Mill, John Stuart, 17, 76, 164
Monkeywrenching, 168, 170, 171, 175
morals, 12, 14–18, 57, 63, 64, 66, 74–77, 121, 122, 124–29, 136, 140, 170–75, 179, 201, 204, 205, 210–12, 214–16, 230, 236, 240, 245, 246, 258, 278, 279
Muldoon, Robert, 21, 123
Murphy, Alex "Lex," 95, 96, 206, 259, 267, 272
Murphy, Tim, 84, 85, 95, 96, 205, 267

Naess, Arne, 15, 16, 170

natural selection, 32, 33, 34, 36, 45, 46, 47, 254, 255
the natural, 3, 6, 7, 8, 9, 12, 14–17, 43, 44–46, 55–60, 74–79, 103, 109, 113, 126, 131, 140, 156, 157, 159, 171, 172, 173, 176, 182, 186, 188–195, 199, 203, 231–36, 239–243, 250, 251, 254, 258, 261, 263, 264, 269, 270
Neanderthal, 16, 30, 130, 164
Nedry, Dennis, 55, 82, 83, 87, 88, 123, 144, 197, 233, 234, 259, 261
Nietzsche, Friedrich, 200, 230–36, 275

Odyssey, 76
Owen, Nick Van, 167–68
Owen, Richard, 31, 32, 144, 146, 150, 167, 168

paleontology, 22, 28, 35, 103, 116, 118, 146, 212, 213
paradoxes, xii, 96, 97, 98, 135, 244, 255
passenger pigeons, xii, 11, 12, 30, 60, 61, 65, 69
personhood, 136–37
Philo (David Hume), 32
Philosophical Essay on Probabilities (Laplace), 250–51
Philosophical Investigations (Wittgenstein), 138
physicalism, 102, 103, 108, 109, 110
Piaget, Jean, 161
Pister, Edwin, 143, 146, 150
Pister's Bucket, 143, 149, 151
playing God, 29, 57, 58, 192, 198, 202, 229
Plessey v. Ferguson, 164

possibility, ix, xii, 7, 37, 54, 64, 70, 144, 147, 151, 184, 193, 237, 264
prudence, 75, 260–65
Pterodactyl, 126, 273, 276

raptors (velociraptors), 6, 11, 13, 14, 15, 17, 19, 23, 24, 27, 29, 33, 35, 56, 57, 58, 69, 70, 87, 88, 93, 95, 104, 105, 111, 113, 115, 116, 118, 121, 122, 124–29, 133–35, 139, 140, 150, 155–165, 171, 172, 177, 178, 189, 191, 209, 220, 221, 223, 229, 234, 242, 253, 271
Read, Rupert, 178
reality, xi, 8, 25, 26, 37, 49, 66, 67, 74, 86, 87, 91, 93, 94, 97, 98, 103, 131, 171, 175, 178, 229, 252; and unreality, 108–120
Red Queen, 268, 269, 272
Regan, Tom, 127–29, 139, 140, 213; *The Case for Animal Rights*, 127, 140
restoration, 14, 18, 55, 77, 78, 79, 80, 144, 146, 147, 175
rights, 15, 16, 17, 77, 87, 121, 122, 123, 124, 125, 126, 127, 128, 129, 132, 140, 144, 145, 148, 149, 158, 160, 164, 172, 175, 201, 204, 206, 207, 212, 213, 214, 215, 216, 246

sabotage, 88, 168, 169, 174, 175
Sattler, Dr. Ellie, xi, 13, 14, 19, 21, 44, 60, 64, 70, 82, 83, 84, 102, 107, 108, 109, 122, 140, 148, 181, 203, 205, 206, 213, 215, 220, 246, 261, 264, 265, 267, 272, 273
sensitive dependence, 252
Simon, Pierre, 250
Singer, Peter, 76, 172, 173, 205

the soul, 6, 9, 40, 41, 42, 43, 102, 109, 110, 134, 141, 210, 214, 220, 221, 222, 223, 224, 226
Stoics, 55
subject-of-a-life, 127, 128

Tembo, Roland, 18, 125, 171, 183, 206
temperance, 260, 263, 265
Tragedy of the Commons, 271, 272, 274
Trevorrow, Colin, 111, 112
Triceratops, 13, 15, 26, 105, 108, 148, 150, 265
twins, 41
Tyrannosaurus rex, ix, xi, xii, 3, 6–9, 21, 23, 24, 26, 29, 30, 56, 61, 65, 66, 69, 76, 81, 84, 85, 88, 89, 91, 94, 96, 97, 101, 105–110, 112, 114–17, 125–28, 131, 135, 136, 137, 140, 143–151, 169, 171–73, 176, 182, 183, 198, 209, 210, 213, 215, 219–221, 223, 235, 236, 249, 257, 259, 264, 277, 279

Übermensch, 231, 233

utilitarianism, 17, 18, 147, 204, 205

Veblen, Thorstein, 84, 85, 145; *The Theory of the Leisure Class*, 84
velociraptors; *see* raptors
vulnerability, 4, 5, 59

warning, 3, 5, 54, 60, 117, 118, 120, 122, 123, 146, 181, 183, 200, 203, 256
Warren, Mary Anne, 136–39
Wittgenstein, Ludwig, 137–39
Wonderful Life (Gould), 255
Wu, Dr. Henry, 25, 27, 55, 56, 64, 69, 70, 117, 119, 123, 202, 241, 242

Yellowstone, 75, 79, 219

zoos, 9, 13, 48, 50, 56, 76, 124–27, 145, 149, 150, 175, 197, 202, 207, 210, 211, 214, 215, 240, 245, 257